C++ LABORATORY MANUAL AND WORKBOOK

Andrew C. Staugaard, Jr.
Brenda Snider

STRUCTURING TECHNIQUES: AN INTRODUCTION USING C++ and STRUCTURING TECHNIQUES: AN INTRODUCTION USING TURBO C++

Andrew C. Staugaard, Jr.

Prentice Hall, Englewood Cliffs, New Jersey 07632

A Simon & Schuster Company
Englewood Cliffs, New Jersey 07632

The author and publisher of this book have used their best efforts in preparing this book. These efforts include the development, research, and testing of the theories and programs to determine their effectiveness. The author and publisher make no warranty of any kind, expressed or implied, with regard to these programs or the documentation contained in this book. The author and publisher shall not be liable in any event for incidental or consequential damages in connection with, or arising out of, the furnishing, performance, or use of these programs.

Printed in the United States of America

10 9 8 7 6 5 4 3 2 1

ISBN 0-13-193061-3

Prentice-Hall International (UK) Limited, London
Prentice-Hall of Australia Pty. Limited, Sydney
Prentice-Hall Canada Inc., Toronto
Prentice-Hall Hispanoamericana, S.A., Mexico
Prentice-Hall of India Private Limited, New Delhi
Prentice-Hall of Japan, Inc., Tokyo
Simon & Schuster Asia Pte. Ltd., Singapore
Editora Prentice-Hall do Brasil, Ltda., Rio de Janeiro

PREFACE

This manual contains laboratory projects intended to guide you through problem solving using the C++ programming language. It is intended to be a supplement to Andrew C. Staugaard's two texts, *Structuring Techniques: An Introduction Using C++* and *TURBO C++*. However, the manual is generic and can be used as a supplement with any good C++ text.

Using this Lab Manual and Workbook

The exercises in this manual have been written and tested using Borland's TURBO C++, however, the exercises are not dependent on a particular implementation of C++. The intention is to provide programming problems that can be developed in many different environments. Instructions for the exercises are generic enough to be used with any C++ compiler. In addition, specific instructions are given for the TURBO C++ for Windows and TURBO C++ for DOS program development environments. The screen print examples are from TURBO C++. If you are using a different implementation of C++, your screen will look similar to, but not exactly like, the ones provided in this manual.

Conventions used in this Manual

This manual uses several conventions to help you identify information. The following table describes these typographical conventions.

Type style	*Used for*
bold	Menu items and commands.
italic	C++ key words, variables, filenames, and other emphasized words.
[K] [E] [Y] [C] [A] [P] [S]	Keys to use on the keyboard.
shaded area	Algorithm and code area for you to complete.
Pre-Lab 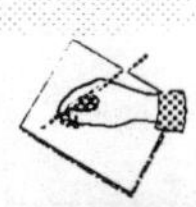	Section to be completed before going to the computer lab.
In-the-Lab 	Section to be completed in the computer lab.

To the Student

This manual has been written as a guide to provide you with a structured, systematic approach to problem solving and programming. You will learn how to define problems, plan their solution, and write C++ programs to implement the planned solution.

Pencil and paper **Pre-Lab** sections have been included to emphasize the importance of thinking through a problem before sitting at the computer to write the program code. The Pre-Labs should be completed before lab time. Make sure that you complete all of the questions and algorithms so that you are prepared for the In-the-Lab section of each problem.

Step-by-step **In-the-Lab** sections are included for each problem to guide you through the process of coding, compiling, linking, debugging, and running the problem solutions. Sample program results are shown for each problem to help you check your solution. The In-the-Lab sections are intended to be hands-on and completed in the computer lab. They are planned to take from one to three hours of time depending upon the computer lab situation, the amount of preparation you have done, and your programming skill.

It is assumed that you have a working knowledge of using the computer's operating system (file maintenance and manipulating directories, for example), how to use a mouse, and the use and location of keys on the keyboard.

The only way to become a good programmer is to start programming. You will never know how to do something unless you give it your best try. *Enjoy!*

To the Instructor

Thank you for using our C++ laboratory manual and workbook. This manual is written to guide the student through a structured, systematic approach to problem solving and programming. Each laboratory exercise has a **Pre-Lab** section and an **In-the-Lab** section. The Pre-Lab section requires the student to formulate a problem definition and algorithm(s) for a given problem outside of the laboratory environment so that they are ready to code the problem solution when they sit down at a machine. Questions are asked within each problem to guide the student through the problem definition and solution planning steps. Space is provided within the manual for the student to answer the questions and write their algorithms. You should emphasize that problem definition and solution planning via algorithms is a Pre-Lab experience so that they are ready to code when they sit down at a machine. The In-the-Lab section directs the student to code, compile, debug, test, and document their program via sample runs and a source code listing. The student codes their program using a generic C++ program shell which relates to the algorithms they developed in the Pre-Lab section.

The first two lab projects are written to get students familiar with their C++ compiler and debugger using pre-written C++ programs. We suggest that these first two projects be assigned the first week or two of the class. After the first two projects, the manual builds on the structured programming paradigm, leading into the object-oriented paradigm and ADTs. We have found this pedagogy to be very workable, especially when accompanied by either of Staugaard's texts: *Structuring Techniques: An Introduction Using C++* or *TURBO C++*.

Special features of this manual include:

- Questions in each problem that guide the student through the problem definition and planning via algorithms.
- A generic C++ program shell for each problem to guide the student through coding.
- Space for answering questions, writing algorithms, and coding.
- Easily identifiable icons for required keystrokes.
- For convenient grading, the student is directed to produce program test runs and source code listings.
- Comprehensive coverage of the TURBO C++ compiler and debugger (DOS and Windows versions) for those using these products.
- A total of 15 lab projects containing 30 problems that cover the major topics of software design using the C++ language.

The solutions to all the lab problems are contained in the solutions manual/disk for Staugaard's text: *Structuring Techniques: An Introduction Using C++*. Please use the following cross reference to obtain the appropriate solution.

Lab Project/Problem Number	Solutions Manual Chapter/Problem Number
Project 1 / Problem 1	Chapter 1 / Problem 3
Project 1 / Problem 2	Chapter 1 / Problem 4

Project 2 / Problem 1	---------------------------
Project 2 / Problem 2	---------------------------
Project 3 / Problem 1	Chapter 3 / Problem 5
Project 3 / Problem 2	Chapter 3 / Problem 11
Project 4 / Problem 1	Chapter 4 / Problem 9
Project 4 / Problem 2	Chapter 4 / Problem 11
Project 5 / Problem 1	Chapter 5 / Problem 5
Project 5 / Problem 2	Chapter 5 / Problem 7
Project 6 / Problem 1	Chapter 6 / Problems 1, 2, 3
Project 6 / Problem 2	Chapter 6 / Problem 7
Project 7 / Problem 1	Chapter 7 / Problem 16
Project 7 / Problem 2	Chapter 7 / Problems 18, 19, 20
Project 8 / Problem 1	Chapter 8 / Problem 4
Project 8 / Problem 2	Chapter 8 / Problems 7, 8, 10
Project 9 / Problem 1	Chapter 9 / Problem 1
Project 9 / Problem 2	Chapter 9 / Problem 15
Project 10 / Problem 1	Chapter 10 / Problem 2
Project 10 / Problem 2	Chapter 10 / Problem 4
Project 11 / Problem 1	Chapter 11 / Problems 1, 2, 3
Project 11 / Problem 2	Chapter 11 / Problems 4, 5, 6, 7, 8, 9, 10, 11
Project 12 / Problem 1	Chapter 12 / Problems 1, 2, 3, 4
Project 12 / Problem 2	Chapter 12 / Problem 5
Project 13 / Problem 1	Chapter 13 / Problem 3
Project 13 / Problem 2	Chapter 13 / Problems 4, 5, 6
Project 14 / Problem 1	Chapter 14 / Problems 4, 5
Project 14 / Problem 2	Chapter 14 / Problem 10
Project 15 / Problem 1	Chapter 15 / Problem 8
Project 15 / Problem 2	Chapter 15 / Problem 8

Enjoy!

Brenda Snider
Andrew C. Staugaard, Jr.

CONTENTS

LAB PROJECT #1
Algorithm Development &
Getting Started in the C++ Environment

Lab Objectives

In this lab, you will . . .

- Develop structured algorithms that are easily converted to C++ code.
- Enter, save, compile, link, print, test, and run programs in your C++ programming environment.

Introduction

The only way to really learn C++ and your program development environment is to get busy and just do it. The instructions and screen prints in this project's In-the-Lab section refer to the TURBO C++ for DOS and TURBO C++ for Windows integrated development environments. If you are using a different implementation of C++, your instructor or lab supervisor should provide you with the details of using your particular C++ programming environment for entering, editing, saving, compiling, linking, running, and printing your C++ programs.

In Problem 1 you will create a problem definition and algorithm for a classic payroll problem. You will then enter the C++ code for the program using an editor. After the code is entered, you will compile, link, run, test, and print the program.

In Problem 2 you will use a problem definition and algorithm for a credit card problem to calculate the interest on a credit card account balance. You will then revise the algorithm that uses two *If/Then* operations so that a single *If/Then/Else* operation can be used. And finally, you will enter, compile, link, run, test, and print the C++ code for this problem.

Problem 1 - Payroll

In this lab you will create a problem definition and algorithm to calculate and report the gross pay for an employee who works 40 hours or less per week. Then you will enter the C++ code to solve the problem, compile, link, run, and print the program.

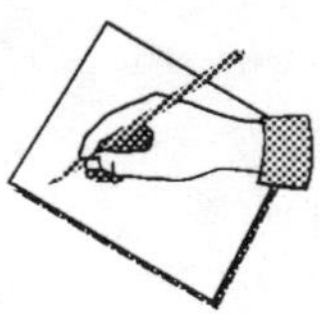

Pre-Lab

PROBLEM STATEMENT

Calculate and report the weekly gross pay for a part time employee.

Procedure & Questions:

PROBLEM DEFINITION

Output: What output is needed according to the problem statement?

____

Input: What input will be needed for processing to obtain the required output?

____

Processing: What processing is required to calculate gross pay from the given input values?

____

____

Discussion:

According to the problem statement you will be calculating the gross pay for an employee that works 40 hours or less per week. This means that you will not have to worry about overtime pay. The output should be the employee's name, rate of pay, hours worked, and the total amount of gross pay. The employee's name, hours worked, and rate of pay are needed as input. To process the gross pay, you would multiply the employee's hours by the pay rate.

Procedure:

THE ALGORITHM

Write a step-by-step algorithm using the input, output, and processing described above.

BEGIN

END

Discussion:

Does your algorithm look similar to the one below?

BEGIN
  Write a program description message to the user.
  Write a user-prompt to enter the employee's name.
  Read (*Name*).
  Write a user-prompt to enter the employee's rate of pay.
  Read (*Rate*).
  Write a user-prompt to enter the employee's hours worked this week.
  Read (*Hours*).
  Assign (*Rate* × *Hours*) to *GrossPay*.
  Write (*Name*, *Rate*, *Hours*, *GrossPay*).
END.

In-the-Lab

Procedure & Discussion:

In order to create C++ programs, you will need to become familiar with a C++ editing environment and compiler. If you are *not* using TURBO C++, complete the steps that follow. Your instructor or lab supervisor should provide you with the details of using your particular C++ programming environment for entering, editing, saving, compiling, linking, running, and printing your C++ programs. *If you are using either the DOS or Windows version of TURBO C++, go directly to their respective discussion to get you started in these programming environments.*

Enter the Source Code

Enter the following C++ source code, being careful to type the code exactly as shown, unless otherwise directed by your instructor or lab supervisor:

```
// LAB 1-1 (L1-1.CPP)
// AUTHOR : type your name here
// DATE WRITTEN : type the date here

#include <iostream.h>
#include <iomanip.h>

void main()
{

// DEFINE VARIABLES
   char Name[22];          // EMPLOYEE NAME
   float Hours;            // WEEKLY HOURS WORKED
   float Rate;             // HOURLY RATE OF PAY
   float GrossPay;         // WEEKLY GROSS PAY
```

```
// DISPLAY PROGRAM DESCRIPTION MESSAGE
cout <<   "This program will calculate the gross pay for a\n"
          "part time employee, given his/her rate of pay\n"
          "and number of weekly hours worked. It is assumed\n"
          "that the employee has worked less than 40 hours.\n\n\n\n";

// OBTAIN USER INPUT DATA
   cout << "Enter employee name:  Name =  ";
   cin.getline(Name,22);
   cout << "\nEnter the rate of pay:  Rate = ";
   cin >> Rate;
   cout << "\nEnter the hours worked this week:  Hours = ";
   cin >> Hours;

// CALCULATE EMPLOYEES GROSS PAY
   GrossPay = Rate * Hours;

// GENERATE OUTPUT TABLE
   cout << "\n\nPAYROLL REPORT FOR: " << Name;
   cout << "\n\n" << setw(20) << "RATE" << setw(20) << "HOURS"
        << setw(20) << "GROSS PAY";
   cout << "\n\n" << setw(17) << "$" << Rate << setw(20) << Hours
        << setw(12) << "$" << setprecision(2) << GrossPay;
}
```

Save the Program

Always save your program onto a disk once it has been entered. While you are working with a program in the editor, it is stored in the computer's primary memory, but not on disk. If the power to the computer should happen to go off, the program would be lost. Saving the program makes a permanent copy of it on disk. If you are entering a long program, you should save it every ten or fifteen minutes. This will keep you from loosing what you have worked so hard to create. Remember, always save and save often!

When you save a program for the first time, you will need to give it a file name. Give our payroll program the name *L1-1.cpp*.

Compile the Program

Now that you have entered and saved the program, it is time to compile it. Compiling a source code program creates an object (*.obj*) file that the computer can understand.

Errors?

If there were any errors in the program, you will have to edit the program code to fix the errors, or "bugs", then compile the program again before you can link and run the program. Make sure that you typed the code exactly as shown earlier in this problem. Be sure to save the program again after you correct any errors.

Link the Program

Once the program is successfully compiled, you need to link it. Linking the object file creates an executable (*.exe*) program that is a combination of all the files needed to run the program properly. The compiler will link your object file and any needed C++ library files to produce an executable (*.exe*) file that is ready to run.

Run the Program

When the program is successfully compiled and linked, you can run it to make sure that it does what it is supposed to do. Run the program and enter the information via the keyboard when prompted to do so. Look at the program listing to answer the following questions.

What C++ statement is causing the program's messages to be displayed on the screen?

____

What C++ statement is causing the computer to wait for information to be entered?

____

What do you think the \n parts of the program code are doing?

____

What C++ statement is causing the *RATE*, *HOURS*, and *GROSS PAY* headers to be placed where they are on the screen?

____

Discussion:

As you run the program, the user messages are displayed on your screen with the *cout* << statements in the program and when input is needed the *cin* >> statements wait for you to enter information from the keyboard and then place the information into a specified variable. As you may have guessed, the \n part of the C++ code is causing the cursor to move to a new line for each \n entered in the program code. Output can be placed where you want it to be displayed by using the *setw()* statement. The *setw()* statement is used to place the *RATE*, *HOURS*, and *GROSS PAY* headers where they are on the screen.

Procedure:

Check the Program Results

Check the program output to make sure that it is correct. Figure 1-1 shows a sample output from the payroll program. If your program results should look similar, congratulations, it worked!

```
This program will calculate the gross pay for a
part time employee, given his/her rate of pay
and number of weekly hours worked.  It is assumed
that the employee has worked less than 40 hours.


Enter employee name:  Name = Brenda

Enter the rate of pay:  Rate = 12.75

Enter the hours worked this week:  Hours = 34


PAYROLL REPORT FOR: Brenda
              RATE                HOURS               GROSS PAY

              $12.75                  34               $433.50
```

Figure 1-1 Sample output from the payroll program.

Test and Print Sample Runs of the Program

Running the program several times with different input information is an important part of program testing. Run the program several times with different values for the *Name, Rate,* and *Hours*. Be sure to check the program output each time.

Printed copies of sample program runs are part of the documentation process in programming. To obtain these, you will need to have access to a printer. Make sure that the printer is on and on-line. Get a print-out of your program runs.

Print the Source Code

A printed copy of the program source code is also an important part of program documentation. Make sure that the printer is ready and then print the source code.

Close the File

When you are finished with a program file make sure that you have saved any final changes and then close the file. It is always good programming practice to close a file when you are finished with it.

TURBO C++ for DOS

If you are using TURBO C++ for DOS, or a similar C++ programming environment, continue with the following procedure and discussion. If you are using TURBO C++ for Windows, skip to the section that describes that environment.

Starting TURBO C++ for DOS

TURBO C++ must be installed on your computer system before you can use it. After it is correctly installed, you can simply type [T] [C] and press [ENTER], as shown in Figure 1-2, to start TURBO C++.

Figure 1-2 Enter [T] [C] at the DOS prompt.

If entering [T] [C] does not work, change to the directory containing the TURBO C++ program files, then type [T] [C] and press [ENTER], as shown in Figure 1-3 (for example, [C] [D] [\] [T] [C] [\] [B] [I] [N] [ENTER] [T] [C] [ENTER]).

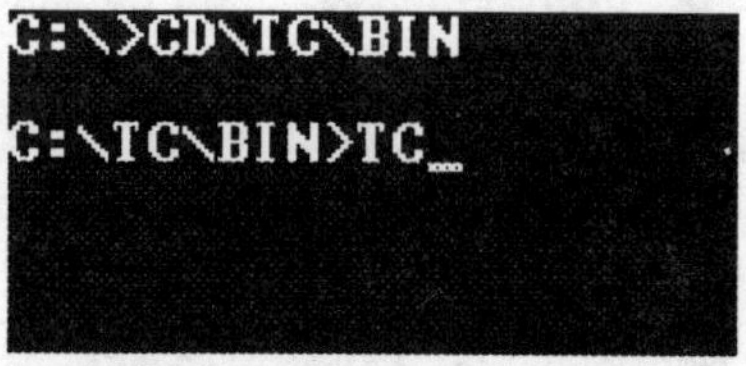

Figure 1-3 Change to the TURBO C++ directory and type [T] [C].

Since TURBO C++ is a compiler for both C and C++ programs, there are some important options that you may need to set to prepare for object-oritented C++ programming. If your compiler has not been configured for C++ programming, Appendix A titled, **"Important Options to Check Before Using the TURBO C++ Compiler"** has some suggestions for setting compiler, directory, and environment options.

Elements of the TURBO C++ for DOS IDE

What you see after starting the TURBO C++ for DOS compiler is the Integrated Development Environment, or IDE, screen. This is the control center and editing environment for TURBO C++. Elements of the IDE are shown in Figure 1-4.

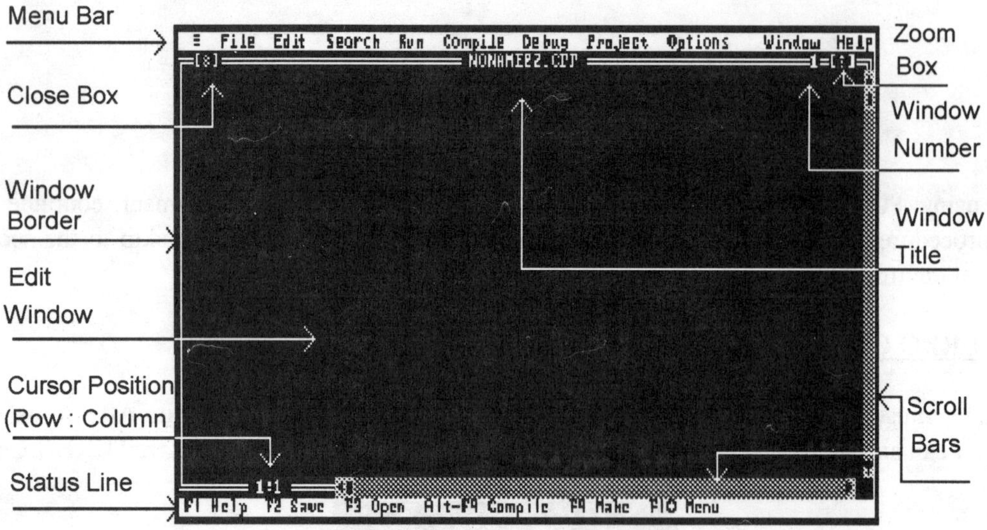

Figure 1-4 TURBO C++ Integrated Development Environment (IDE) desktop.

Make sure that a new file is open in the **Edit** window. If you need to open a new file, press ALT + F for the **File** menu and then press N for a new file.

Locate each of the important TURBO C++ IDE elements, shown in Figure 1-4, on your computer screen.

The Menu Bar

The Menu Bar shown in Figure 1-5 is the primary access to all the commands available in TURBO C++. It is always at the top of the screen except when you are viewing your program's output in the user screen. The F10 key activates the Menu Bar and the cursor control arrow keys can be used to move to the menu items needed. You can also click the mouse on any menu item to activate its pull down menu.

Figure 1-5 The Menu Bar.

If you choose an item in a pull down menu that is followed by an ellipsis (...), a Dialog box will be displayed allowing you to enter needed information, as shown in Figure 1-6.

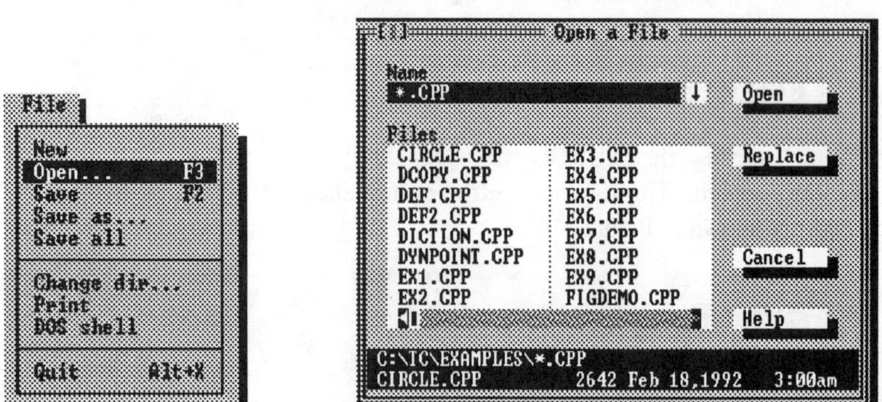

Figure 1-6 Before and after choosing a menu item with ellipsis (...).

To see what happens when you select a menu item with ellipsis (...), activate the **File** pull down menu shown in Figure 1-6 by clicking on **File** in the Menu bar or by pressing the ALT + F Hot Key combination. Select the **Open...** item to see the **Open a file** dialog box shown in Figure 1-6. Since you are not ready to use the options presented, click the **Cancel** button or press the ESC key to close the dialog box.

If you choose an item in a pull down menu that is followed by an arrow (▶) the command leads to a secondary menu, as shown in Figure 1-7.

Figure 1-7 Before and after choosing a menu item with an arrow (▶).

To see what happens when you select a menu item with an arrow (▶), activate the **Options** pull down menu by clicking on **Options** in the Menu bar or by pressing the ALT + O Hot Key combination. Select the **Compiler** ▶ command to see the secondary menu shown in Figure 1-7. Since you are not ready to use the options presented, press the ESC key to close the menus.

Notes

Here are some things to note that will help you understand the TURBO C++ menu system:

- If you choose a command in a pull down menu that doesn't have an ellipsis (...) or arrow (▶), the action will be performed as soon as you choose the command.
- Commands in a pull down menu that are not presently available for use will be lighter and cannot be selected until they can be actively applied by the IDE.
- To choose a command from a pull down menu, simply move the highlight bar to the desired command with the arrow keys and press ENTER or click the command with the mouse.
- To cancel an unwanted pull down menu or close an unneeded dialog box, press the ESC key.

Hot Keys

- A Hot Key, or shortcut, method to a Menu bar item is to hold the ALT key and press the first letter of the needed item. For example, Hold the ALT key down and press F for the **File** menu. An alternate shortcut is to press the F10 key to activate the Menu Bar, then press the first letter of the needed menu item. For example, press F10 then F for the **File** menu.

- A Hot Key shortcut to choosing a command in a pull down menu is pressing the underlined, highlighted letter of the needed command in the pull down menu. For example to print the active file, you can simply press ALT + F for the **File** menu then press P for the print option.

- Learning the Hot Keys and shortcuts available in the TURBO C++ IDE can save valuable programming time. It is a good idea to learn them and make a habit of using them. A summary of the TURBO C++ Hot Keys is located in Appendix B.

The Status Line

The Status Line, shown in Figure 1-8, is displayed at the bottom of the screen. It shows basic keystrokes and shortcuts, or Hot Keys, that are available at that moment in the active window. The items in the Status Line will change as the active option in the window changes. It offers on-line hints on any selected menu command and dialog box item. Always take note of the information that the Status Line is displaying, since it will keep you informed as to what is going on.

F1 Help F2 Save F3 Open Alt - F9 Compile F9 Make F10 Menu

Figure 1-8 An example Status Line.

What information is currently displayed in the Status Line on your screen?

____

The Edit Window

Most of what you see and do in the TURBO C++ IDE takes place in a window. The Edit window, shown in Figure 1-9, will be the one that you use to write and edit your programs. For more information about using the windows in TURBO C++ refer to the TURBO C++ reference manuals.

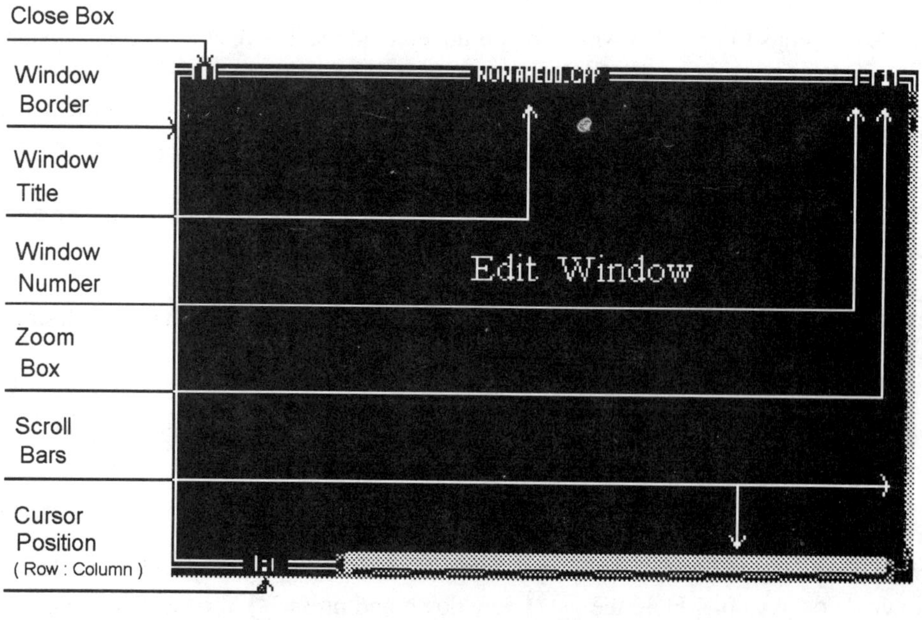

Figure 1-9 The TURBO C++ Edit window.

Creating Your First Program

Now that you are somewhat familiar with the C++ programming environment, it's time to enter the code for the payroll program from the algorithm developed in the Pre-Lab exercise.

Opening a New File

If you haven't already opened a new file, you will need to open one for your program. This can be done in the TURBO C++ IDE, as shown in Figure 1-10 , by selecting the File menu from the Menu Bar then selecting the New menu item from the pull down menu. Pressing [ALT] + [F] then [N] will also accomplish this task.

Figure 1-10 Opening a **New** file.

Enter the Source Code

After you have a new file window open, you can enter the program source code. Enter the following C++ code, being careful to type the code exactly as shown, unless otherwise directed by your instructor or lab supervisor.

```
// LAB 1-1 (L1-1.CPP)
// AUTHOR : type your name here
// DATE WRITTEN : type the date here

#include <iostream.h>
#include <iomanip.h>
#include <conio.h>          // FOR DOS BASED COMPILERS ONLY

void main()
{
// DEFINE VARIABLES
   char Name[22];           // EMPLOYEE NAME
   float Hours;             // WEEKLY HOURS WORKED
   float Rate;              // HOURLY RATE OF PAY
   float GrossPay;          // WEEKLY GROSS PAY

// DISPLAY PROGRAM DESCRIPTION MESSAGE
   clrscr();                // CLEARS THE SCREEN IN DOS BASED COMPILERS
   cout <<    "This program will calculate the gross pay for a\n"
              "part time employee, given his/her rate of pay\n"
              "and number of weekly hours worked. It is assumed\n"
              "that the employee has worked less than 40 hours.\n\n\n\n";
```

```
// OBTAIN USER INPUT DATA
   cout << "Enter employee name:  Name =  ";
   cin.getline(Name,22);
   cout << "\nEnter the rate of pay:  Rate = ";
   cin >> Rate;
   cout << "\nEnter the hours worked this week:  Hours = ";
   cin >> Hours;

// CALCULATE EMPLOYEES GROSS PAY
   GrossPay = Rate * Hours;

// GENERATE OUTPUT TABLE
   cout << "\n\nPAYROLL REPORT FOR: " << Name;
   cout << "\n\n" << setw(20) << "RATE" << setw(20) << "HOURS"
        << setw(20) << "GROSS PAY";
   cout << "\n\n" << setw(17) << "$" << Rate << setw(20) << Hours
         << setw(12) << "$" << setprecision(2) << GrossPay;
}
```

Your screen should look similar to the one in Figure 1-11.

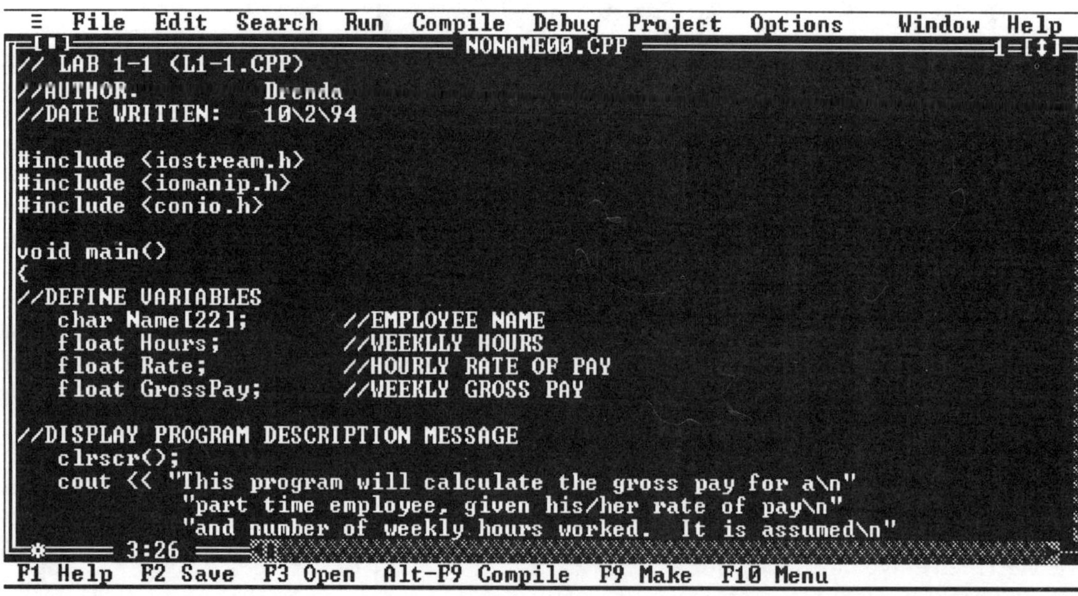

Figure 1-11 The payroll program displayed in the Edit window of the TURBO C++ IDE.

Saving the Program

Always save your program onto a disk once it has been entered. While you are working with a program in the editor, it is stored in the computer's primary memory, but not on disk. If the power to the computer should happen to go off, the program would be lost. Saving the program makes a permanent copy of it on disk. If you are entering a long program, you should save it every ten or fifteen minutes. This will keep you from loosing what you have worked so hard to create. Remember, always save and save often!

Saving the program can be done in TURBO C++ , as shown in Figure 1-12, by selecting the **File** menu from the Menu Bar, then selecting the **Save** command from the pull down menu. Another way is to simply press the F2 Hot Key from anywhere within the TURBO C++ IDE.

Figure 1-12 Choosing the **Save** command (F2).

When you save a program for the first time, you will need to give it a file name, as shown in Figure 1-13. Remember that if you are working with DOS, you must follow DOS's file naming rules. The most important of these are that a file name can be up to eight characters in length and cannot contain any spaces. When programming in C++, your source program files should have a *.cpp* extension. Give our payroll program the name *L1-1.cpp* , as shown in Figure 1-13.

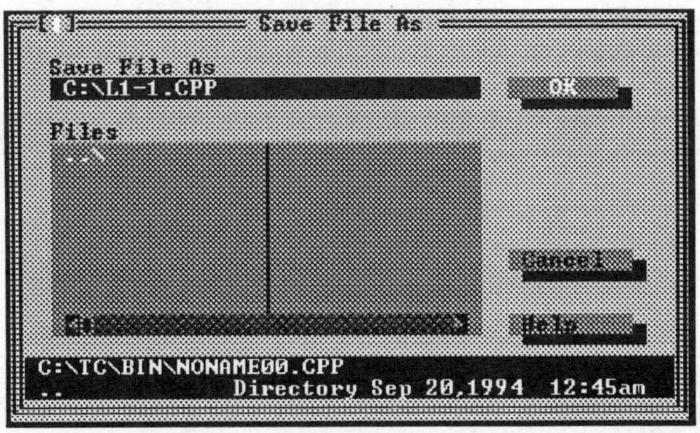

Figure 1-13 Naming a C++ file.

Compiling the Program

Now that you have entered and saved the program, it is time to compile it. You can compile the source code program in the TURBO C++ IDE, as shown in Figure 1-14, by selecting the **Compile** menu from the Menu Bar then selecting the **Compile** command from the pull down menu. Or press the ALT + F9 Hot Key combination without having to access the Menu Bar. Compiling a source code program creates an object (*.obj*) file that the computer can understand.

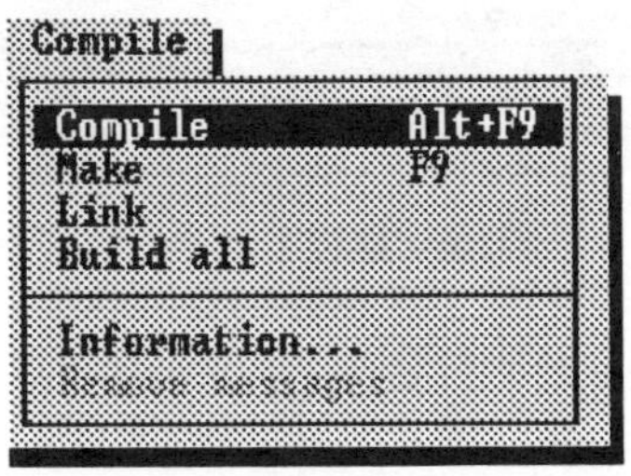

Figure 1-14 Choosing the **Compile** command (ALT + F9).

Figure 1-15 shows the status box that you will see as your program compiles. Notice the message at the bottom of the box, **"Ctrl-Break to quit."** This means that if you need to terminate the compile process at any time, you can hold the CTRL key and press the BREAK key. This will terminate the compile process immediately.

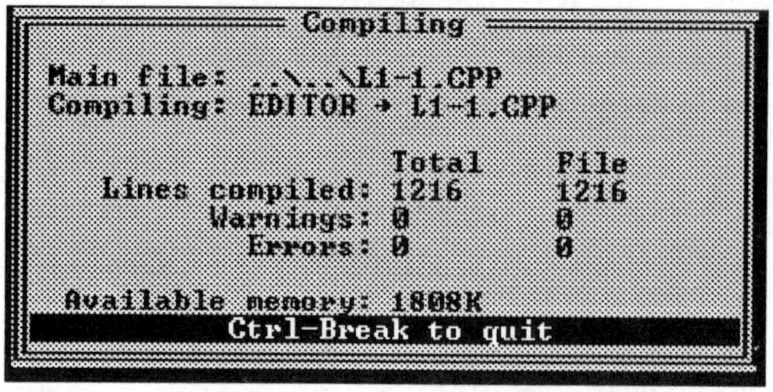

Figure 1-15 Compiling a program.

If there were no errors in the program, the message **"Success : press any key"** will be displayed, as shown in Figure 1-16. It's always a great feeling to see this message, since it means that you typed in the program code correctly and the compiler found all the files necessary to compile the program.

Figure 1-16 Success!

Errors?

If there were any errors in the program, the message, **"Errors : Press any key"** will be displayed, as shown in Figure 1-17. You will have to edit the program code to fix the errors, or "bugs", then compile the program again before you can link and run the program. Make sure that you typed the code exactly as shown earlier in this problem. Be sure to save the program again after you correct any errors.

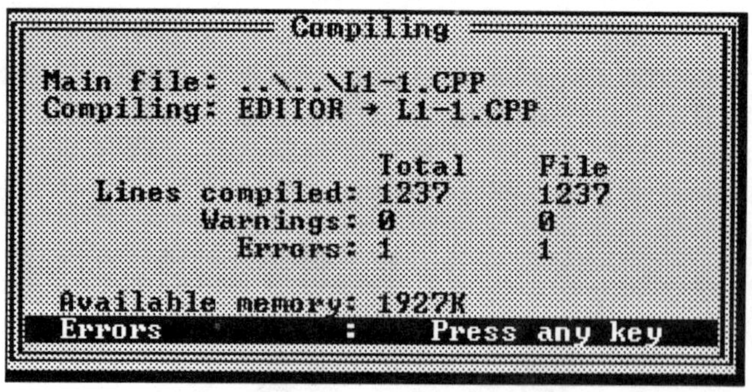

Figure 1-17 Errors!

If the TURBO C++ compiler has detected an error, pressing any key will produce an Errors Message window at the bottom of the screen. A highlight bar will then show where the errors are located in your program. A simple statement about the nature of the error and its line number is displayed in the Errors Message window.

TURBO C++ also offers Help screens with a more detailed explanation of a particular error. To activate a Help screen, position the highlight bar on an error message in the Error Message window that you need more information about, then press the F1 key.

When an error is highlighted in the Errors Message window, pressing ENTER will position the cursor in the Edit window just after the error. You can then correct the error. After correcting all errors, you must save and compile the program again.

Linking the Program

Once the program is successfully compiled, you need to link it. Linking the object file creates an executable (*.exe*) program that is a combination of all the files needed to run the program properly. Select the **Compile** menu from the TURBO C++ Menu Bar, then select the **Link** command from the pull down menu, as shown in Figure 1-18. The Hot Key combination for this action is ALT + C then L.

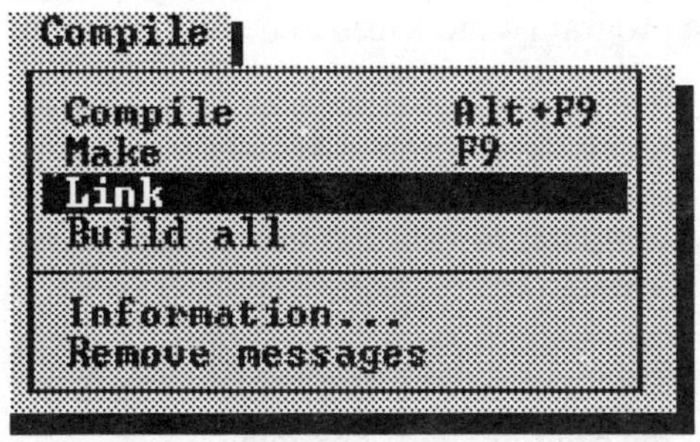

Figure 1-18 Choosing the **Link** command.

The compiler will link your object file and any needed C++ library files to produce an executable (*.exe*) file that is ready to run. See Figure 1-19 for a look at the TURBO C++ status box that is displayed while a program is linking. Notice the **"Ctrl-Break to quit"** message. Use this key combination if you need to terminate the linking process.

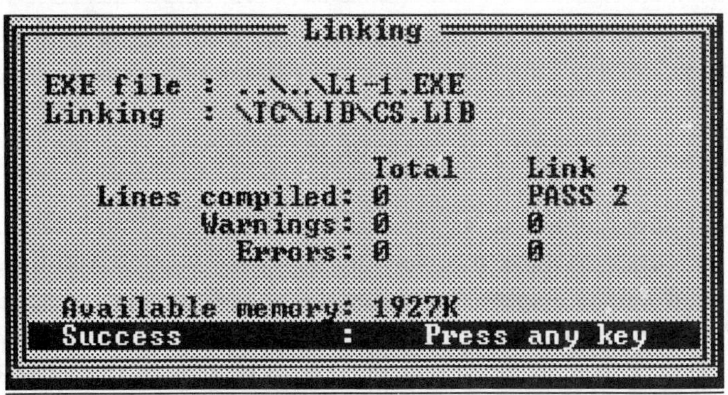

Figure 1-19 Linking a program.

Running the Program

When the program is successfully compiled and linked, you can run it to make sure that it does what it is supposed to do. Select the **Run** menu from the Menu Bar, then select the **Run** command from the pull down menu, as shown in Figure 1-20. The Hot Key combination of CTRL + F9 will also perform this action. By the way, pressing CTRL + F9 will also compile, link, and run the program from the Edit window, so that you don't have to do each step separately.

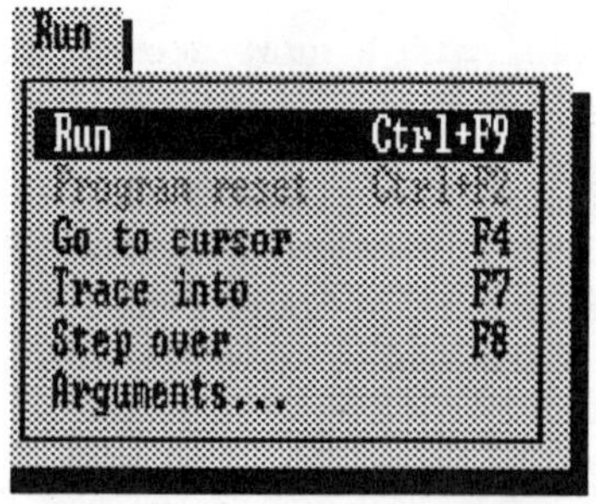

Figure 1-20 Choosing the **Run** command ([CTRL] + [F9]).

Run the program and enter the information via the keyboard when prompted to do so. Look at the program source code listing to answer the following questions.

What C++ statement is causing the program's messages to be displayed on the screen?

____

What C++ statement is causing the computer to wait for information to be entered?

____

What do you think the *\n* parts of the program code are doing?

____

What C++ statement is causing the *RATE*, *HOURS*, and *GROSS PAY* headers to be placed where they are on the screen?

____

Discussion:

As you run the program, the user messages are displayed on your screen with the *cout* << statements in the program and when input is needed the *cin* >> statements wait for you to enter information from the keyboard and then place the information into a specified variable. As you may have guessed, the *\n* part of the C++ code is causing the cursor to move to a new line for each *\n* entered in the program code. Output can be placed where you want it to be displayed by using the *setw()* statement. The *setw()* statement is used to place the *RATE*, *HOURS*, and *GROSS PAY* headers where they are on the screen.

After you run the program, you will notice that the screen returns to the TURBO C++ Edit window. The information that was sent out by the program is on the User screen.

Procedure:

Checking the Program Results

To see the results of the program run you must check the User screen. To do this you can select the **Window** menu from the Menu Bar and then select the **User screen** menu item from the pull down window, as shown in Figure 1-21. Or you can use the Hot Key combination of [ALT] + [F5] without having to access the Menu Bar.

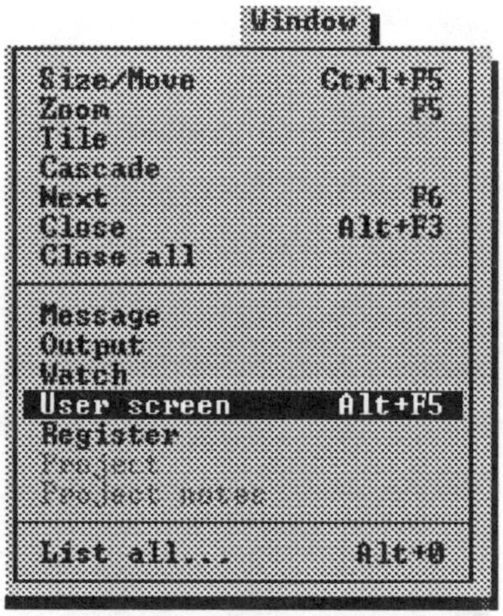

Figure 1-21 Choosing the **User screen** option (ALT + F5).

The output of our payroll program is shown in Figure 1-22. If your screen looks like Figure 1-22, congratulations, it worked! From the User screen, you can press any key to return to the TURBO C++ Edit window in the IDE.

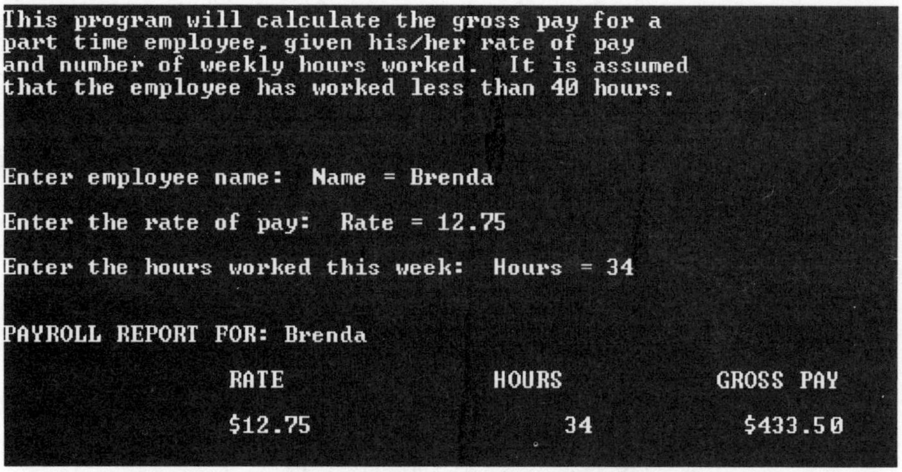

Figure 1-22 The **User screen** generated by the payroll program.

Test and Print Sample Runs of the Program

Run the program again with different values for the *Name, Rate,* and *Hours*. Be sure to check the User screen each time.

Running the program several times with different input information is an important part of program testing. Printed copies of sample program runs are part of the documentation process in programming. To obtain these, you will need to have access to a printer. Make sure that the printer is on and on-line.

You can get a print-out of your sample runs by doing the following:

1. Run the program (CTRL + F9 in TURBO C++).
2. Input the appropriate information.
3. Switch to the User screen (ALT + F5 in TURBO C++).
4. Make sure that the printer is ready.
5. Press the **PRINT SCREEN** key on the keyboard.

Print the Source Code

A printed copy of the program source code is also an important part of program documentation. Make sure that the printer is ready and then print the source code by selecting the **Print** command. In TURBO C++ **Print** is found in the **File** menu, as shown in Figure 1-23.

Figure 1-23 Selecting the **Print** command to print the current program in the Edit window.

Closing the File

When you are finished with a program file make sure that you have saved any final changes (F2) and then close the file. Select the **Window** menu from the Menu Bar, then select the **Close** command from the pull down menu to close the active window, as shown in Figure 1-24. Alternatively, you can use the Hot Key combination of ALT + F3 without having to access the Menu Bar. Clicking the Close Box in the upper left corner of the window will also close the window.

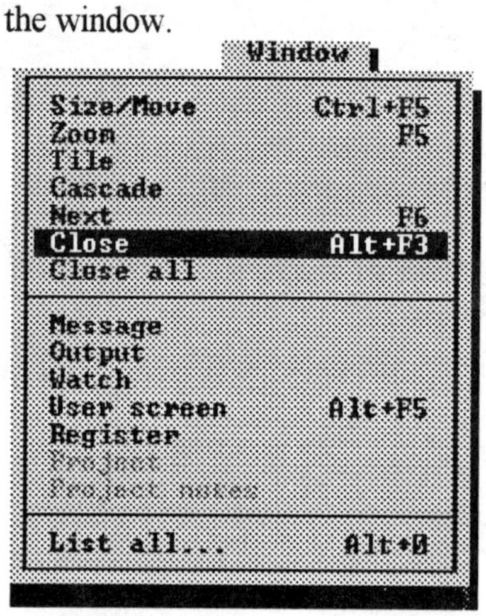

Figure 1-24 Closing a **File** (ALT + F3).

If you leave any file window open when you exit from TURBO C++, that file window will open when you start TURBO C++ again. It is always good programming practice to close a file window when you are finished with it.

TURBO C++ for Windows

If you are using the TURBO C++ for Windows programming environment, continue with the following procedure and discussion.

Starting TURBO C++ for Windows

TURBO C++ for Windows must be installed on your computer system before you can use it. To start TURBO C++ for Windows, simply double-click the  icon from the Program Manager. Click the maximize button in the upper right corner to give yourself the largest possible work area.

Since TURBO C++ is a compiler for both C and C++ programs, there are some important options that you may need to set to prepare for object-oriented C++ programming. If your compiler has not been configured for C++ programming, Appendix A , titled **"Important Options to Check Before Using the TURBO C++ Compiler"**, has some suggestions for setting compiler and directory options. In addition, make sure that your command set options are set to the *Alternate* command set for the purposes of this discussion. Select the *Alternate* command set by choosing the following commands from the Menu bar: **Options | Environment | Preferences**. And finally, click the **Alternate** button in the Command Set category. Setting this option will allow you to use the standard TURBO C++ Hot Key shortcuts.

Elements of the TURBO C++ for Windows IDE

What you see after starting the TURBO C++ for Windows program is the Integrated Development Environment, or IDE, window. This is the control center and editing environment for TURBO C++ for Windows. The IDE window is shown in Figure 1-25.

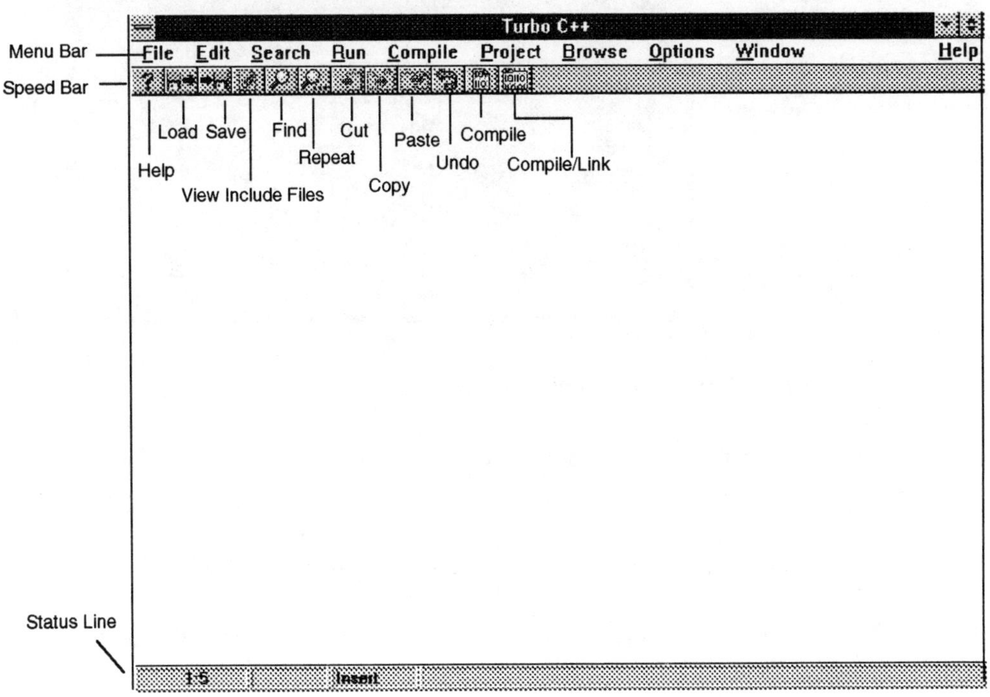

Figure 1-25 The TURBO C++ Integrated Development Environment (IDE) window.

Locate each of the important TURBO C++ IDE elements, shown in Figure 1-25, on your computer.

The Menu bar

The Menu bar shown in Figure 1-26 is the primary access to all the commands available in TURBO C++. It is always at the top of the screen. The F10 key activates the Menu bar and the cursor control arrow keys can be used to move to the menu items needed. You can also click the mouse on any menu item to activate its pull down menu.

Figure 1-26 The Menu bar.

If you choose an item in a pull down menu that is followed by an ellipsis (...), a Dialog box will be displayed allowing you to enter needed information, as shown in Figure 1-27.

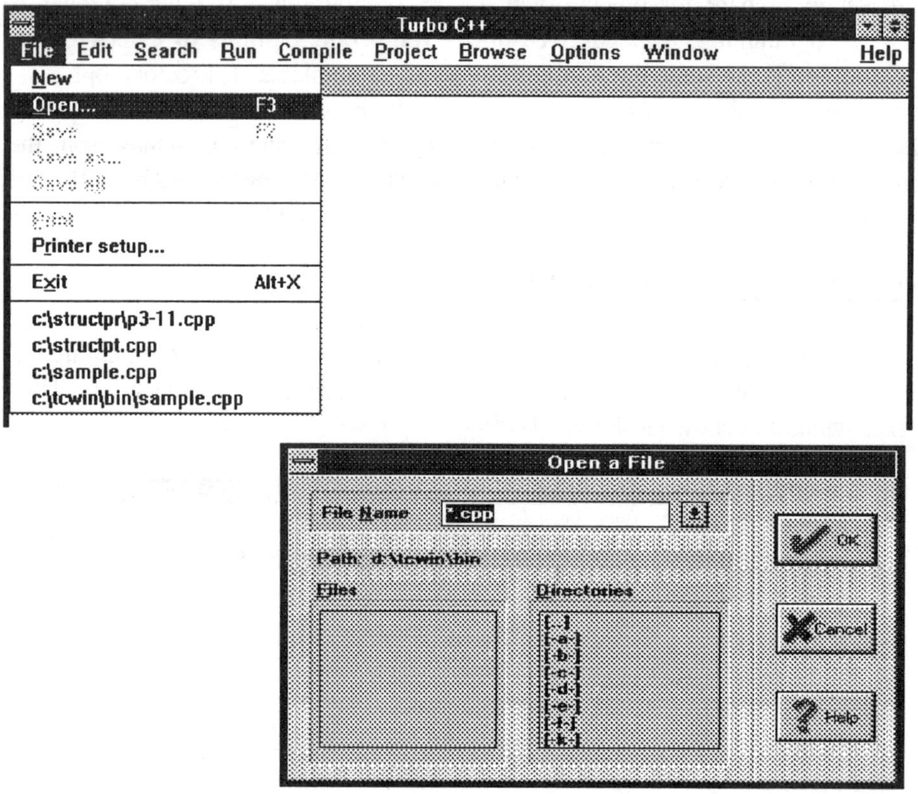

Figure 1-27 Before and after choosing a menu item with ellipsis (...).

To see what happens when you select a menu item with ellipsis (...), activate the **File** pull down menu shown in Figure 1-27 by clicking on **File** in the Menu bar or by pressing the ALT + F Hot Key combination. Select the **Open...** item to see the **Open a file** dialog box shown in Figure 1-27. Since you are not ready to use the options presented, click the **Cancel** button or press the ESC key to close the dialog box.

If you choose an item in a pull down menu that is followed by an arrow (▶) the command leads to a secondary menu, as shown in Figure 1-28.

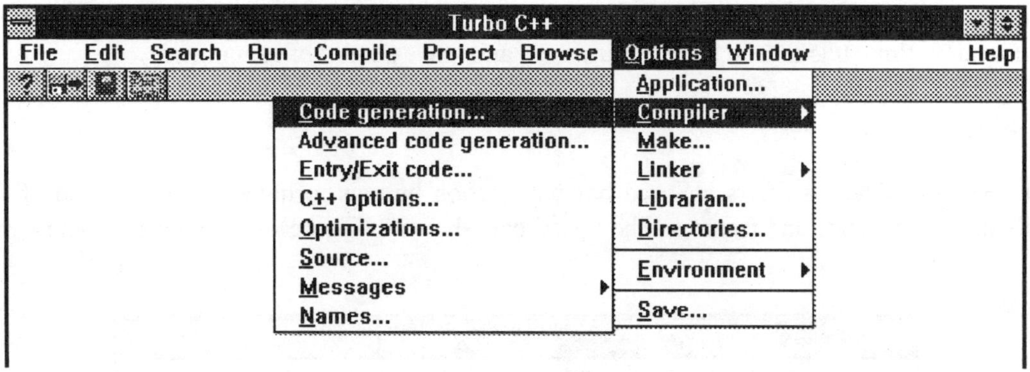

Figure 1-28 Before and after choosing a menu item with an arrow (▶).

To see what happens when you select a menu item with an arrow (▶), activate the **Options** pull down menu by clicking on **Options** in the Menu bar or by pressing the [ALT] +[O] Hot Key combination to see the secondary menu shown in Figure 1-28. Since you are not ready to use the options presented, press the [ESC] key to close the menus.

Notes

Here are some things to note that will help you understand the TURBO C++ menu system:

- If you choose a command in a pull down menu that doesn't have an ellipsis (...) or arrow (▶), the action will be performed as soon as you choose the command.
- Commands in a pull down menu that are not presently available for use will be lighter and cannot be selected until they can be actively applied by the IDE.
- To choose a command from a pull down menu, simply move the highlight bar to the desired command with the arrow keys and press [ENTER] or click the command with the mouse.
- To cancel an unwanted pull down menu or close an unneeded dialog box, press the [ESC] key.

Hot Keys

- To use the standard TURBO C++ Hot Key shortcuts, make sure that your command set options are set to the *Alternate* command set. Select the *Alternate* command set by choosing the following commands from the Menu bar: **Options | Environment | Preferences.** And finally, click the **Alternate** button in the Command Set category.
- A Hot Key, or shortcut, method to a Menu bar item is to hold the [ALT] key and press the first letter of the needed item. For example, Hold the [ALT] key down and press [F] for the **File** menu. An alternate shortcut is to press the [F10] key to activate the Menu bar, then press the first letter of the needed menu item. For example, press [F10] then [F] for the **File** menu.
- A Hot Key shortcut to choosing a command in a pull down menu is pressing the underlined, highlighted letter of the needed command in the pull down menu. For example to print the active file, you can simply press [ALT] +[F] for the **File** menu then press [P] for the print option.

- Learning the Hot Keys and shortcuts available in the TURBO C++ IDE can save valuable programming time. It is a good idea to learn them and make a habit of using them.

The Speed Bar

TURBO C++ for Windows offers a Speed bar with action buttons to quickly access some of the most commonly used commands and features. The Speed bar, shown in Figure 1-29, is located below the Menu bar.

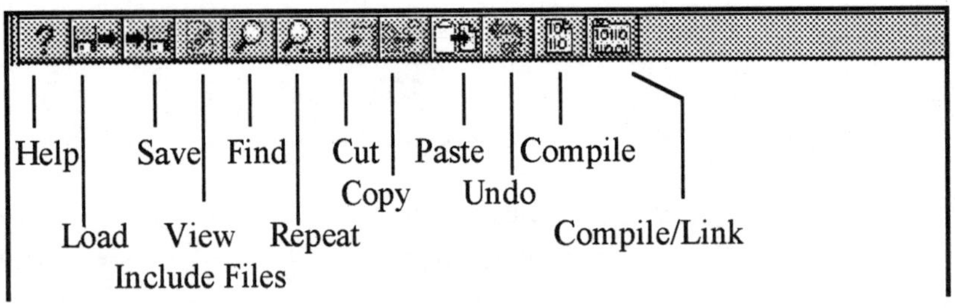

Figure 1-29 The Speed Bar.

The Status Line

The Status Line, shown in Figure 1-30, is displayed at the bottom of the window. It shows basic keystrokes and shortcuts, or Hot Keys, that are available at that moment in the active window. The items in the Status Line will change as the active option in the window changes. It offers on-line hints on any selected menu command and dialog box item. Always take note of the information that the Status Line is displaying, since it will keep you informed as to what is going on.

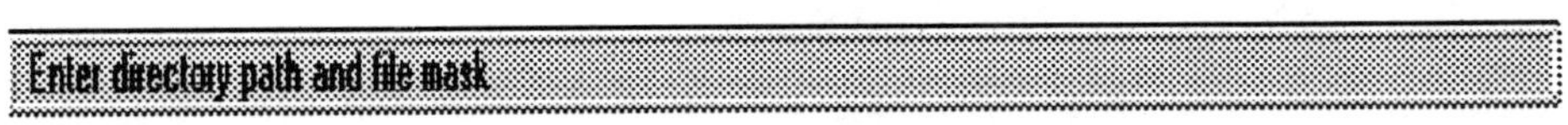

Figure 1-30 An example Status Line.

What information is currently displayed in the Status Line on your computer screen?

____

The Edit Window

All of what you see and do in the TURBO C++ for Windows IDE takes place in a window. The Edit window, shown in Figure 1-31, will be the one that you use to write and edit your programs. Take special note of the action buttons on the Speed bar, since using them will save you time when editing your programs.

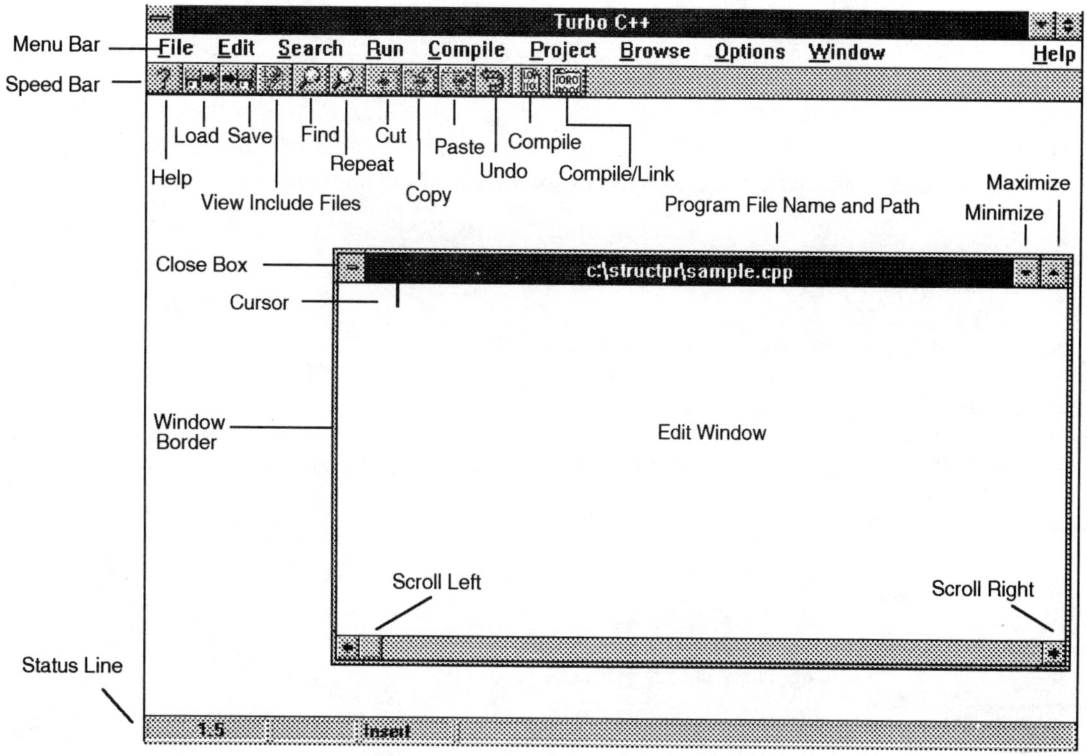

Figure 1-31 The TURBO C++ Edit window.

Creating Your First Program

Now that you are somewhat familiar with the C++ programming environment, it's time to enter the code for the payroll program from the algorithm developed in the Pre-Lab exercise.

Opening a New File

If you haven't already opened a new file, you will need to open one for your program. This can be done in the TURBO C++ IDE, as shown in Figure 1-32 , by selecting the **File** menu from the Menu bar then selecting the **New** menu item from the pull down menu. Pressing ALT + F then N will also accomplish this task.

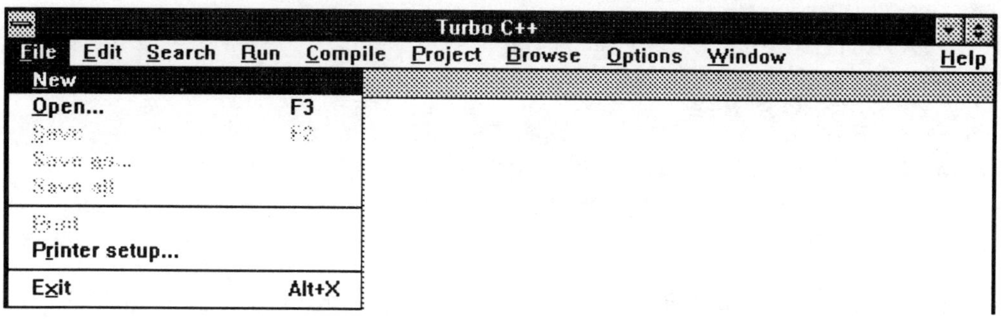

Figure 1-32 Opening a **New** file.

Typing in the Program

After you have a new file Edit window open, click the maximize  button in the upper right corner to give yourself the largest edit area possible. Enter the following C++ code, being careful to type the code exactly as shown, unless otherwise directed by your instructor or lab supervisor.

```
// LAB 1-1 (L1-1.CPP)
// AUTHOR : type your name here
// DATE WRITTEN : type the date here

#include <iostream.h>
#include <iomanip.h>
#include <conio.h>          // FOR USERS OF DOS BASED COMPILERS

void main()
{
// DEFINE VARIABLES
  char Name[22];            // EMPLOYEE NAME
  float Hours;              // WEEKLY HOURS WORKED
  float Rate;               // HOURLY RATE OF PAY
  float GrossPay;           // WEEKLY GROSS PAY

// DISPLAY PROGRAM DESCRIPTION MESSAGE
  clrscr();                 // CLEARS THE SCREEN IN DOS BASED COMPILERS
  cout <<     "This program will calculate the gross pay for a\n"
              "part time employee, given his/her rate of pay\n"
              "and number of weekly hours worked. It is assumed\n"
              "that the employee has worked less than 40 hours.\n\n\n\n";

// OBTAIN USER INPUT DATA
  cout << "Enter employee name:  Name =  ";
  cin.getline(Name,22);
  cout << "\nEnter the rate of pay:  Rate = ";
  cin >> Rate;
  cout << "\nEnter the hours worked this week:  Hours = ";
  cin >> Hours;

// CALCULATE EMPLOYEES GROSS PAY
  GrossPay = Rate * Hours;

// GENERATE OUTPUT TABLE
  cout << "\n\nPAYROLL REPORT FOR: " << Name;
  cout << "\n\n" << setw(20) << "RATE" << setw(20) << "HOURS"
       << setw(20) << "GROSS PAY";
  cout << "\n\n" << setw(17) << "$" << Rate << setw(20) << Hours
       << setw(12) << "$" << setprecision(2) << GrossPay;
}
```

Once you type in the program, your Edit window should appear like that shown in Figure 1-33.

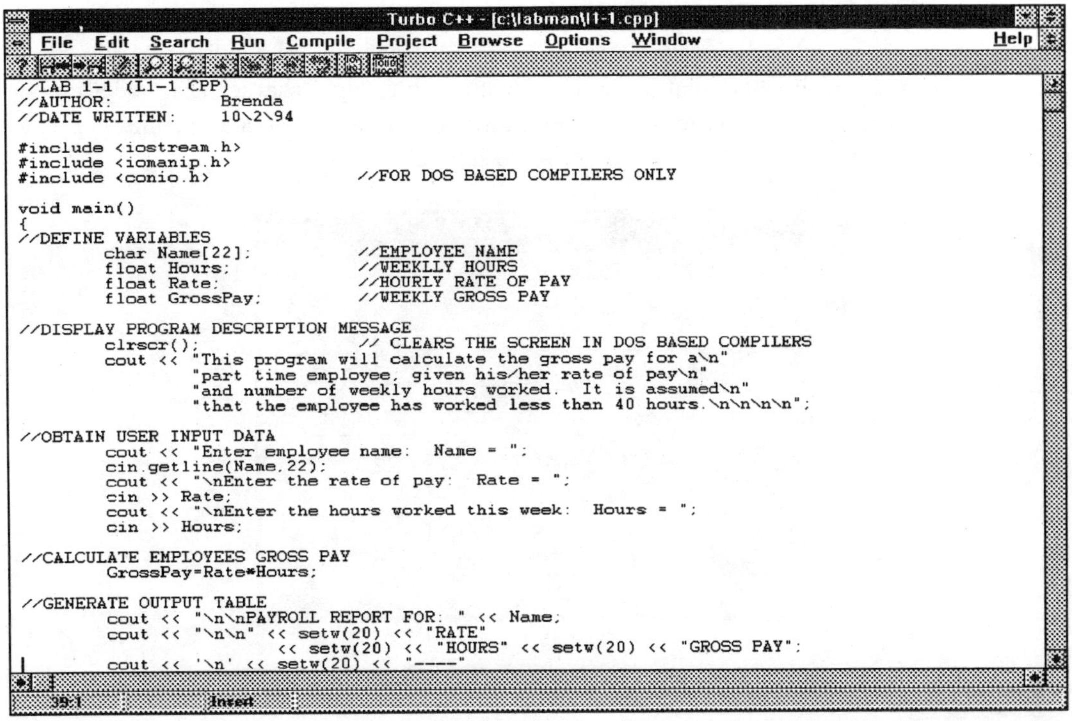

Figure 1-33 The payroll program displayed in the Edit window of the TURBO C++ IDE.

Saving the Program

Always save your program onto a disk once it has been entered. While you are working with a program in the editor, it is stored in the computer's primary memory, but not on disk. If the power to the computer should happen to go off, the program would be lost. Saving the program makes a permanent copy of it on disk. If you are entering a long program, you should save it every ten or fifteen minutes. This will keep you from loosing what you have worked so hard to create. Remember, always save and save often!

Saving the program can be done in TURBO C++ , as shown in Figure 1-34, by selecting the **File** menu from the Menu bar, then selecting the **Save** command from the pull down menu. Another way to save the program, is to simply press the F2 Hot Key from anywhere within the IDE or press the action button on the IDE Speed bar.

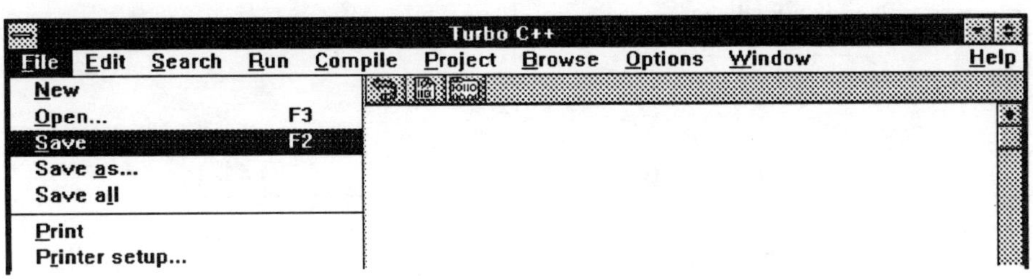

Figure 1-34 Choosing the **Save** command (F2).

When you save a program for the first time, you will need to give it a file name, as shown in Figure 1-35. Remember, if you are working with the DOS operating system, you must follow DOS's file naming rules. The most important of these are that a file name can be up to eight characters in length and cannot contain any spaces. When programming in C++, your source program files should have a *.cpp* extension. Give our payroll program the name *L1-1.cpp* , as shown in Figure 1-35.

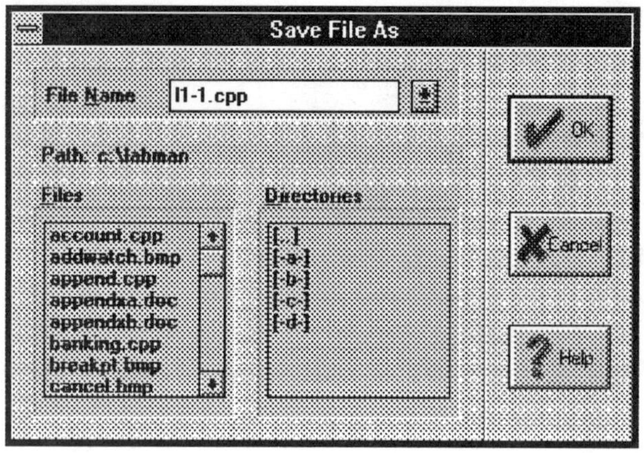

Figure 1-35 Naming a C++ file.

Compiling the Program

Now that you have entered and saved the program, it is time to compile it. You can compile the source code program in the TURBO C++ IDE, as shown in Figure 1-36, by selecting the **Compile** menu from the Menu bar then selecting the **Compile** command from the pull down menu. Another way to activate the compile command is to press the [ALT] + [F9] Hot Key combination without having to access the Menu bar, or click the action button on the IDE Speed bar. Compiling a source code program creates an object (*.obj*) file that the computer can understand.

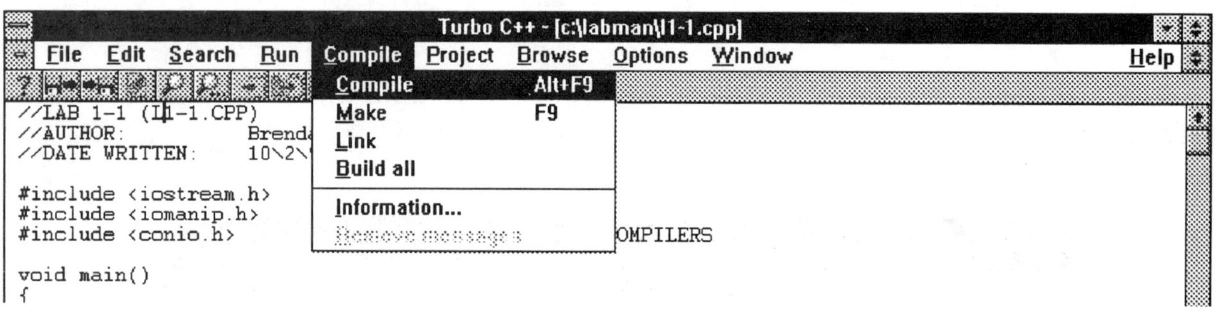

Figure 1-36 Choosing the **Compile** command ([ALT] + [F9]).

Figure 1-37 shows the status box that you will see as your program compiles. While the program is compiling , a [Cancel] button will appear at the bottom of the status box. Clicking this button at any time will terminate the compile process immediately.

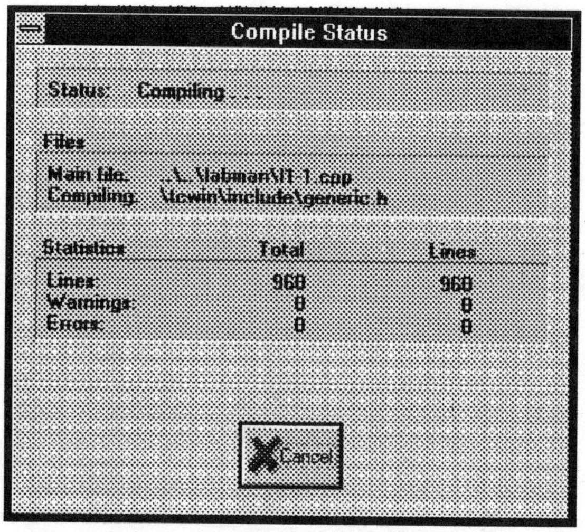

Figure 1-37 Compiling a program.

If there were no errors in the program, the message **"Success"** will be displayed in the status box, as shown in Figure 1-38. It's always a great feeling to see this message, since it means that you typed in the program code correctly and the compiler did not find any errors. After the program has compiled, click the  button to go on.

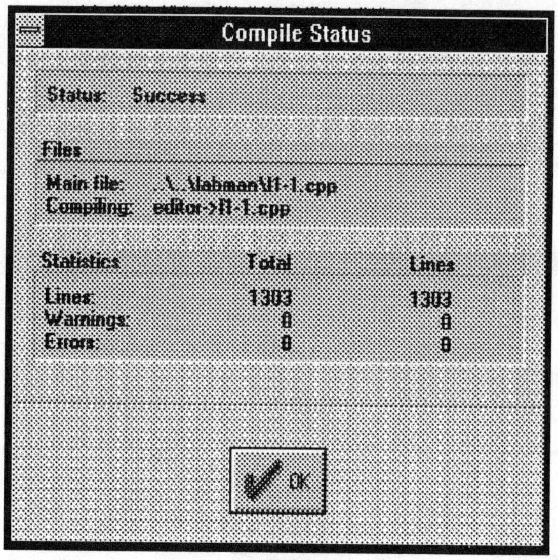

Figure 1-38 Success!

Errors?

If there were any errors in the program, the message, **"There are Errors"** will be displayed in the status box, as shown in Figure 1-39. You will have to edit the program code to fix the errors, or "bugs", then compile the program again before you can link and run the program. Make sure that you typed the code exactly as shown earlier in this problem. Be sure to save the program again after you correct any errors.

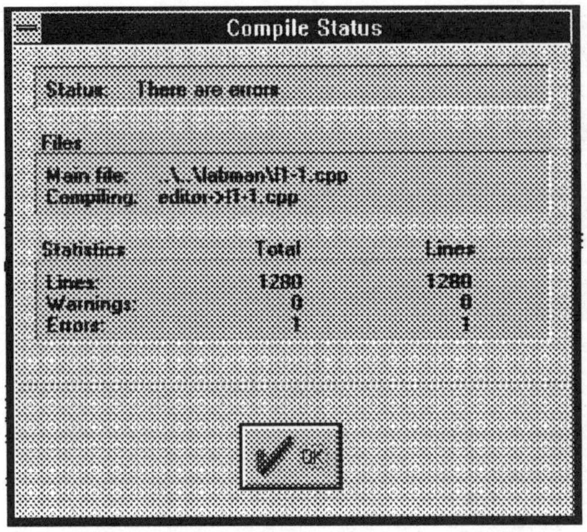

Figure 1-39 Errors!

If the TURBO C++ compiler has detected an error, clicking the  button will produce a Message window, as shown in Figure 1-40. A simple statement about the nature of the error and its line number is displayed in the Message window. In addition, a highlight bar will show the approximate location of the indicated error in your program. If there are multiple errors, clicking on a given error in the Message window will cause the highlight bar to move to the approximate location of the indicated error in your program. *Note*: The highlight bar is sometimes positioned one line beyond the actual program line containing the error as is the case in Figure 1-40. Here, the missing semicolon is *not* in the highlighted line, but on the previous line.

When an error is highlighted in the Errors Message window, pressing  will position the cursor in the Edit window at the approximate error location. You can then correct the error. After correcting all errors, you must save and compile the program again.

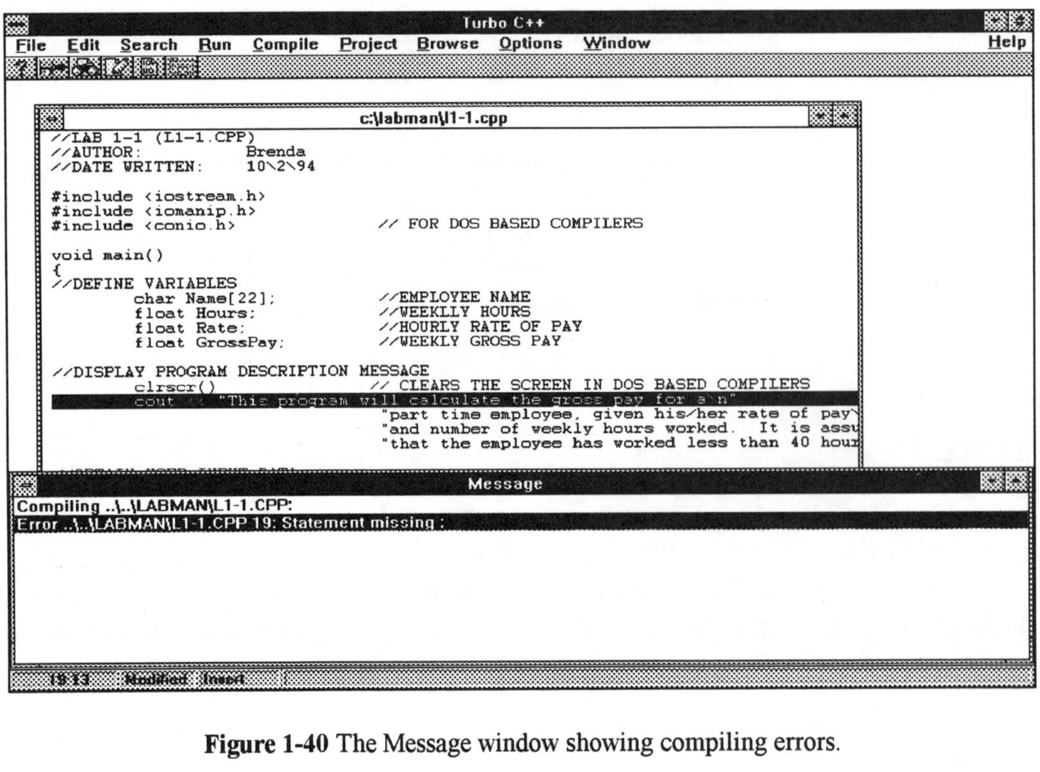

Figure 1-40 The Message window showing compiling errors.

TURBO C++ also offers Help windows with a more detailed explanation of a particular error. To activate a Help window, position the highlight bar on an error in the Error Message window, then press the [F1] key, or click the [?] button on the Speed bar. Once you read the help message, you must close the Help window to go on. To close the window when it is active, simply double-click the close button in the upper left corner of the Help window.

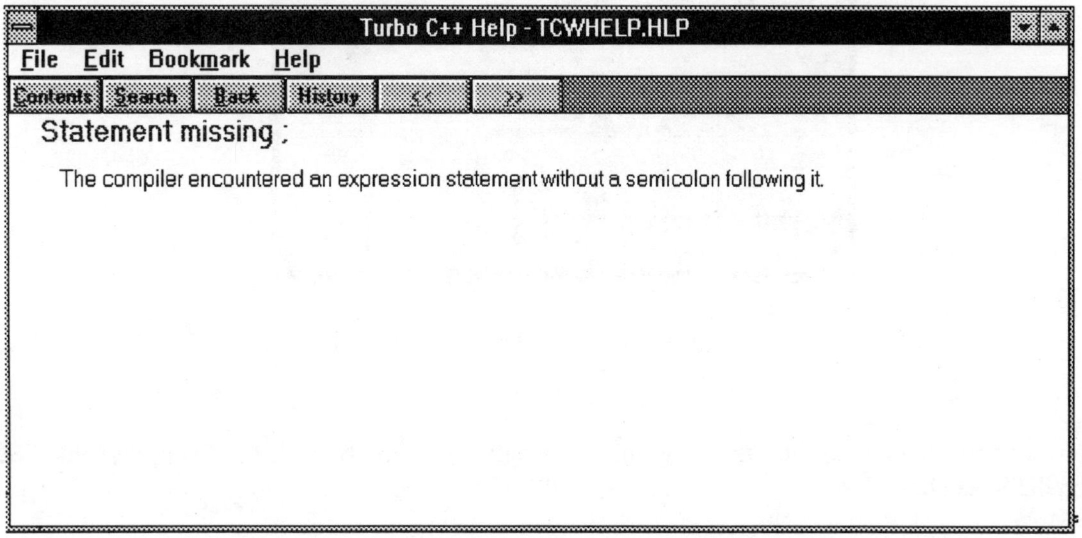

Figure 1-41 Error messages and **Help** window example.

Linking the Program

Once the program is successfully compiled, you need to link it. Linking the object file creates an executable (*.exe*) program that is a combination of all the files needed to run the program properly. Select the **Compile** menu from the Menu bar, then select the **Link** command from the pull down menu, as shown in Figure 1-42. The Hot Key combination for this action is [ALT] + [C] then [L].

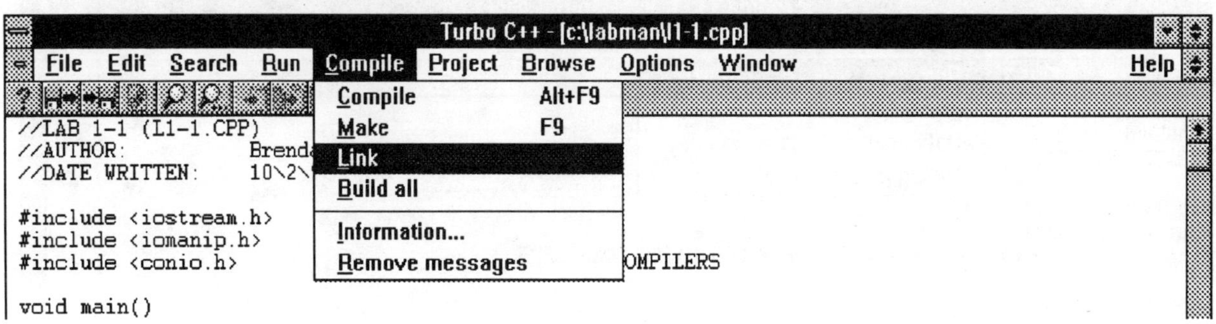

Figure 1-42 Choosing the **Link** command.

The compiler will link your object file and any needed C++ library files to produce an executable (*.exe*) file that is ready to run. See Figure 1-43 for a look at the TURBO C++ status box that is displayed while a program is linking.

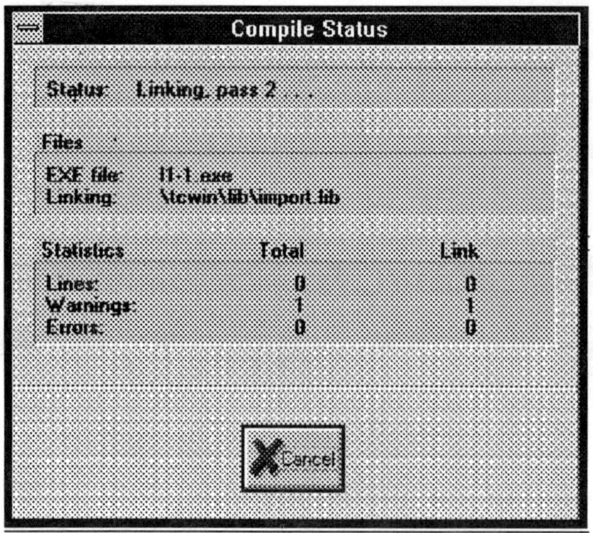

Figure 1-43 Linking a program.

If you want to compile and link the program in a single step, simply click the **Compile/Link** button on the Speed bar.

Running the Program

When the program is successfully compiled and linked, you can run it to make sure that it does what it is supposed to do. Select the **Run** menu from the Menu bar, then select the **Run** command from the pull down menu, as shown in Figure 1-44. The Hot Key combination of CTRL + F9 will also perform this action. By the way, pressing CTRL + F9 will also compile, link, and run the program from the Edit window, so that you don't have to do each step separately. Remember, these shortcuts are for the TURBO C++ IDE and the Command Set must be set to *Alternate* to use the Hot Keys in the Windows environment.

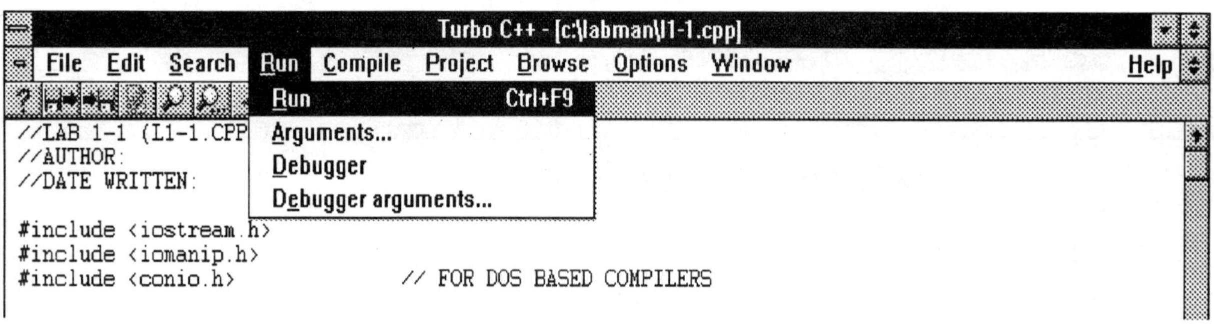

Figure 1-44 Choosing the **Run** command (CTRL + F9).

When you run the program, an Execution window is produced that allows you to interact with the program and shows the results of the program run.

Run the program and enter the information via the keyboard when prompted to do so. Sample output of the payroll program is shown in Figure 1-45. If your screen looks like Figure 1-45, congratulations, it worked!

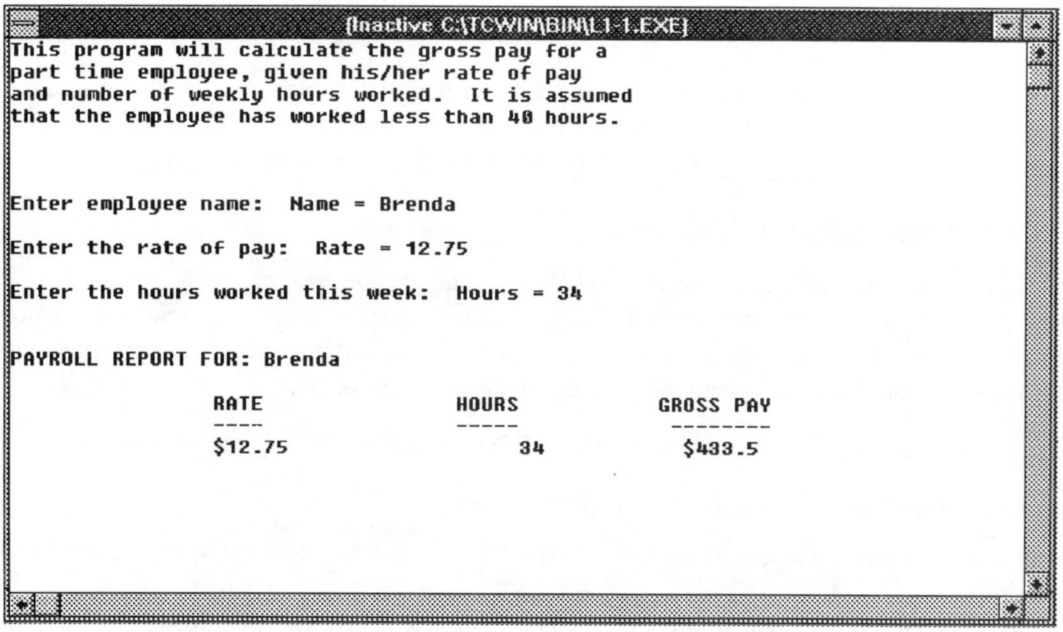

Figure 1-45 The Execution window showing the results of the payroll program.

Look at the program source code listing to answer the following questions.

What C++ statement is causing the program's messages to be displayed on the screen?

____

What C++ statement is causing the computer to wait for information to be entered?

____

What do you think the *\n* parts of the program code are doing?

____

What C++ statement is causing the *RATE*, *HOURS*, and *GROSS PAY* headers to be placed where they are on the screen?

____

Discussion:

As you run the program, the user messages are displayed on your screen with the *cout* << statements in the program and when input is needed the *cin* >> statements wait for you to enter information from the keyboard and then place the information into a specified variable. As you may have guessed, the *\n* part of the C++ code is causing the cursor to move to a new line for each *\n* entered in the program code. Output can be placed where you want it to be displayed by using the *setw()* statement. The *setw()* statement is used to place the *RATE*, *HOURS*, and *GROSS PAY* headers where they are on the screen.

Procedure:

After you run the program, you *must* close the Execution window before you can run the program again. To close the window when it is active, simply double-click the close button in the upper left corner. If another window is active, use ALT + (tab) to sequence to the Execution window then close it.

Test and Print Sample Runs of the Program

Run the program again with different values for the *Name, Rate,* and *Hours*.

Running the program several times with different input information is an important part of program testing. Printed copies of sample program runs are part of the documentation process in programming. To obtain these, you will need to have access to a printer. Make sure that the printer is on and on-line.

You can get a print-out of your sample runs in TURBO C++ for Windows by doing the following:

1. Make sure that the Execution window is displayed on the screen.
2. Maximize the Execution window by clicking on its maximize button in the upper right corner of the window.
3. Press the PRTSC key on the keyboard to place a copy of the screen on the clipboard.
4. Use ALT + (tab) to switch to the Program Manager.
5. Activate the Write program.
6. Place the copy of the screen print into the Write window by selecting **Edit | Paste** from the Menu bar in Write.
7. Print the screen print by selecting **File | Print** from the Menu bar in Write.
8. Close Write when you are finished printing. This releases the computer memory used by Write.
9. Switch back to TURBO C++

Print the Source Code

A printed copy of the program source code is also an important part of program documentation. Make sure that the printer is ready and then print the source code by selecting the **Print** command. In TURBO C++ **Print** is found in the **File** menu, as shown in Figure 1-46.

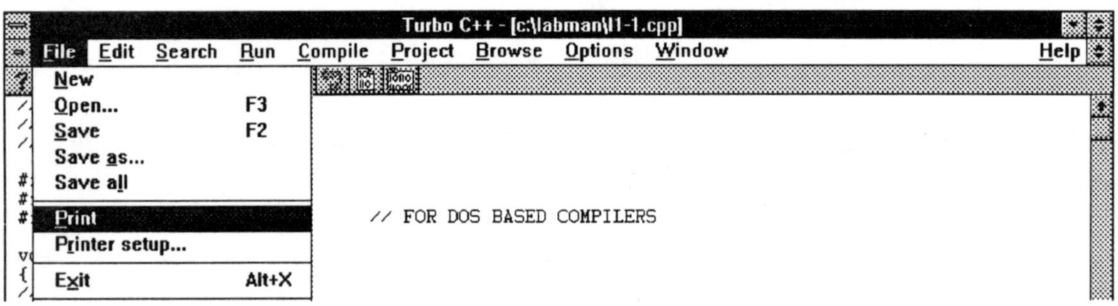

Figure 1-46 Selecting the **Print** command to print the current program in the Edit window.

Closing the File

When you are finished with a program file make sure that you have saved any final changes (F2) and then close the file. To close the file, simply double-click the close button in the upper left-hand corner of the active source file window. If you have several files active, you can close them all by selecting the **Window** menu and choosing the **Close All** command.

If you leave any file window open when you exit from TURBO C++, that file window will open when you start TURBO C++ again. So it is good programming practice to close a file window when you are finished with it.

Problem 2 - Credit Card Interest

In this problem you will create a problem definition for and use an algorithm for a credit card problem to calculate the interest on a credit card account balance. Then you will enter the code for the problem, compile, link, run, test, and print the program.

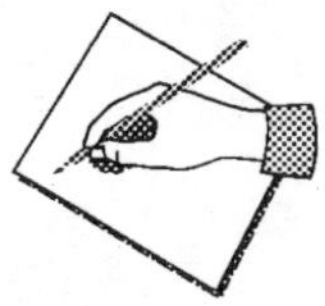

Pre-Lab

Read the following problem statement, complete the problem definition, and revise the algorithm that follows to use a single *If/Then/Else* operation in place of the two *If/Then* operations.

PROBLEM STATEMENT

The interest charged on a credit card account depends on the remaining balance according to the following criteria:

> Interest charged is 18 percent of the balance up to $500 and 15 percent of the balance for any amount over $500.

Define the problem and develop an algorithm to find the total amount of interest due on any given account balance.

Procedure & Questions:

PROBLEM DEFINITION

<u>*Output:*</u> What output is needed according to the problem statement?

____

<u>*Input:*</u> What input will be needed for processing to obtain the required output?

____

<u>*Processing:*</u> According to the criteria defined in the problem statement, the amount of interest is divided into two cases.

Case 1: What processing is required *if* the balance is less than or equal to $500?

____

Case 2: What processing is required *if* the Balance is greater than $500?

____

Discussion:

According to the problem statement, the output will be the total amount of interest due. The account balance is needed as input for processing. If the balance is less than or equal to $500, the balance must be multiplied by 0.18. If the balance is greater than $500, the first $500 must be multiplied by 0.18 and the portion of the balance that is over $500 must be multiplied by 0.15. See the following algorithm to help you understand the separate processing required to calculate the interest.

THE ALGORITHM

```
BEGIN
    Write a program description message to the user.
    Write a user-prompt to enter the account balance.
    Read (Balance).
    If Balance <= 500 Then
        Assign (0.18 × Balance) to Interest.
    If Balance > 500 Then
        Assign (0.18 × 500) + [0.15 × (Balance - 500)] to Interest.
    Write (Interest).
END.
```

Procedure:

Revise the algorithm for this problem to combine the two shaded *If/Then* operations into a single *If/Then/Else* operation.

BEGIN

END.

Discussion:

An *If/Then/Else* operation performs the statements that follow the *If* when the test condition is TRUE. The statements that follow the *Else* are performed when the test condition is FALSE. The *If/Then/Else* operation is a two-way selection process. The condition to test in this problem is whether the *Balance* is $500 or less. If this is FALSE, then the *Balance* is greater than $500. Since this condition is either TRUE or FALSE, the two *If/Then* operations from the previous algorithm can be written as:

If *Balance* <= 500 Then
    Assign (0.18 × *Balance*) to *Interest.*
Else
    Assign (0.18 × 500) + [0.15 × (*Balance* - 500)] to *Interest.*

This algorithm says that (0.18 × *Balance*) will be assigned to *Interest* if the *Balance* is less than or equal to $500; otherwise (0.18 × 500) + [0.15 × (*Balance* - 500)] will be assigned to *Interest.*

In-the-Lab 

Procedure & Discussion:

Open a New File

Open a new file for this program. You can select the **File** menu from the Menu bar then select the **New** command. If you are not using TURBO C++ locate the command for opening a new file and select it.

Enter the Program Code

Type the following program code into your C++ editor, being very careful to type the code exactly as shown.

```
// LAB 1-2 (L1-2.CPP)
// AUTHOR : type your name here
// DATE WRITTEN : type the date here

#include <iostream.h>
#include <iomanip.h>
#include <conio.h>              // FOR DOS BASED COMPILERS ONLY

void main()
{
// DECLARE CONSTANTS AND DEFINE VARIABLES
  float Interest;               // AMOUNT OF INTEREST
  float Balance;                // AMOUNT OF ACCOUNT BALANCE

// DISPLAY PROGRAM DESCRIPTION MESSAGE
  clrscr();                     // CLEARS THE SCREEN IN DOS BASED COMPILERS
  cout << "This program will calculate total interest due for a credit card account.\n\n\n";

// OBTAIN USER INPUT DATA
  cout <<"Enter the credit card account balance:  Balance = $ ";
  cin >> Balance;

// CALCULATE INTEREST
  if (Balance <= 500)
    Interest = 0.18 * Balance;
  else
    Interest = (0.18 * 500) + (0.15 * (Balance - 500));
```

```
// DISPLAY RESULTS
   cout << "\n\nThe total interest for the account balance of $ " << Balance
         << " is $ "<<Interest;
}
```

Save the Program

Remember, always save your program onto a disk once it has been entered. When you save a program for the first time, you will need to give it a file name. Give this program the name *L1-2.cpp*.

Compile the Program

Now that you have entered and saved the program, compile it. Locate and select the compile command in your programming environment.

Errors?

If there were any errors in the program, you will have to edit the program code to fix the errors. You will have to compile the program again before you can link and run it. Save the program again after you correct any errors.

Link the Program

Once the program is successfully compiled, you need to link it. Locate and select the link command in your compiler.

Running the Program

When the program is successfully compiled and linked, you can run and test it. Locate and select the run command in your programming environment. Enter a value for *Balance* when prompted to do so.

Discussion:

As you run the program, the user messages are displayed on your screen with the *cout* << statements in the program and when input is needed the *cin* >> statements wait for you to enter information from the keyboard. The *cin* >> statement assigns the information to the specified variable.

Procedure:

Check the Program Output

Check your program output. The output generated for an input *Balance* of $725 is shown in Figure 1-47.

For TURBO C++ users, you must check the User screen or Execution window. To do this in TURBO C++ for DOS, you can select the **Window** menu from the Menu bar and then select the **User screen** menu item from the pull down window. Or, you can use the Hot Key combination of ALT + F5 without having to access the Menu bar. From the DOS User screen, you can press any key to return to the TURBO C++ Edit window in the IDE. If you are using TURBO C++ for Windows, the Execution window appears after the program has run. You *must* close the Execution window before you can run the program again.

```
This program will calculate total interest due for a credit card account.

Enter the credit card account balance:  Balance = $ 725

The total interest for the account balance of $ 725 is $ 123.75
```

Figure 1-47 Sample output for the credit card program.

Test and Print Sample Runs of the Program

Run the program again with a different value for the *Balance*. Be sure to check the program output each time for correct results.

Get a print out of 3 sample program runs as follows:
- One with the *Balance* less than $500.
- One with the *Balance* equal to $500.
- One with the *Balance* greater than $500.

You get a print-out of your sample runs in *TURBO C++ for DOS* by doing the following:

1. Run the program ([CTRL] + [F9] in TURBO C++).
2. Input the appropriate information.
3. Switch to the User Screen ([ALT] + [F5] in TURBO C++).
4. Make sure that the printer is ready.
5. Press the **PRINT SCREEN** key on the keyboard.

You get a print-out of your sample runs in *TURBO C++ for Windows* by doing the following:

1. Make sure that the Execution window is displayed on the screen.
2. Maximize the Execution window by clicking on its maximize button in the upper right corner of the window.
3. Press the [PRTSC] key on the keyboard to place a copy of the screen on the clipboard.
4. Use [ALT] + [⇆] (tab) to switch to the Program Manager.
5. Activate the Write program.
6. Place the copy of the screen print into the Write window by selecting **Edit | Paste** from the Menu bar in Write.
7. Print the Screen print by selecting **File | Print** from the Menu bar in Write.
8. To free up computer memory, close Write when you are finished printing.
9. Switch back to TURBO C++

Print the Source Code

Get a print out of your source code.

Closing the File

When you are finished with a program file make sure that you have saved any final changes.

Exit Your C++ Compiler

Exit your compiler when you are finished with the lab exercises. If you are using TURBO C++, select the **File** menu from the Menu bar, then select the **Quit** command from the pull down menu. Or you can use the Hot Key combination of [ALT] + [X] without having to access the Menu bar.

Programming Steps Summary

The steps required to complete a C++ program are:

- Define the problem.
- Plan the solution with one or more related algorithms.
- Type the solution code into an editor, being sure to comment the code as you go.
- Save the program onto a disk.
- Compile the program.
- Correct any errors and save the program again.
- Link the program files.
- Run and test the program.
- Print the program source code and sample program runs.
- Close the program file when you are finished.

LAB PROJECT #2
Modifying a Program & Using a Debugger

Lab Objectives

In this lab, you will . . .

- Open an existing file.
- Modify the program code.
- Use the debugger in your C++ programming environment.
- Set program breakpoints and watches on variables.
- Step over and trace into the program code.

Introduction

In Problem 1 you will modify the problem definition and algorithm from Project #1, Problem 1 for the payroll problem. You will then open the program source code file, edit the C++ code, recompile, link, run, test, and print the modified program.

Bugs are errors in your program that are due to the incorrect use of the C++ language (syntax errors) or incorrect programming logic (logic errors). Removing these errors from your program is called *debugging*. There is no absolute correct procedure to debug a program, but a systematic approach can help make the process easier. The basic steps of debugging are:

1. Realizing that you have an error.
2. Locating the error.
3. Determining the cause of the error.
4. Fixing the error.

First of all you have to realize that you have an error. Sometimes, this is very obvious when your computer freezes up or crashes. At other times, the program might work fine until certain unexpected information is entered by someone using the program. The most subtle errors occur when the program is running fine and the results look correct, but when you examine the results closely, they are not quite right.

The next step in the debugging process is finding the error. Isolating the location of the error is sometimes the most difficult part of debugging.

Syntax errors will be found and displayed when you compile your program. These errors must be fixed before you are able to run and test your program. Your compiler's reference manual should contain a complete list of error messages and suggestions of how to fix the errors.

Logic errors are a little more difficult to find. Your program may be running fine and producing results, but if the results are not correct, the cause must be found. If you have used a structured, modular approach in writing your program, the job of finding the error will be easier.

A *debugger* is a software tool that allows you to step over functions that you know are working properly and trace into functions that you need to examine more closely as you run and test your program.

Finding the cause of the error is the next step in debugging. After finding the error, it is relatively easy to determine what is causing the program to not perform correctly. Using a watch window to monitor variables and display their changing values during debugging will help show you when the error occurs and what kind of input causes the program to misbehave.

Fixing the error is the final step in debugging. Knowing where the error is, your knowledge of the C++ language, your text, this lab manual, on-line help, the debugger, and the reference manuals are all valuable tools in fixing the error and removing the "bug" from your program.

In Problem 2 you will use a debugger to execute the program one line at a time. This will allow you to find program errors, watch the contents of the program variables and help you understand what the program statements are doing. A debugger is a very valuable tool in program development.

Problem 1 - Modifying the Payroll Problem

In this exercise you will modify the problem definition and algorithm from the payroll problem given in Project #1 so that it will calculate gross and net pay including the option for overtime pay for employees working more than 40 hours. You will then modify the C++ code to solve the expanded problem, recompile, link, run, test, and print the program.

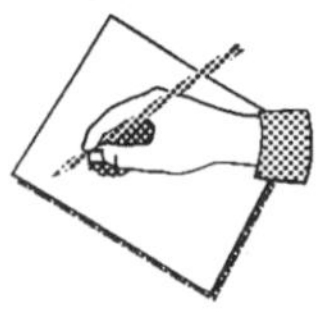

Pre-Lab

PROBLEM STATEMENT

Calculate and report the weekly gross and net pay for a full time employee, including the option for overtime hours at 1.5 times the regular pay rate. The net pay will be the gross pay minus deductions. The deductions for net pay in this problem will be 18 percent of the gross pay.

Procedure & Questions:

PROBLEM DEFINITION

Output: What output is needed according to the problem statement?

____

Input: What input will be needed for processing to obtain the required output?

____

Processing: According to the problem statement, there could be two cases for calculating the employee's gross pay depending on if the employee works 40 hours or less, or if the employee works more than 40 hours.

Case 1: What processing is required to calculate the gross pay if the employee worked 40 hours or less?

____

Case 2: What processing is required to calculate the gross pay if the employee worked more than 40 hours?

____

What processing is required to calculate the net pay if the deductions are 18% of the gross pay?

____

Discussion:

According to the problem statement the output will be a report of the employee's earnings. The employee name, pay rate, and hours worked are needed as input. To process the gross pay, you need to determine if the hours worked are 40 or less or if the hours worked are more than 40. If the hours worked are 40 or less, the gross pay is simply the pay rate multiplied by the hours worked. If the hours worked are more than 40, the gross pay is regular earnings plus overtime earnings. The regular earnings are the pay rate multiplied by 40 regular hours, and the overtime earnings are the hours over 40 multiplied by one and one-half times the pay rate. According to the problem statement, the net pay is the gross pay minus deductions. Deductions are gross pay multiplied by 0.18.

Procedure:

THE ALGORITHM

Modify the shaded portion of the following algorithm to include the input, output, and processing described in the problem definition. *Hint*: Use an *If/Then/Else* operation for the two cases of calculating gross pay.

BEGIN
  Write a program description message to the user.
  Write a user-prompt to enter the employee's name.
  Read (*Name*).
  Write a user-prompt to enter the employee's rate of pay.
  Read (*Rate*).
  Write a user-prompt to enter the employee's hours worked this week.
  Read (*Hours*).
  Assign (*Rate* × *Hours*) to *GrossPay*.
  Write (*Name*, *Rate*, *Hours*, *GrossPay*).
END.

BEGIN

END.

Discussion:

Does your algorithm look similar to the one below?

BEGIN
  Write a program description message to the user.
  Write a user-prompt to enter the employee's name.
  Read (*Name*).
  Write a user-prompt to enter the employee's rate of pay.
  Read (*Rate*).
  Write a user-prompt to enter the employee's hours worked this week.
  Read (*Hours*).
  If (*Hours <= 40)* then
    Assign (*Rate* × *Hours*) to *GrossPay*.
  Else
    Assign (*Rate* × 40) + [(*Hours* - 40) × (*Rate* × 1.5)] to *GrossPay*.
  Assign [*GrossPay* - (*GrossPay* × 0.18)] to *NetPay*.
  Write (*Name*, *Rate*, *Hours*, *GrossPay*, *NetPay*).
END.

In-the-Lab

Procedure & Discussion:

Start Your Compiler

Start your C++ program development environment.

Open the Program File

Open the program source code file for the payroll program, *L1-1.cpp*. If you are using TURBO C++, you can select the **File** menu from the Menu bar then select the **Open** command. Alternatively, you could use the TURBO C++ Hot Key, F3, to activate the **Open a file** dialog box. Move the highlight bar in the dialog box to the *L1-1.cpp* filename and press ENTER to select and open the file. If you are not using TURBO C++ locate the command for opening a program source code file and select it.

Make the following modifications to the payroll program into your C++ editor being very careful to enter the code exactly as shown. *Note*: The required modifications are shown on a shaded background in the following code.

```
// LAB 2-1 (L2-1.CPP)
// AUTHOR : type your name here
// DATE WRITTEN : type the date here

#include <iostream.h>
#include <iomanip.h>
#include <conio.h>          // FOR USERS OF DOS BASED C++ COMPILERS ONLY

void main()
```

```
{
// DEFINE VARIABLES
   char Name[22];          // EMPLOYEE NAME
   float Hours;            // WEEKLY HOURS WORKED
   float Rate;             // HOURLY RATE OF PAY
   float GrossPay;         // WEEKLY GROSS PAY
   float NetPay;           // WEEKLY NET PAY

// DISPLAY PROGRAM DESCRIPTION MESSAGE
   clrscr();               // FOR USERS OF DOS BASED C++ COMPILERS
   cout <<"This program will calculate and report \n"
          "the gross and net pay for an employee, \n"
          "given his/her rate of pay and \n"
          "number of weekly hours worked. \n\n\n\n";

// OBTAIN USER INPUT DATA
   cout << "Enter employee name:  Name =  ";
   cin.getline(Name,22);
   cout << "\nEnter the rate of pay:  Rate = $";
   cin >> Rate;
   cout << "\nEnter the hours worked this week:  Hours = ";
   cin >> Hours;

// CALCULATE EMPLOYEES GROSS PAY
   if (Hours <= 40)
     GrossPay = Rate * Hours;
   else
     GrossPay = (Rate * 40) + ((Hours - 40) * (Rate * 1.5));

// CALCULATE EMPLOYEES NET PAY
   NetPay = (GrossPay - (GrossPay * 0.18));

// GENERATE OUTPUT TABLE
   cout << "\n\nPAYROLL REPORT FOR: " << Name;
   cout << "\n\n" << setw(10) << "RATE" << setw(20) << "HOURS"
        << setw(20) << "GROSS PAY" <<setw(20) << "NET PAY";
   cout << "\n\n" << setw(7) << "$" << Rate << setw(18) << Hours
        << setw(15) << "$" << setprecision(2) << GrossPay
        << setw(15) << "$"  << NetPay ;
}
```

Save the Program with a New Name

After you have made the necessary modifications to the source code, you need to save the program again. Since this program solves a different problem than *L1-1.cpp*, name this one *L2-1.cpp.* Saving the program with a new name can be done in TURBO C++ by selecting the **File** menu from the Menu bar, then selecting the **Save as . . .** command from the pull down menu.

Compile the Program

Now that you have modified and saved the program, compile it.

Errors?

If there were any errors in the program, the errors message will be displayed. You will have to edit the program code to fix the errors then compile the program again before you can link and run the program. Be sure to save the program again after you correct any errors.

Link the Program

Once the program is successfully compiled, you need to link it with the C++ library files needed by the program.

Run the Program

When the program is successfully compiled and linked, you can run it to make sure that it does what it is supposed to do. Enter the required information as you run the program.

Check the Program Output

Examine the program output. A sample output is shown in Figure 2-1.

```
This program will calculate and report
the gross and net pay for an employee,
given his/her rate of pay and
number of weekly hours worked.


Enter employee name:  Name = Jason

Enter the rate of pay:  Rate = $9.45

Enter the hours worked this week:  Hours = 43

PAYROLL REPORT FOR: Jason
      RATE              HOURS               GROSS PAY              NETPAY
      $9.45               43                 $420.52               $344.83
```

Figure 2-1 Sample output generated by the new payroll program.

Test and Print Sample Runs of the Program

Running the program several times with different input information is an important part of testing. To obtain printed copies of program runs, you will need to have access to a printer. Make sure that the printer is on and on line.

Print 3 different sample program runs as follows:
- One with the employee working less than 40 hours per week.
- One with the employee working 40 hours.
- One with the employee working more than 40 hours.

Print the Source Code

Get a printed copy of your source code for program documentation.

Leave the program file open and go on to **Problem 2 - Using a Debugger.**

Problem 2 - Using a Debugger (TURBO C++ Users Only)

In this exercise you will use a debugger to single step the execution of the payroll program code in Problem 1. You will also watch the contents of the variable expressions to see when the input information is placed in them.

The examples and screen prints in this problem are from the TURBO C++ integrated debugger. An integrated debugger is one that is available within the program development environment. If you are not using TURBO C++, you may not have access to an integrated debugger. There are stand alone debuggers that can be used to single step the execution of your program code and watch the contents of the variable expressions. Check with your instructor or lab supervisor to find out about the debugger in your computer lab.

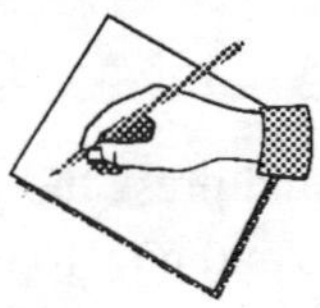

Pre-Lab

If you have completed Problem 1, then you are ready to begin the In-the-Lab section in this exercise. If not, then you need to return to Problem 1 and complete it before continuing.

In-the-Lab

Procedure & Discussion:

Using the Debugger

The debugger is one of the best tools to deal with bugs, or errors, that creep into your programs. An integrated debugger, such as the one in TURBO C++, allows you to do source-level debugging without leaving the convenience of the Integrated Development Environment. It helps with the two hardest parts of debugging: finding the error and finding the cause of the error. It does this by allowing you to *trace* into your programs and their functions one step at a time. This slows down the program execution so that you can examine the contents of the individual data elements and program output at any given point in the program. You can also set *breakpoints* that allow you to run your program up to the place where you have determined that an error has occurred, then step through and inspect the portion of the program that isn't producing correct results.

The rest of this lab is divided into two parts: one for TURBO C++ for DOS beginning on page 45 and one for TURBO C++ for Windows beginning on page 52. Refer to the respective section that most closely matches your programming environment.

TURBO C++ for DOS

If you are using TURBO C++ for Windows, skip to the section in this project for TURBO C++ for Windows.

The commands for the TURBO C++ for DOS debugging features are found in the **Debug** and **Run** menus on the Menu bar, as shown in Figure 2-2.

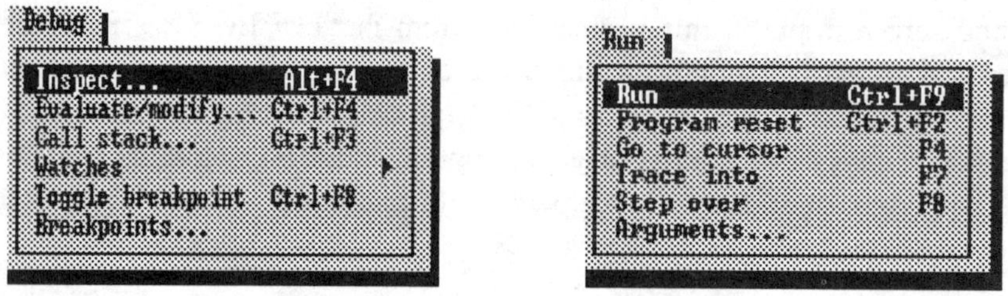

Figure 2-2 The **Debug** and **Run** menus.

It would be a good idea to highlight the commands on these menus and press the F1 key to activate the on-line help feature and read the description of what these commands do and how to use them.

You will use the payroll program from Problem 1 to demonstrate the use of the **Watch** window, single step through program execution, reset the program, and set a breakpoint. Open program *L2-1.cpp* at this time, if it is not already opened.

Using the Watch Window

Watch windows allow you to view the contents of variable expressions that you want to examine closely. This allows you to see what is happening inside of your program as it executes.

To open a **Watch** window and add a variable expression to examine, select the **Watches** item from the **Debug** menu, then select the **Add watch ...** command from the sub-menu, as shown in Figure 2-3, or press the Hot Key combination of CTRL + F7 .

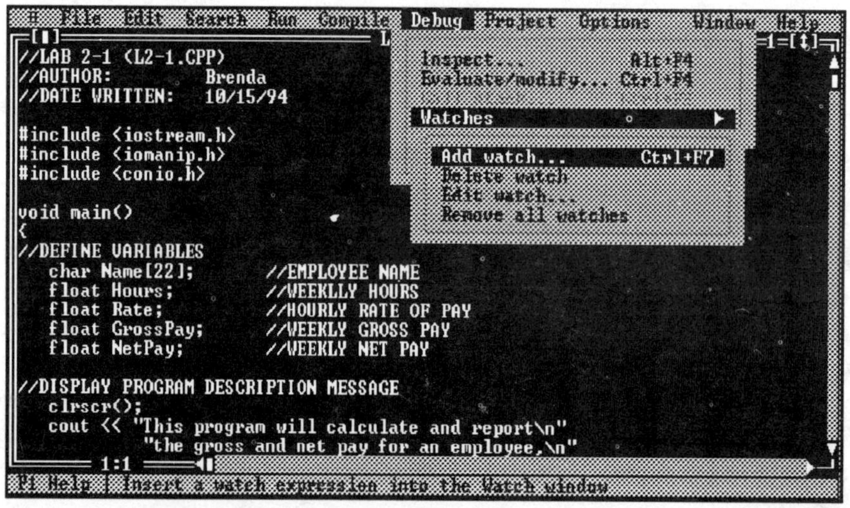

Figure 2-3 Adding a **Watch** window.

Figure 2-4 shows the **Add Watch** Dialog box that allows you to type in the name of the variable expression to watch. Be very careful that you enter the variable name *exactly* as it is in the program code. C++ is case-sensitive, so upper- or lowercase does matter.

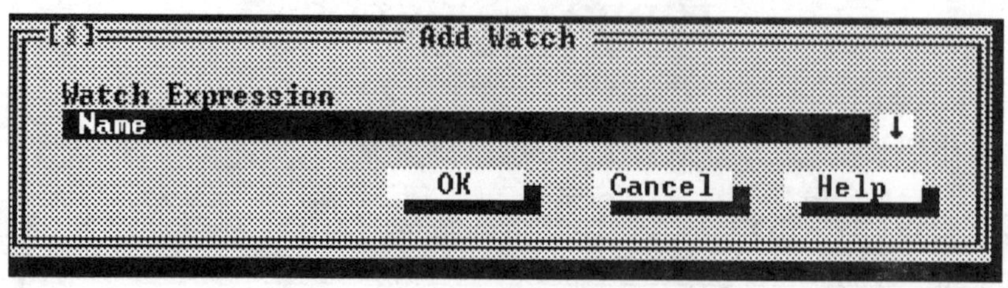

Figure 2-4 Adding a variable expression to watch.

In this exercise, you will watch *Name, Rate, Hours, GrossPay,* and *NetPay*. Type *Name* in the **Watch Expression** input box. Click **OK** or press [ENTER] to add the specified expression to the **Watch** window. Add *Rate, Hours, GrossPay,* and *NetPay* to the **Watch** window the same way.
Since only one window is active at a time in TURBO C++, it is a good idea to tile the windows so that you can view the program in the **Edit** window and the variable expressions in the **Watch** window. Select the **Tile** command from the **Window** menu, as shown in Figure 2-5.

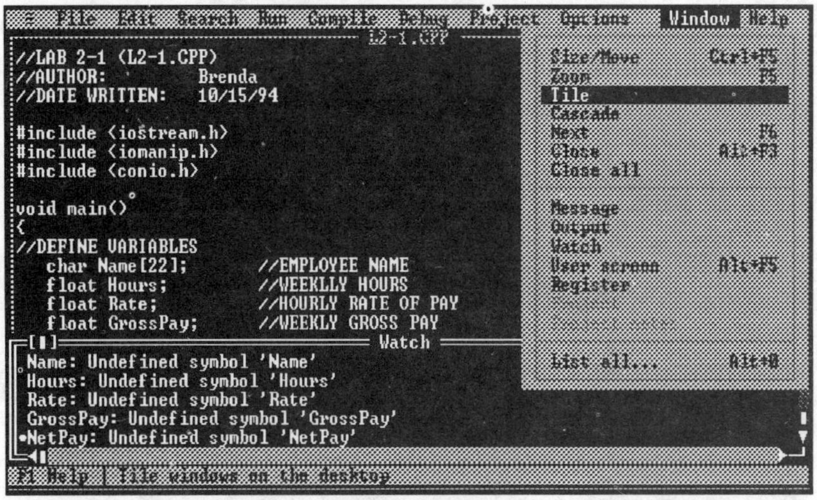

Figure 2-5 Choosing the **Tile** command.

The windows are shown tiled in Figure 2-6. Notice that before the debugger is activated, the message in the **Watch** window shows that the variables are undefined. A variable is not recognized until after it has been declared within the program execution.

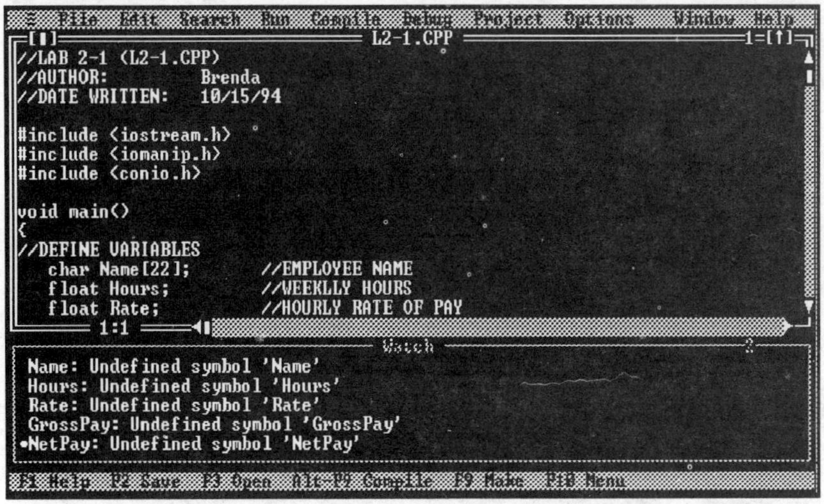

Figure 2-6 The **Edit** and **Watch** windows tiled.

There are now two windows open and only one of them can be active at a time. To switch between them, you can use the short cut of holding the **Alt** key down and pressing the number of the window you want to make active. For example, if the **Watch** window is active and you want to switch to the **Edit** window, you can press [ALT] +[1] (assuming that the number is the upper right corner of the **Edit** window is **1**). The **Edit** window must be active to continue with the next section.

Single Stepping and Tracing

There are two options for single stepping the program execution, **Trace into** F7 and **Step over** F8. **Trace into** single steps and executes each statement of your program, including all of the functions and include files that your program calls. This method may be needed when you have isolated the portion of the program or function that contains an error. To **Trace into** functions, press the F7 key for each statement of code to execute. **Step over** traces the high-level flow of your program by single stepping and executing each statement of code in function *main()*, stepping over the details of the other functions. To **Step over** functions, press the F8 key for each statement of code to execute. The **Step over** and **Trace into** commands are in the **Run** menu as shown in Figure 2-7.

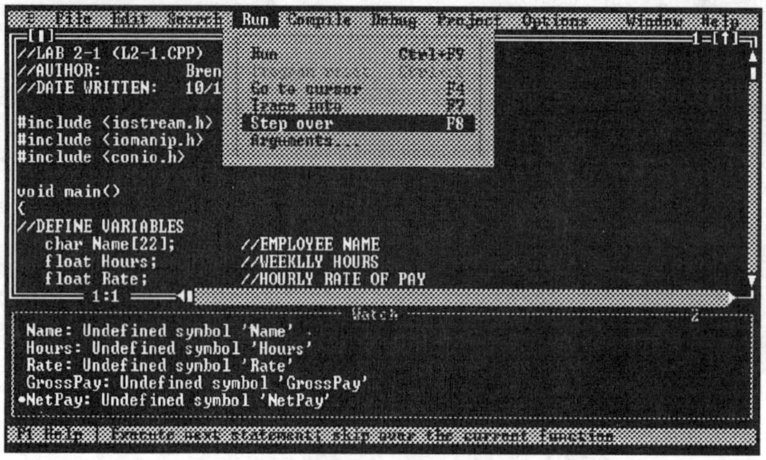

Figure 2-7 Choosing **Step over (F8)**

Press F8 at this time to start single stepping through the program.

After selecting **Step over** F8, the highlighted run bar is positioned at the beginning of function *main()* in the **Edit** window. This marks the execution position, as shown in Figure 2-8, indicating the *next* statement to be executed.

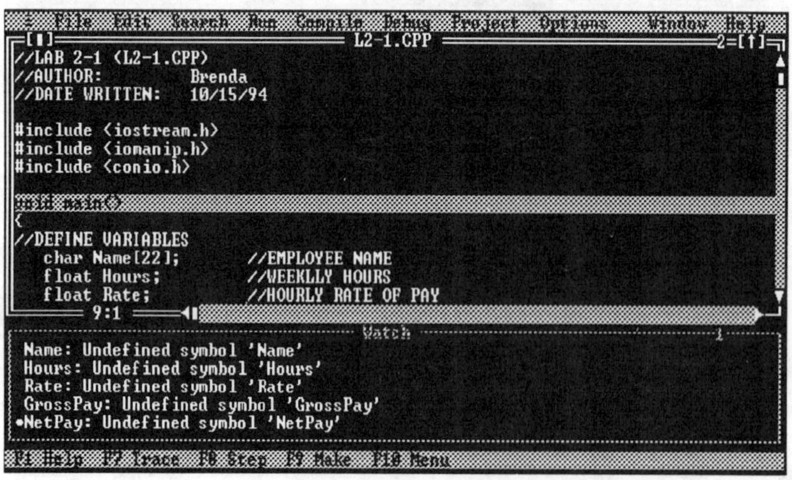

Figure 2-8 The Run bar positioned at function *main()*.

Press [F8] enough times to execute the statements of code and to bring the highlighted run bar to the *cin.getline (Name,22);* statement shown in Figure 2-9. Before pressing [F8] to execute this statement, notice that the message in the **Watch** window now shows that the variable *Name* is defined and contains garbage. Now, press [F8] again to execute the *cin.getline* statement.

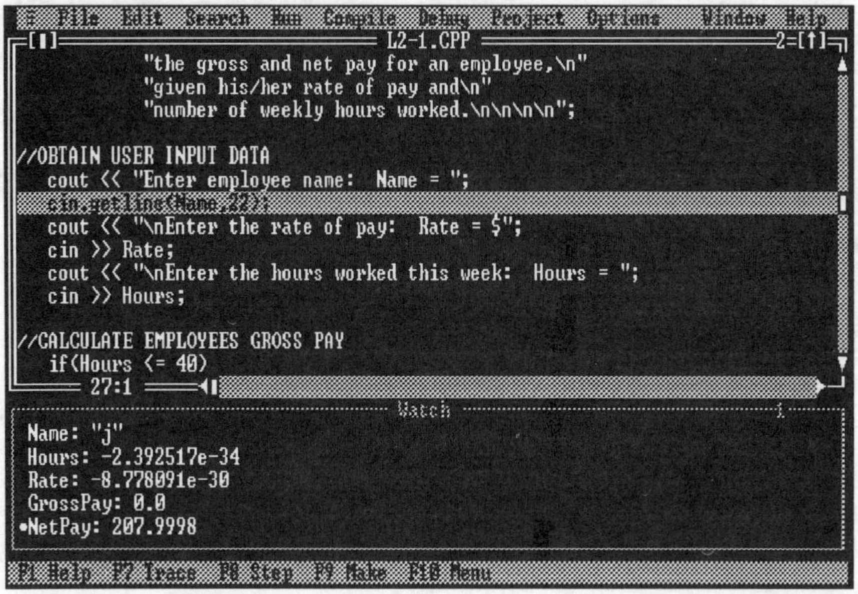

Figure 2-9 Ready to execute the *cin.getline* statement.

Figure 2-10 shows the User screen that is displayed after pressing [F8] to execute the *cin.getline* statement. Control is passed to the User screen to accept input into the variable *Name*.

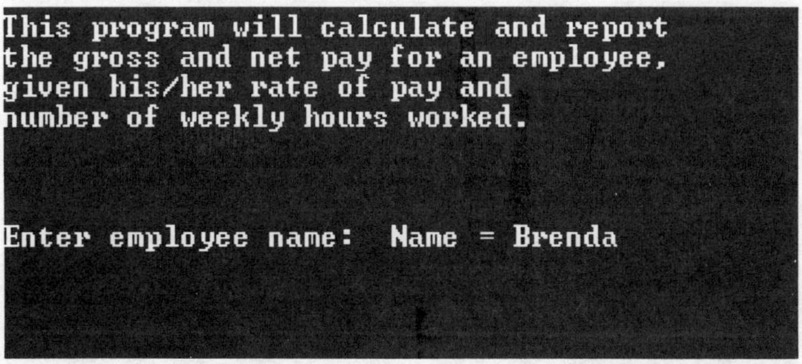

Figure 2-10 The *cin.getline* User screen.

Type in your name and press [ENTER]. After typing your name and pressing the [ENTER] key, you are returned to the **Edit** window and the run bar is on the next statement ready to execute it, as shown in Figure 2-11.

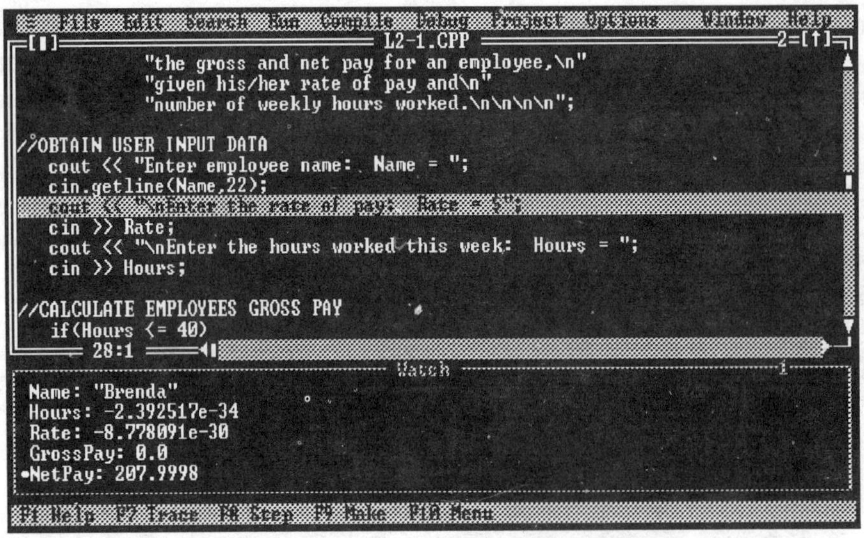

Figure 2-11 Ready to execute the *cout* statement.

Notice that the message in the **Watch** window now shows that the contents of the *Name* variable is the name you entered from the User screen. This means that this portion of the program is working correctly. If the contents of *Name* did not match what was entered, you would know that there was an error, or bug, at this point. Always check to make sure that the variable contents are what you expect them to be when debugging your programs.

Press [F8] again to execute the *cout* statement.

Continue executing the lines of the program using the **Step over** command ([F8]). Observe the variables in the **Watch** window.

Discussion:

Resetting the Program

There may be times that you need to start single stepping a program from the beginning before you have reached the end. The **Program reset** ([CTRL] + [F2]) command in the **Run** menu will reposition the run bar back at the beginning of the program for you, as shown in Figure 2-12.

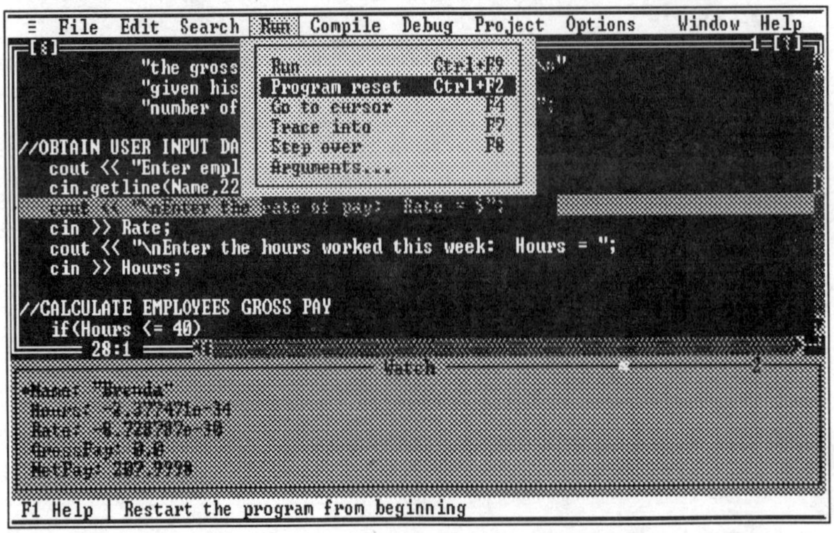

Figure 2-12 Resetting the program ([CTRL] + [F2]).

Setting a Breakpoint

If you have determined that your program is running correctly up to a certain point, a breakpoint can be set so that you can run the program and then start single stepping at the portion of the program that needs closer inspection. A breakpoint is a place in your program where you want execution to stop, or "break". To set a breakpoint, move the cursor to the line of code where you want execution to stop, then select the **Toggle breakpoint** command in the **Debug** menu, as shown in Figure 2-13, or press the CTRL + F8 Hot Key Combination.

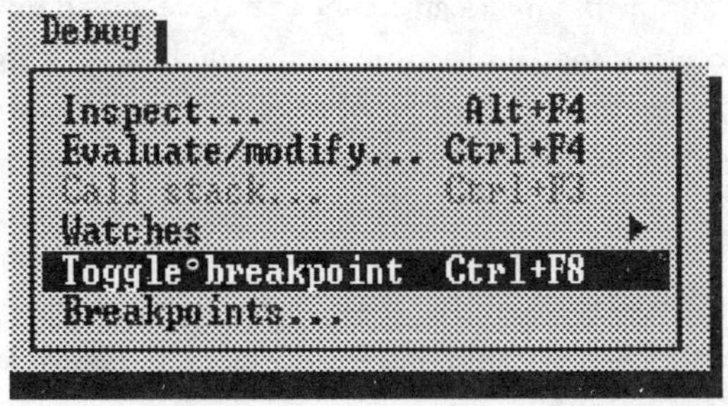

Figure 2-13 Setting a breakpoint (CTRL + F8)

A breakpoint bar, like the one shown in Figure 2-14, will be placed on the line where the cursor is currently located in the program. Once a breakpoint is set, running the program (CTRL + F9) will cause the program to stop executing at the breakpoint and return you to the debugger. At this point you can single step the remainder of the program allowing you to inspect the execution of each statement.

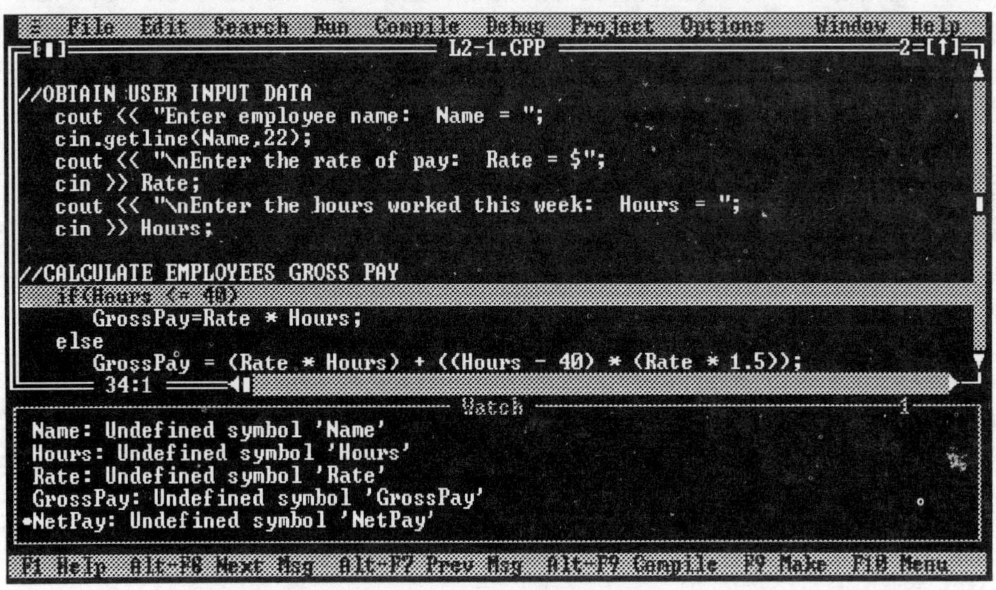

Figure 2-14 The breakpoint position.

Procedure & Discussion:

1. Reset the program (CTRL + F2).
2. Move the cursor to the *if (Hours <= 40)* line in the program code and set a breakpoint (CTRL + F8).
3. Run the program (CTRL + F9).
4. When the program stops at the breakpoint, single step (F8) the remainder of the program observing the execution of the *If/Else* statements.

A breakpoint can be removed by placing the cursor on the line where the breakpoint is located and pressing CTRL + F8 again, since CTRL + F8 toggles a breakpoint on or off.

5. Remove the breakpoint from your program. Position the cursor on the *if (Hours <= 40)* line in the program code and press CTRL + F8 to remove the breakpoint.

Close the File

When you are finished with a program file make sure that you have saved any final changes (F2) and then close the file. The fastest way to close the file is to make the window to close active (ALT + the # of the window) and then use the Hot Key combination of ALT + F3 to close the window. Clicking the Close Box in the upper left corner of the window will also close the window.

Exit your Compiler

Exit your compiler when you are finished with the lab exercises. The fastest way to exit TURBO C++ is to use the Hot Key combination of ALT + X.

TURBO C++ for Windows

If you are using TURBO C++ for Windows, continue from this point to the end of the lab project.

You will use the payroll program from Problem 1 to demonstrate the use of the **Watch** window, single step through program execution, reset the program, and set a breakpoint. Open program *L2-1.cpp* at this time, if it is not already opened.

Starting the Debugger

To start the debugger, select the **Run** menu on the Menu bar and click on the **Debugger** option. TURBO C++ will compile your program and load the debugger. Notice that your program source code appears in a **Module** window at the top of the screen and a **Watch** window appears at the bottom of the screen. In particular, notice that an *execution pointer* appears on the left side of the **Module** window and is pointing to function *main()*. The execution pointer locates the *next* program statement to be executed. Thus, function *main()* is ready to be executed.

You see the main Menu bar at the top of the debugger window. When using the debugger for the first time, it would be a good idea to highlight each of the commands in these menus and press the F1 key to activate the on-line help feature. Read the description of what these commands do and how to use them.

Using the Watch Window

Watch windows allow you to view the contents of variable expressions that you want to examine closely. This allows you to see what is happening inside of your program as it executes.

To open a **Watch** window and add a variable expression to examine, select the **Data** menu, then select the **Add watch ...** command from the sub-menu, or press the Hot Key combination of CTRL + F7.

The **Add Watch** dialog box allows you to type in the name of the variable expression to watch. Be very careful that you enter the variable name *exactly* as it is in the program code. C++ is case-sensitive, so upper- or lowercase does matter.

In this exercise, you will watch *Name, Rate, Hours, GrossPay,* and *NetPay*. Type *Name* in the **Watch Expression** input box. Click **OK** or press [ENTER] to add the specified expression to the **Watch** window. Add *Rate, Hours, GrossPay,* and *NetPay* to the **Watch** window the same way.

Notice that before the debugger is activated, the message in the **Watch** window shows that the variables are undefined. The debugger doesn't recognize a variable until after it has been declared within the program execution.

There are now two windows open and only one of them can be active at a time. To switch between them, you can use the short cut of holding the **Alt** key down and pressing the number of the window you want to make active. For example, if the **Watch** window is active and you want to switch to the **Module** window, you can press [ALT] + [1] (assuming that the number is the upper right corner of the **Module** window is **1**). Another way to switch between windows is to click in the window. The **Module** window must be active to continue with the next section.

If the **Watch** window is not big enough to view the variable expressions, re-size it by selecting the **Size/Move** command in the **Window** menu. Use the arrow keys to size the window and press [ENTER] to finish the process.

Single Stepping and Tracing

There are two options for single stepping the program execution, **Trace into** [F7] and **Step over** [F8]. **Trace into** single steps and executes each statement of your program, including all of the functions and include files that your program calls. This method may be needed when you have isolated the portion of the program or function that contains an error. To **Trace into** functions, press the [F7] key for each statement of code to execute. **Step over** traces the high-level flow of your program by single stepping and executing each statement of code in function *main()*, stepping over the details of the other functions. To **Step over** functions, press the [F8] key for each statement of code to execute.

Press [F8] at this time to start single stepping through the program.

After selecting **Step over** [F8], the execution pointer is positioned at the *clrscr();* statement in the **Module** window. This marks the execution position indicating the *next* statement to be executed.

Press [F8] enough times to execute the statements of code and to bring the execution pointer to the *cin.getline (Name,22);* statement. Before pressing [F8] to execute this statement, notice that the message in the **Watch** window now shows that the variable *Name* is defined and contains garbage. Now, press [F8] again to execute the *cin.getline* statement.

The Execution window is displayed after pressing [F8] to execute the *cin.getline* statement. Control is passed to the Execution window to accept input into the variable *Name*.

Type in your name and press [ENTER]. After typing your name and pressing the [ENTER] key, you are returned to the debugger **Module** window and the execution pointer indicates that the next statement is ready to execute.

Notice that the message in the **Watch** window now shows that the contents of the *Name* variable is the name you entered from the Execution window. This means that this portion of the program is working correctly. If the contents of *Name* did not match what was entered, you would know that there was an error, or bug, at this point. Always check to make sure that the variable contents are what you expect them to be when debugging your programs.

Press [F8] again to execute the *cout* statement.

Continue executing the lines of the program using the **Step over** command ([F8]). Observe the variables in the **Watch** window. A final Execution window is displayed when you reach the end of the program. At this point, you must close the Execution window to return to the debugger. Double-click the close button in the upper left corner of the Execution window and a dialog box will appear. Click **OK** to return to the debugger. To terminate the debugger at any time, select the **Quit** option in the **File** menu or use the ALT + X Hot Key combination. Finish the rest of the lab exercise before exiting from the debugger.

<u>**Resetting the Program**</u>

There may be times that you need to start single stepping a program from the beginning before you have reached the end. The **Program reset (CTRL + F2)** command in the **Run** menu will reposition the execution pointer back at the beginning of the program.

<u>**Setting a Breakpoint**</u>

If you have determined that your program is running correctly up to a certain point, a breakpoint can be set so that you can run the program and then start single stepping at the portion of the program that needs closer inspection. A breakpoint is a place in your program where you want execution to stop, or "break". To set a breakpoint, move the cursor to the line of code where you want execution to stop, then select the **Toggle breakpoint** command in the **Breakpoints** menu, or press the F2 Hot Key.

A breakpoint bar will be placed on the line where the cursor is currently located in the program. Once a breakpoint is set, running the program (F9) will cause the program to stop executing at the breakpoint. At this point you can single step the remainder of the program.

Procedure & Discussion:

1. Reset the program (CTRL + F2).
2. Move the cursor to the *if (Hours <= 40)* line in the program code and set a breakpoint (F2).
3. Run the program (F9).
4. When the program stops at the breakpoint, single step (F8) the remainder of the program observing the execution of the *If/Else* statements.

A breakpoint can be removed by placing the cursor on the line where the breakpoint is located and pressing F2 again, since F2 toggles a breakpoint on or off.

5. Remove the breakpoint from your program. Position the cursor on the *if (Hours <= 40)* line in the program code and press F2 to remove the breakpoint.

<u>**Exit the Debugger**</u>

When you have finished debugging in TURBO C++ for Windows, you must exit the debugger. Select the **Quit** option in the **File** menu or use the ALT + X Hot Key combination.

<u>**Close the File**</u>

When you are finished with a program file make sure that you have saved any final changes (F2) and then close the file. The fastest way to close the file is to make the window to close active (ALT + the # of the window) and then use the Hot Key combination of ALT + F3 to close the window. Clicking the Close Box in the upper left corner of the window will also close the window.

<u>**Exit your Compiler**</u>

Exit your compiler when you are finished with the lab exercises. The fastest way to exit TURBO C++ is to use the Hot Key combination of ALT + X.

LAB PROJECT #3
Getting Things In and Out

Lab Objectives

In this lab, you will . . .

- Generate output messages on the display monitor.
- Obtain input from the keyboard.
- Use special codes to format and manipulate program output.

Introduction

In this project you will be displaying information on the display monitor. Generating output from your program is called ***writing***. In C++ you will use the *cout* << statement for displaying information. You will also be accepting input from the keyboard. Accepting input into your program is called ***reading.*** You will use the *cin* >> statement for program input. The *iostream.h* header file must be included in your program to use the *cin* >> and *cout* << statements.

The ***I/O manipulators*** listed in Table 3-1 and ***escape sequences*** listed in Table 3-2 are used with the *cout* << statement to format your output. To use the I/O manipulators in Table 3-1, you must include the *iomanip.h* header file in your program. To use the escape sequences in Table 3-2, you must included the *iostream.h* header file which, of course, must be included to use the *cout* << object.

TABLE 3-1 I/O STREAM MANIPULATORS FOR C++

Manipulator	**Action**
setw(*n*)	Set field width to *n.*
setprecision(*n*)	Set floating point precision to *n*.
setfill(*n*)	Set fill character to *n.*
dec	Decimal output.
hex	Hexadecimal output.
oct	Octal output.
ws	Extract whitespace characters.
endl	Inserts a new line in the output stream then flushes the output stream.
ends	Adds a null terminator to the output stream.
flush	Flushes the output stream.

Any of the manipulators in Table 3-1 can be inserted in the *cout* << statement just like any other output item.

TABLE 3-2 ESCAPE SEQUENCES DEFINED FOR C++

Sequence	Action
\a	Bell
\b	Backspace
\f	Formfeed
\n	CRLF
\r	CR
\t	Horizontal Tab
\v	Vertical Tab
\\	Backslash
\’	Single quote
\”	Double quote
\?	Question mark
\O	O = a string of up to three octal digits
\xH	H = a string of hex digits

To use any of the escape sequences, simply include it as part of a string or enclose it within single quotes in the output stream in your program. Each escape sequence is treated as a separate character by the compiler.

In Problem 1 you will develop a problem definition and algorithm to calculate simple interest on a loan.

In Problem 2 you will develop a problem definition, algorithm, and user friendly C++ program to obtain test scores from the keyboard and calculate the average of the test scores.

In both problems, you will write the source code program that produces a formatted output. You will compile, link, run, test, and print your program.

Problem 1 - Loan Interest Report

In this exercise you will develop a problem definition and algorithm to calculate simple interest on a loan. You will then write the source code program that produces a formatted output. You will compile, link, run, test, and print your program.

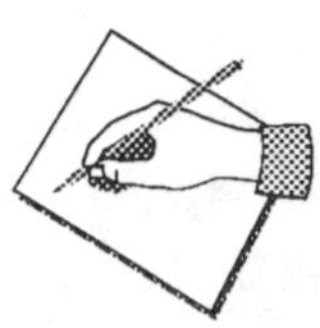

Pre-Lab

PROBLEM STATEMENT

Write a program to calculate simple interest on a $2,000 loan for a term of two years at a rate of 12.5 percent. Format your output appropriately, showing the amount of the loan, the term, interest rate, and interest amount.

Procedure & Questions:

PROBLEM DEFINITION

Output: What output is needed according to the problem statement?

____

Input: What input will be needed for processing to obtain the required output?

____

Will the program user be required to enter the input or can you hard-code the needed input as constant amounts?

____

Processing: What processing is required to calculate the loan interest?

____

Discussion:

According to the problem statement the output will be a formatted report showing the amount of the loan, the term, interest rate, and interest amount. The amount of the loan, the term, and interest rate are needed as input. These items can be hard-coded into the program as constants. To calculate the loan interest, you need to multiply the loan amount by the rate and by the term.

Procedure:

THE ALGORITHM

Write an algorithm to include the input, output, and processing that you developed in the problem definition.

BEGIN

END.

In-the-Lab 

Procedure & Discussion:

Start Your Compiler

Start your C++ program development environment.

Open a new File

Make sure that a new file is open.

Enter the Source Code

Using the algorithm that you developed, complete the following program shell for the loan interest program.

```
// LAB 3-1 (L3-1.CPP)
// AUTHOR : type your name here
// DATE WRITTEN : type the date here

#include <iostream.h>
#include <iomanip.h>
#include <conio.h>                    // FOR USERS OF DOS BASED C++ COMPILERS ONLY

void main()
{
// DEFINE VARIABLES




// DISPLAY PROGRAM DESCRIPTION MESSAGE
  clrscr();                           // FOR USERS OF DOS BASED C++ COMPILERS




// CALCULATE INTEREST




// DISPLAY RESULT TABLE




}
```

Save the Program

After you have entered the source code, you need to save the program. Name this program *L3-1.cpp*.

Compile the Program

Now that you have entered and saved the program, compile it.

Errors?

If there were any errors in the program you will have to edit the program code to fix the errors then compile the program again before you can link and run the program. Be sure to save the program again after you correct any errors.

Link the Program

Once the program is successfully compiled, you need to link it with the C++ library files needed by the program.

Run the Program

When the program is successfully compiled and linked, run it to make sure that it does what it is supposed to do.

Check the Program Output

A sample output of the loan interest program is shown in Figure 3-1. If your output does not look similar to the one shown in Figure 3-1, edit your program code so that you obtain the correct output. You may need to adjust the *setw()* statements or *setprecision()* statements.

```
This program will calculate simple interest.

      LOAN       TERM        INTEREST RATE    INTEREST AMOUNT
      ----       ----        -------------    ---------------

     $2000       2 YR.           12.5%             $500
```

Figure 3-1 Sample output for the loan interest program.

Test and Print a Sample Run of the Program

Get a print-out of the program run.

Print the Source Code

Get a print-out of the program source code. A printed copy of the program source code is also an important part of program documentation.

Close the File

When you are finished with the program file make sure that you have saved any final changes and then close the file.

Problem 2 - Test Scores and Average

In this exercise you will develop a problem definition and algorithm to accept a student name, course name, and test scores from the program user. You will calculate the test average, and generate a report of the student name, course, test scores, and test average. You will then write the source code program that produces a formatted output. You will compile, link, run, test, and print your program.

Pre-Lab

PROBLEM STATEMENT

Write a user-friendly program that will allow a student to enter his/her name, course, and calculate the test average from *four* test scores. Generate a display of the student's name, course name, individual test scores, and test average.

Procedure & Questions:

PROBLEM DEFINITION

Output: What output is needed according to the problem statement?

____

Input: What input will be needed for processing to obtain the required output?

____

Will the program user be required to enter the input or can you hard-code the needed input as constant amounts?

____

Processing: What processing is required to calculate the test average?

____

Discussion:

According to the problem statement, the output will be a formatted report showing the student's name, course name, individual test scores, and test average. The student's name, course name, and test scores are needed as input. These items can *not* be hard-coded into the program as constants and must be accepted as variable input from the keyboard. To calculate the test average, you need to add the test scores and divide by 4.

Procedure:

THE ALGORITHM

Write a step-by-step algorithm using the input, output, and processing that you developed in the problem definition.

BEGIN

END.

In-the-Lab

Procedure & Discussion:

Start Your Compiler

Start your C++ program development environment.

Open a new File

Make sure that a new file is open.

Enter the Source Code

Using the algorithm that you developed, complete the following program shell for the test average program. *Note*: The *cin.getline()*, *gets()*, or *fgets()* statements should be used to accept character string input and *cin* >> should be used to accept numeric or single character input.

```
// LAB 3-2 (L3-2.CPP)
// AUTHOR : type your name here
// DATE WRITTEN : type the date here

#include <iostream.h>
#include <iomanip.h>
#include <conio.h>          // FOR USERS OF DOS BASED C++ COMPILERS ONLY

void main()
{

// DEFINE VARIABLES



// DISPLAY PROGRAM DESCRIPTION MESSAGE
   clrscr();                // FOR USERS OF DOS BASED C++ COMPILERS



// OBTAIN STUDENT NAME, COURSE, AND TEST SCORES



// CALCULATE TEST AVERAGE



// GENERATE OUTPUT TABLE



}
```

Save the Program

After you have entered the source code, you need to save the program. Name this program *L3-2.cpp*.

Compile the Program

Now that you have entered and saved the program, it is time to compile it.

Errors?

If there were any errors in the program you will have to edit the program code to fix the errors then compile the program again before you can link and run the program. Be sure to save the program again after you correct any errors.

Link the Program

Once the program is successfully compiled, you need to link it with the C++ library files needed by the program.

Run the Program

When the program is successfully compiled and linked, run it to make sure that it does what it is supposed to do.

Check the Program Output

A sample output of the loan interest program is shown in Figure 3-2. Your output screen does not have to look exactly like the one on Figure 3-2, but should look similar. If your output does not look similar to the screens shown in Figure 3-2, edit your program code so that you obtain the correct output. You may need to adjust your *setw()* statements or *setprecision()* statements.

```
This program will calculate the average of four test
scores that you must enter.


Enter student name:  Athena

Enter course name:  CS 101

Enter test score #1:  84

Enter test score #2:  92

Enter test score #3:  79

Enter test score #4:  94
```

```
          STUDENT:  Athena
           COURSE:  CS 101

       TEST SCORES
       -----------

           84
           92
           79
           94


TEST AVERAGE:  87.25
```

Figure 3-2 Sample output for the test average program.

Observe the Program Execution with the Debugger

Use a debugger to single step the program execution and observe the operation of the input and output statements in your program. Set a watch on your student, course, scores, and average variables using a watch window. Refer to Problem 2 in Project #2 for specific instructions for single stepping the program execution and using the watch window.

Print the Source Code and Sample Runs of the Program

Get a print-out of the program source code. Obtain a printed copy of 3 sample program runs, entering different values for the test scores for each sample run.

Close the File

When you are finished with the program file make sure that you have saved any final changes.

A Programming Challenge

Change the program to employ each of the following three string input functions:

cin.getline()
gets()
fgets()

First, observe any difference in program execution. Then, use your debugger to watch the string variable values as they are read using each of the above input functions.

When should you use any one of these input functions over the other two?

____

____

____

When should you *not* use a given string input function?

____

____

____

Exit C++

When you are finished with the lab exercises, exit your C++ programming environment.

LAB PROJECT #4
Simple Straight-Line Programs

Lab Objectives

In this lab, you will . . .

- Use C++ arithmetic operations.
- Use C++ assignment operations.
- Use special codes to format and manipulate output.

Introduction

In this project you will be using arithmetic operations to calculate sale prices for Ma & Pa's General Store. Arithmetic operations in C++ include the add, subtract, multiply, and divide operations. Table 4-1 lists the basic arithmetic operations and the C++ symbols used to represent those operations.

TABLE 4-1 ARITHMETIC OPERATORS DEFINED IN C++

Operation	Symbol
Add	+
Subtract	–
Multiply	*
Divide	/
Remainder (Modulus)	%

Refer to your text for information on using the arithmetic operators and the order of priority of the operators.

Assignment operators store a value in memory. Once the value is stored, it is accessed by the variable on the left side of the assignment operator. Another way to say this is that the variable on the left side of the operator is set to the value on the right side of the operator. Table 4-2 lists the C++ assignment operators.

TABLE 4-2 ASSIGNMENT OPERATORS USED IN C++

Operation	Symbol
Simple Assignment	=
Compound Addition Assignment	+=
Compound Subtraction Assignment	–=
Compound Multiplication Assignment	*=
Compound Division Assignment	/=
Compound Remainder Assignment (integers only)	%=

Refer to your text for information on using the assignment operators. Remember that the = operator does not mean "equal to." In C++, the variable on the left side of the = is set to the value of the expression on the right side of the =.

In Problem 1 you will develop a problem definition and algorithm to calculate and display the regular price and sale price of certain items in Ma & Pa's General Store.

In Problem 2 you will develop a problem definition, algorithm, and user friendly C++ program for Ma & Pa that will calculate their payroll and produce a formatted report.

In both problems, you will write the source code program that produces a formatted output. You will compile, link, run, test, and print your program.

Problem 1 - Calculate Sale Prices

In this exercise you will develop a problem definition and algorithm to calculate and display the regular price and sale price of certain items in Ma & Pa's General Store. You will then write the source code program that produces a formatted output. You will compile, link, run, test and print your program. You will then modify the program to allow Ma or Pa to enter any percentage of sales discount.

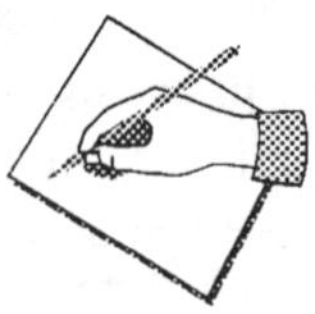

Pre-Lab

PROBLEM STATEMENT

Here is the inventory and price list of the Health and Beauty Aids department in Ma & Pa's General Store.

Item	Price
Grandma's Lye Soap	0.49
Bag Bahm	1.29
Chicken Soup	0.29
Liniment	2.35
Baking Soda	0.63

Ma and Pa want to run a "big" sale and reduce all Health and Beauty Aid items by 5 percent. Write a program that will print a listing of all the Health and Beauty Aid items, showing the regular and sale price. Assume that Ma or Pa will enter the above item and price list. Format your output, showing all of the items, regular prices, and sale prices.

Procedure & Questions:

PROBLEM DEFINITION

Output: What output is needed according to the problem statement?

____

Input: What input will be needed for processing to obtain the required output?

____

Will the program user be required to enter all of the input or can you hard-code some of the needed input as constant amounts?

____

Processing: What processing is required to calculate the sale prices?

____

Discussion:

According to the problem statement the output will be a formatted report showing the item, regular price, and sale price. The item name, regular price, and sale percentage are needed as input. The sale percentage can be hard-coded into the program as a constant. To calculate the sale price, you need to subtract the discount from the regular price. The discount is the regular price multiplied by the decimal equivalent of the sale percentage.

Procedure:

THE ALGORITHM

Write an algorithm to include the input, output, and processing that you developed in the problem definition.

BEGIN

END.

In-the-Lab 

Procedure & Discussion:

Start Your Compiler

Start your C++ program development environment.

Write the Program

Make sure that a new file is open. Using the algorithm that you developed, complete the following program shell for the Ma & Pa sale program. *Hint:* Declare DISCOUNT as a constant value of 0.05 and calculate the sale price as *SalePrice = RegularPrice* ∗ (1 – *DISCOUNT*); *Note:* the *gets()* statement can be used to accept character string input and *cin* >> should be used to accept numeric or single character input.

In order to display a result table of all the sale items, you will need to define multiple variables to hold each of the sales items, regular prices, and sale prices. On the other hand, if you accepted and displayed the results of each sale item as it is processed, you could define only one sale item variable, one regular price variable, and one sale price variable. With this method, you would have to perform the section of code that accepts the input, processes the sale price, and displays the output as many times as you have sale items.

The following program shell assumes that you will be displaying a formatted result table on the screen.

```
// LAB 4-1 (L4-1.CPP)
// AUTHOR : type your name here
// DATE WRITTEN : type the date here

#include <iostream.h>
#include <iomanip.h>
#include <stdio.h>
#include <conio.h>                          // FOR DOS BASED C++ COMPILERS ONLY

void main()
{

// DECLARE CONSTANTS AND DEFINE VARIABLES




// DISPLAY PROGRAM DESCRIPTION MESSAGE
   clrscr();                                // FOR USERS OF DOS BASED C++ COMPILERS



// GET ITEM INFORMATION
```

```
// CALCULATE SALE PRICES



// DISPLAY HEADINGS



// DISPLAY RESULT TABLE



}
```

Save the Program

After you have entered the source code, you need to save the program. Name this program *L4-1.cpp*.

Compile the Program

Now that you have entered and saved the program, it is time to compile it.

Errors?

If there were errors in the program, you will have to edit the code to fix the errors. You will then have to compile the program again before you can link and run it. Be sure to save the program after you correct the errors.

Link the Program

Once the program is successfully compiled, you need to link it with the C++ library files needed by the program.

Run the Program

When the program is successfully compiled and linked, run it to make sure that it does what it is supposed to do. Use the inventory information in the problem statement as input.

Check the Program Output

Sample output screens of the sale program for Ma and Pa are shown in Figure 4-1 and Figure 4-2. Your output screens should look similar to these. If your output does not look similar to the ones shown in Figure 4-1 and Figure 4-2, edit your program code so that you obtain the correct output. You may need to adjust the *setw()* statements or *setprecision()* statements in your program to obtain similar results.

```
Dear Ma or Pa

You will be asked to enter five sale items, one at
a time.  With each item you will be asked to enter
the item name and the regular price of the item.
The computer will then calculate the sale prices and
display a listing of the sale prices.

Please enter the item name:  Grandma's Lye Soap

Please enter the regular price of Grandma's Lye Soap :  $0.49

Please enter the item name:  Bag Bahm

Please enter the regular price of Bag Bahm :  $1.29

Please enter the item name:  Chicken Soup

Please enter the regular price of Chicken Soup :  $0.29

Please enter the item name:  Liniment

Please enter the regular price of Liniment :  $2.35
```

Figure 4-1 The input screen for the sale price program.

```
              ITEM           REGULAR PRICE              SALE PRICE
              ----           -------------              ----------
Grandma's Lye Soap               $0.49                     $0.47
          Bag Bahm               $1.29                     $1.23
      Chicken Soup               $0.29                     $0.28
          Liniment               $2.35                     $2.23
       Baking Soda               $0.63                     $0.60
```

Figure 4-2 The output screen for the sale price program.

Print a Sample Run of the Program

Get a print-out of the program run.

Print the Source Code

Print a source code listing of your program.

Modify the Program

Modify the sale price program for Ma & Pa so that you only have to define one sale item variable, one regular price variable, and one sale price variable. Remember that the output display *cannot* be a formatted table of all the sale items. You will perform the section of code that accepts the input, processes the sale price, and displays the output for each sale item entered.

Why can't the display be a formatted table of all the sale items, if you have only one variable for each of the sale item, regular price, and sale price?

____

____

Since there is only one variable for the sale item, one for the regular price, and one for the sale price, the variable contents are changed each time that your program accepts input and displays output. Therefore, a formatted report of all the sales items would be impossible.

Name this modified program *L4-1a.cpp* when you save it. Compile, link, run, test, and print this program.

What is the difference in the two versions of the sale price program?

Is there an advantage of one method over the other? What if the output table were to be printed? Explain.

Close the File

When you are finished with the program file, make sure that you have saved any final changes and then close the file.

Problem 2 - Ma and Pa's Payroll

In this exercise you will develop a problem definition, algorithm, and user friendly C++ program for Ma and Pa that will calculate their payroll and produce a formatted report.

Pre-Lab

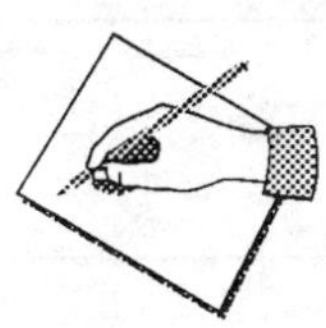

PROBLEM STATEMENT

Ma and Pa were so elated with the last program you wrote for them that they want to expand their computer operations to the payroll department. Write Ma and Pa a payroll program that will calculate Herb's (their only employee) net pay given the following information:

Employee's name
Number of weekly hours worked
Hourly rate of pay
FICA (7.15%)
Federal withholding (16%)
State withholding (4.75)

Assume that Ma or Pa will only be required to enter the first three items when running the program. Provide a report using the following format.

```
Employee Name: XXXXXXXXXXXXXXXXXXX

Rate of Pay:                    $XXX.XX
Hours Worked:                    XX.XX
Gross Pay:                                   $XXXX.XX
Deductions:
      FICA                       $XXX.XX
      Fed. Withholding            XXX.XX
      State Withholding           XXX.XX
                                 _______
      Total Deductions           $XXX.XX

Net Pay:                                     $XXXX.XX
```

Procedure & Questions:

PROBLEM DEFINITION

Output: What output is needed according to the problem statement?

___

Input: What input will be needed for processing to obtain the required output?

___

Will the program user be required to enter the input or can you hard-code the needed input as constant amounts?

___

Processing: What processing is required to calculate the gross pay?

___

What processing is required to calculate the FICA?

___

What processing is required to calculate the federal withholdings?

___

What processing is required to calculate the state withholdings?

___

What processing is required to calculate the total deductions?

___

What processing is required to calculate the net pay?

___

Discussion:

According to the problem statement, the output will be a formatted report showing the employee's name, rate of pay, hours worked, gross pay, itemized deductions, and net pay. The employee's name, pay rate, and hours worked are needed as input. These items can not be hard-coded into the program as constants and must be accepted as variable input from the keyboard. The FICA, Federal Withholding percentages, and State Withholdings can be declared as constants. To calculate the gross pay, you need to multiply the pay rate by the hours worked. The FICA, Federal, and State Withholdings each need to be multiplied by the gross pay. Add the itemized deductions together to calculate the total deductions. The net pay is simply the gross pay minus the total deductions.

Procedure:

THE ALGORITHM

Write a step-by-step algorithm using the input, output, and processing that you developed in the problem definition.

BEGIN

END.

In-the-Lab 

Procedure & Discussion:

Start Your Compiler

Start your C++ program development environment.

Write the Program

Make sure that a new file is open. Using the algorithm that you developed, complete the following program shell for Ma and Pa's payroll program. *Note:* the *gets()* statement can be used to accept character string input and *cin >>* should be used to accept numeric or single character input.

```
// LAB 4-2 (L4-2.CPP)
// AUTHOR : type your name here
// DATE WRITTEN : type the date here

#include <iostream.h>
#include <iomanip.h>
#include <stdio.h>
#include <conio.h>                    // FOR DOS BASED C++ COMPILERS ONLY

void main()
{
// DECLARE CONSTANTS AND DEFINE VARIABLES



// DISPLAY PROGRAM DESCRIPTION MESSAGE
   clrscr();                          // FOR USERS OF DOS BASED C++ COMPILERS



// GET EMPLOYEE DATA FROM MA OR PA



// MAKE PAYROLL CALCULATIONS



// DISPLAY FORMATTED PAYROLL DATA



}
```

Save the Program

After you have entered the source code, you need to save the program. Name this program *L4-2.cpp*.

Compile the Program

Now that you have entered and saved the program, it is time to compile it.

Errors?

If there were errors in the program, you will have to edit the code to fix the errors. You will then have to compile the program again before you can link and run it. Be sure to save the program after you correct errors.

Link the Program

Once the program is successfully compiled, you need to link it with the C++ library files needed by the program.

Run and Test the Program

When the program is successfully compiled and linked, run and test it to make sure that it does what it is supposed to do.

Check the Program Output

Sample output screens of the payroll program for Ma and Pa are shown in Figure 4-3 and Figure 4-4. Your output screens should look similar to these. If your output does not look similar to the ones shown in Figure 4-3 and Figure 4-4, edit your program code so that you obtain the correct output. You may need to adjust your *setw()* statements or *setprecision()* statements. You can also use the \t escape sequence to format your output. *Note:* since the pay rate is declared as a floating point variable and the $ is a character, you cannot enter the $ as part of the pay rate. To avoid incorrect output, you must include the $ as a part of your *cout* << formatting.

```
Dear Ma or Pa

This is a payroll program that will calculate an employee's
gross pay, deductions, and net pay.


Please enter the employee's name:  Herb

Please enter the number of hours that Herb worked:  38

Please enter the rate of pay for Herb:  $5.65
```

Figure 4-3 The user input screen for Ma and Pa's payroll program.

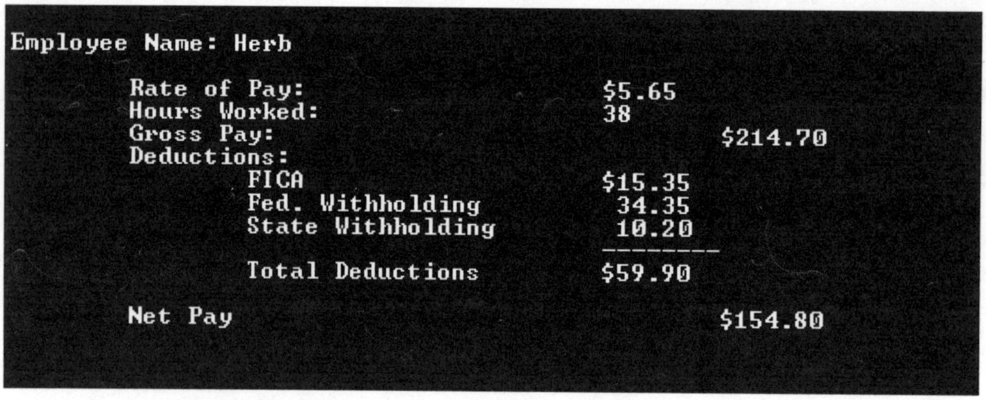

Figure 4-4 The output screen for Ma and Pa's payroll program.

Print Sample Runs of the Program

Run the program using the following test data.

Employee name	Hours worked	Rate of pay
<your name>	40	12.75
Herb	0	7.34
Herb	24	13.71

Get a print-out of each program run.

Print the Source Code

Print a source code listing of your program.

Close the File

When you are finished with the program file make sure that you have saved any final changes and then close the file.

A Programming Challenge

Develop a problem definition, algorithm, and user friendly C++ program to solve the following problem and produce a formatted report. Refer to Figure 4-5 for the problem.

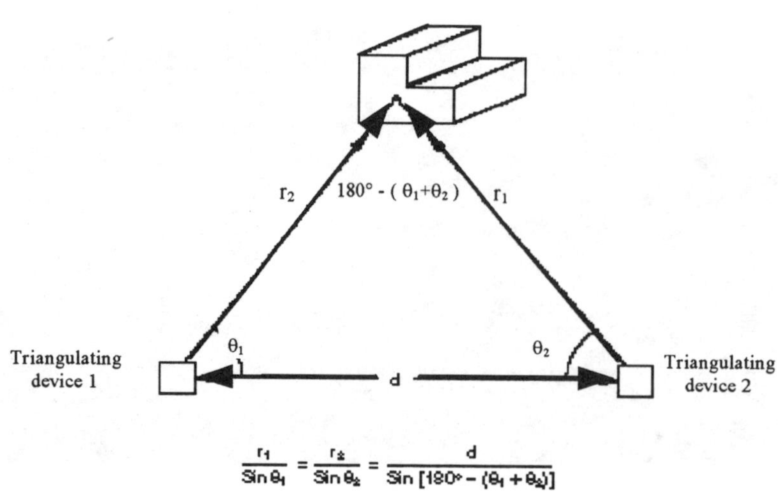

Figure 4-5 A triangulation diagram for the programming challenge.

The diagram in Figure 4-5 illustrates how triangulation is used to find the distance to an object. Here's the idea: Two triangulating devices are positioned a certain distance apart and both devices get a "fix" on an object. The two triangulating devices and the object form a triangle whose one leg, *d*, and two angles $\theta 1$ and $\theta 2$ are known. The third angle is easily found by subtracting the two known angles from 180 degrees. The distance from each triangulating device to the object is then found using the Law of Sines, which states:

$$r1 / Sin\,\theta 1 = r2 / Sin\,\theta 2 = d / Sin(180 - (\theta 1 + \theta 2))$$

Write a user friendly program to find the distance that the object is from each triangulation device. Assume that the user will enter the distance (*d*) between the devices and the two angles ($\theta 1$ and $\theta 2$) that the object makes with the triangulating devices.

Exit C++

When you are finished with the lab exercises, exit your C++ programming environment.

LAB PROJECT #5
Decision Making

Lab Objectives

In this lab, you will . . .

- Use the C++ *if*, *if/else* and *switch* statements for decision making.
- Use nested decision making.
- Use a print routine to produce a printed output.

Introduction

In this project you will be using the C++ *if*, *if/else* and *switch* statements for decision making. The *if*, *if/else*, and *switch* statements are used to control the flow of your program based upon the outcome of a conditional test.

When using the *if* statement, the statements that follow the *if* will be executed if the condition is TRUE. Otherwise, if the condition is FALSE, the statements following the *if* will be skipped.

When using the *if/else* statement, the statements that follow the *if* will be executed if the condition is TRUE. Otherwise, if the condition is FALSE, the statements following the *else* will be executed.

The *switch* statement enables the program to select one of many options or *cases*. A selector variable is evaluated and is compared to a series of cases. If the selector value matches one of the case values, the corresponding case statements are executed. If no match is made, the program simply continues in a straight-line fashion, with the first statement following the *switch* statement.

A valuable protection feature to the *switch* statement is the *default* option that allows a series of statements to be executed if no match is found within the *switch* statement. For example, if the user enters incorrect input information, the *default* option allows you to notify the user that an error was made and that no match will be found. This feature is often used in menu-driven programs.

In Problem 1 you will develop a problem definition and use nested *if/else* statements to develop an algorithm to convert a numeric grade to a letter grade. You will then write the source code program that accepts the input and produces an output report. You will compile, link, run, test and print your program.

In Problem 2 you will develop a problem definition, algorithm, and user friendly C++ program that will use a *switch* statement to project the profit for Ma and Pa's Sporting Goods department. You will then produce a printed report.

Problem 1 - Converting a Numeric Grade to a Letter Grade

In this exercise you will develop a problem definition and algorithm that employs nested *if/else* statements to convert a numeric grade to a letter grade. You will then write the source code program that produces a user friendly output. You will compile, link, run, test, and print your program.

Pre-Lab

PROBLEM STATEMENT

Use nested *if/else* statements to convert a numeric grade to a letter grade according to the following scale:

90 - 100 :	A
80 - 89 :	B
70 - 79 :	C
60 - 69 :	D
Below 60 :	F

Write a user friendly program that will accept a student's name and numeric grade then display the letter grade.

Procedure & Questions:

PROBLEM DEFINITION

Output: What output is needed according to the problem statement?

____

Input: What input will be needed for processing to obtain the required output?

____

Will the program user be required to enter all of the input or can you hard-code some of the needed input as constant amounts?

____

Processing: What processing is required to determine the letter grade? Remember to use nested *if/else* statements.

____

____

____

____

Discussion:

According to the problem statement the output will report the letter grade. The student's name and numeric grade are needed as input. There is not any input for this problem that can be hard-coded into the program as constants. To determine the letter grade, you need to use nested *if/else* statements to make the correspondence between the numeric and letter grade.

Procedure:

THE ALGORITHM

Write an algorithm to include the input, output, and processing that you developed in the problem definition.

BEGIN

END.

In-the-Lab 

Procedure & Discussion:

Start Your Compiler

Start your C++ program development environment.

Write the Program

Make sure that a new file is open. Using the algorithm that you developed, complete the following program shell for the grade conversion program.

```
// LAB 5-1 (L5-1.CPP)
// AUTHOR : type your name here
// DATE WRITTEN : type the date here

#include <iostream.h>
#include <stdio.h>
#include <conio.h>            // FOR DOS BASED C++ COMPILERS ONLY
```

```
void main()
{
// DEFINE VARIABLES




// DISPLAY PROGRAM DESCRIPTION MESSAGE
   clrscr();                    // FOR USERS OF DOS BASED C++ COMPILERS




// GET NAME AND SCORE FROM USER




// DETERMINE AND REPORT THE LETTER GRADE




}
```

Save the Program

After you have entered the source code, you need to save the program. Name this program *L5-1.cpp.*

Compile the Program

Now that you have entered and saved the program, compile it.

Errors?

If there were errors in the program, edit the code to fix the errors. You will then have to compile the program again before you can link and run it. Be sure to save the program after you correct errors.

Link the Program

Once the program is successfully compiled, link it with the C++ library files needed by the program.

Run the Program

When the program is successfully compiled and linked, run it to make sure that it does what it is supposed to do.

Check the Program Output

Observe your program output. A sample output screen of the grade conversion program is shown in Figure 5-1. Your output screen should look similar to this. If not, edit your program code so that you obtain the correct output.

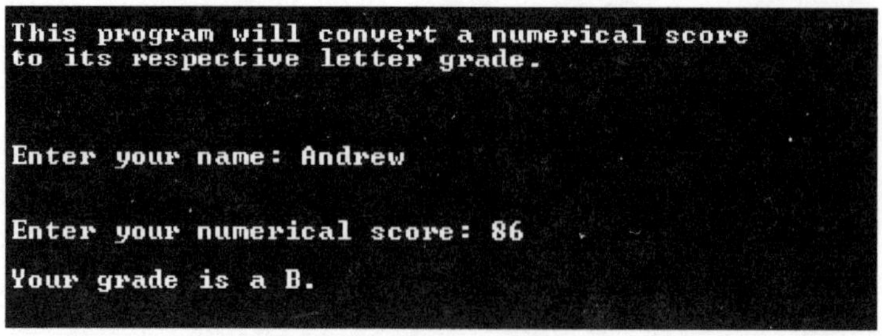

Figure 5-1 Output generated by the letter grade conversion program.

Observe the Program Execution with the Debugger

Use a debugger to single step the program execution and observe the operation of the *if/else* statements in your program. Set a watch of your name and score variables using a watch window. If you are using TURBO C++, refer to Problem 2 in Project #2 for specific instructions for single stepping the program execution and using the watch window.

Print Sample Runs of the Program

Run your program using the following test data:

Student name	Numeric Grade
<any name>	83
<any name>	50
<any name>	74
<any name>	95

Get a print-out of each program run.

Print the Source Code

Print the source code listing.

Close the File

When you are finished with the program file, make sure that you have saved any final changes and then close the file.

A Programming Challenge

Suppose that C++ did not have an *if/else* statement, but only an *if* statement. Rewrite the algorithm and program using only *if* statements.

Problem 2 - Projecting Profits for Ma and Pa

In this exercise you will develop a problem definition, algorithm, and user friendly C++ program for Ma and Pa that will project the profit of their Sporting Goods department and produce a formatted printed report.

Pre-Lab

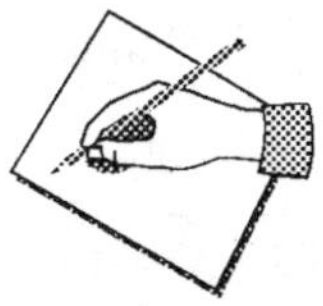

PROBLEM STATEMENT

Ma and Pa are at it again. This time they need a program that will project the profit of their Sporting Goods department. The items in the department are coded with a 1, 2, or 3, depending on the amount of profit for the item. An item with a profit code of 1 produces a 10 percent profit, a code of 2 produces a 12 percent profit, while an item with a code of 3 generates a 15 percent profit. Write a program that will project the profit of the following inventory:

Item	Quantity	Price	Profit Code
Fishing Line	132 spools	$3.95	1
Fish Hooks	97 packages	$0.89	2
Sinkers	123 packages	$0.49	2
Fish Nets	12 each	$8.75	1
Spinner Baits	256 each	$2.49	3
Jigs	49 each	$0.29	3

The program should generate a *printed* report of the item, quantity, price, total expected profit in dollars per item, and total expected profit for all items. *Hint:* use a *switch* statement to determine how much profit will be made on each item.

Procedure & Questions:

PROBLEM DEFINITION

Output: What output is needed according to the problem statement?

____

Input: What input will be needed for processing to obtain the required output?

____

Will the program user be required to enter the input or can you hard-code the needed input as constant amounts?

____

Processing: What processing is required to calculate the expected total profit per item?

____

What processing is required to calculate the expected total profit?

____

How will you determine which profit level to use for calculating the profit of each item?

____

Discussion:

According to the problem statement, the output will be a formatted *printed* report showing the item, quantity, price per item, total expected profit per item, and expected total profit for all items. The item, quantity, price, and profit code are needed as input. Prompt the user to enter the items, quantities, prices and profit codes via the keyboard. To calculate the total expected profit per item, you need to check the profit code. Depending upon the profit code, you will either multiply the price by the quantity by 0.10 for code 1, multiply the price by the quantity by 0.12 for code 2, or multiply the price by the quantity by 0.15 for code 3 to calculate the total profit per item. Since the profit per item depends on the profit code, this is an ideal application for the *switch* statement. The total expected profit for all items will be the sum of each item's profit.

Procedure:

THE ALGORITHM

Write a step-by-step algorithm using the input, output, and processing that you developed in the problem definition.

BEGIN

END.

In-the-Lab 

Procedure & Discussion:

Start Your Compiler

Start your C++ program development environment.

Write the Program

Make sure that a new file is open. Using the algorithm that you developed, complete the following program shell for Ma and Pa's profit projection program.

The following C++ code contains segments that will clear the screen for DOS based C++ compilers. There is also a segment defining "print" as an object pointing to the printer port PRN. This print segment is also for DOS based compilers. Using *print* << in the place of *cout* << will allow you to send output from your program to the printer. If your compiler is not DOS based, check with your instructor or lab supervisor for instructions on clearing the display screen and sending output to the printer.

```
// LAB 5-2 (L5-2.CPP)
// AUTHOR : type your name here
// DATE WRITTEN : type the date here

#include <iostream.h>
#include <iomanip.h>
#include <stdio.h>
#include <fstream.h>
#include <process.h>          // FOR DOS USERS ONLY
#include <conio.h>            // FOR DOS USERS ONLY

void main()
{
// DEFINE VARIABLES




// ***********************************************************************************************
//
//     THIS SEGMENT OF CODE DEFINES   "print"   AS AN OUTPUT FILE POINTING
//     TO YOUR PRINTER PORT  (PRN)                ***** (DOS ONLY) *****
//
//***********************************************************************************************
   ofstream print;                    // DEFINE print AS AN OUTPUT FILE STREAM
   print.open("PRN");                 // OPEN PRINT FILE AND POINT TO PRN
   if (!print)                        // MAKE SURE PRINTER IS READY
   {
      cout << "There is a problem with the printer.\n";
      exit(1);
   }
   clrscr();                          // CLEARS THE SCREEN IN DOS C++ COMPILERS
```

// DISPLAY PROGRAM DESCRIPTION MESSAGE

// PRINT HEADINGS

// GET ITEM INFORMATION FROM MA OR PA FOR ITEM 1

// CALCULATE AND PRINT PROFIT FOR ITEM 1

// GET ITEM INFORMATION FROM MA OR PA FOR ITEM 2

// CALCULATE AND PRINT PROFIT FOR ITEM 2

// GET ITEM INFORMATION FROM MA OR PA FOR ITEM 3

// CALCULATE AND PRINT PROFIT FOR ITEM 3

// GET ITEM INFORMATION FROM MA OR PA FOR ITEM 4

// CALCULATE AND PRINT PROFIT FOR ITEM 4

// GET ITEM INFORMATION FROM MA OR PA FOR ITEM 5

// CALCULATE AND PRINT PROFIT FOR ITEM 5

// GET ITEM INFORMATION FROM MA OR PA FOR ITEM 6

```
// CALCULATE AND PRINT  PROFIT FOR ITEM 6



// CALCULATE AND PRINT THE TOTAL PROFIT



// CLOSE THE PRINT FILE



} // END main()
```

Save the Program

After you have entered the source code, you need to save the program. Name this program *L5-2.cpp.*

Compile the Program

Now that you have entered and saved the program, it is time to compile it.

Errors?

If there were errors in the program, edit the code to fix the errors. Compile the program again before you link and run it. Be sure to save the program after you correct errors.

Link the Program

Once the program is successfully compiled, you need to link it with the C++ library files needed by the program.

Run the Program

When the program is successfully compiled and linked, run it to make sure that it does what it is supposed to do. For those using a DOS based compiler, **make sure that the printer is ready, since the output is directed to the printer instead of the display monitor.** If you are not able to send the output directly to the printer, obtain a print out of the program results using the same method as for earlier lab exercises.

Use the following inventory as input for the program:

Item	Quantity	Price	Profit Code
Fishing Line	132 spools	$3.95	1
Fish Hooks	97 packages	$0.89	2
Sinkers	123 packages	$0.49	2
Fish Nets	12 each	$8.75	1
Spinner Baits	256 each	$2.49	3
Jigs	49 each	$0.29	3

A sample input screen of the profit projection program for Ma and Pa is shown in Figure 5-2. Your input screen should look similar to this. The table in Figure 5-3 shows what the printed output should look like. If your output is not similar, edit the code so that it produces the correct output.

```
Dear Ma or Pa

This program will tell you how much profit that you can
expect from the six items in your sporting goods department

Please enter the item name:  Fishing Line

Please enter the quantity of Fishing Line: 132

Please enter the price of Fishing Line:  $3.95

Please enter the profit code for Fishing Line: 1
```

Figure 5-2 The input screen for Ma and Pa's profit projection program.

EXPECTED PROFIT REPORT

ITEM	QUANTITY	PRICE	PROFIT
-------	---------------	--------	----------
Fishing Line	132	$3.95	$52.14
Fish Hooks	97	$0.89	$10.36
Sinkers	123	$0.49	$7.23
Fish Nets	12	$8.75	$10.50
Spinner Baits	256	$2.49	$95.62
Jigs	49	$0.29	$2.13

TOTAL EXPECTED PROFIT: $177.98

Figure 5-3 The printed output for Ma and Pa's profit projection program.

Print the Source Code

Print a source code listing of your program.

Close the File

When you are finished with the program file make sure that you have saved any final changes and then close the file.

A Programming Challenge

Suppose that C++ did not have a *switch* statement, but only an *if* statement. Rewrite the algorithm and program using only *if* statements.

Exit C++

When you are finished with the lab exercises, exit your C++ programming environment.

LAB PROJECT #6
Looping Operations : Iteration

Lab Objectives

In this lab, you will . . .

- Use the C++ *while*, *do/while*, and *for* looping statements to perform repetitive operations.

Introduction

In this project you will be controlling the flow of your programs using iteration. Iteration simply means to do something repeatedly. In programming, this is called looping.

It is important to provide a way to exit from a loop or the computer would perform the loop forever. To prevent *infinite* looping, all iteration control structures test a condition to determine when to exit the loop. ***Pretest*** loops test a condition each time before the loop is executed. ***Posttest*** loops test a condition after each loop execution. ***Fixed repetition*** loops cause the loop to be executed a predetermined number of times.

You will be using the C++ *while*, *do/while*, and *for* statements to perform looping operations. The difference between these statements is found in the way they control the executing of the loop. The *while* is a pretest loop, the *do/while* is a posttest loop, and the *for* is a fixed repetition loop.

In Problem 1 you will develop a problem definition and use the *while* loop in an algorithm and program to compute the average of any number of test scores. You will revise the algorithm and program to employ a *do/while* loop, then revise the algorithm and program again to use a *for* loop.

In Problem 2 you will develop a problem definition, algorithm, and program to generate a Celsius table for all even temperatures from 32 degrees to 212 degrees Fahrenheit using a *for* loop.

In both problems, you will write the source code program that accepts the input and produces an output report. You will compile, link, run, test, and print your programs.

Problem 1 - Average Any Number of Test Scores

In this exercise you will develop a problem definition, algorithm, and program that employs a *while* statement to average any number of test scores. You will write the source code program that produces a user friendly output. You will compile, link, run, test, and print your program. You will revise the algorithm and program to employ a *do/while* statement to solve the problem and then revise the algorithm and program again using a *for* statement.

Pre-Lab 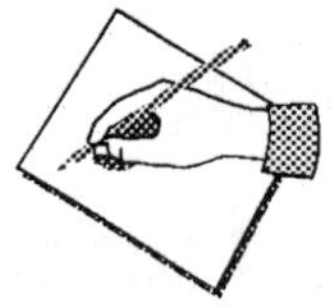

PROBLEM STATEMENT

Write a user friendly program using a *while* statement to compute the average of any number of test scores and report the result to the user.

Procedure & Questions:

PROBLEM DEFINITION

Output: What output is needed according to the problem statement?

____

Input: What input will be needed for processing to obtain the required output?

____

Will the program user be required to enter all of the input or can you hard-code some of the needed input as constant amounts?

____

Processing: What processing is required to calculate the test scores average?

____

Discussion:

According to the problem statement the output will report the average of the test scores. The number of tests and test scores are needed as input. You need to prompt the user for the number of tests to average. Then, use a *while* statement to accept the scores and accumulate a total. There is not any input for this problem that can be hard-coded into the program as constants. To determine the average of the test scores you will need to keep an accumulating total of the test scores then divide this total by the number of test scores entered.

Procedure:

THE ALGORITHM

Write an algorithm to include the input, output, and processing that you developed in the problem definition.

BEGIN

END.

In-the-Lab

Procedure & Discussion:

Start Your Compiler

Start your C++ program development environment.

Write the Program

Make sure that a new file is open. Using the algorithm that you developed, complete the following program shell for the test scores average program.

```
// LAB 6-1a (L6-1a.CPP)
// AUTHOR : type your name here
// DATE WRITTEN : type the date here

#include <iostream.h>
#include <iomanip.h>
#include <conio.h>                    // FOR DOS BASED C++ COMPILERS ONLY

void main()
{

// DEFINE VARIABLES
```

```
// DISPLAY PROGRAM DESCRIPTION MESSAGE
   clrscr();                                  // FOR USERS OF DOS BASED C++ COMPILERS



// GET NUMBER OF SCORES FROM USER AND CHECK FOR INVALID ENTRY



// LOOP TO GET INDIVIDUAL SCORES FROM USER AND ADD TO SUM



// CALCULATE AVERAGE



// DISPLAY RESULTS



} // END PROGRAM
```

Save the Program

After you have entered the source code, you need to save the program. Name this program *L6-1a.cpp.*

Compile the Program

Now that you have entered and saved the program, it is time to compile it.

Errors?

If there were errors in the program, edit the code to fix the errors. You will then have to compile the program again before you can link and run it. Be sure to save the program after you correct errors.

Link the Program

Once the program is successfully compiled, link it with the C++ library files needed by the program.

Run the Program

When the program is successfully compiled and linked, run it to make sure that it does what it is supposed to do.

Check the Program Output

A sample output screen of the test scores average program is shown in Figure 6-1. Your output screen should look similar to this. If not, edit your program code so that you obtain the correct output.

```
This program will compute the average of any number
of test scores using a while loop.


Enter the number of test scores that you wish to average:  4

Enter test score #1: 82

Enter test score #2: 91

Enter test score #3: 93

Enter test score #4: 76


The average of the scores entered is: 85.5
```

Figure 6-1 Sample output for the test scores average program.

Observe the Program Execution with the Debugger

Use a debugger to single step the program execution and observe the operation of the *while* statement in your program. Set a watch on your loop counter, test score, and sum variables using a watch window. If you are using TURBO C++, refer to Problem 2 in Project #2 for specific instructions for single stepping the program execution and using the watch window.

Print Sample Runs of the Program

Use the following data to test your program:

Number of Test Scores	Test Scores						
3	83	79	94				
0							
7	53	72	91	82	75	62	94
4	74	98	89	93			

Get a print-out of each program run.

Did your program check for an invalid entry on the number of test scores? ______________________

Print the Source Code

Print a source code listing.

Modify the Program Code

Revise the program from problem 1 to employ a *do/while* loop statement to accept the test scores instead of the *while* loop statement.

Save, Compile, and Link the Program

After you have revised the source code, you need to save the modified program. Name this program *L6-1b.cpp.* Now that you have saved the program, it is time to compile it. Once the program is successfully compiled, link it with the C++ library files needed by the program.

Run the Program

When the program is successfully compiled and linked, run it to make sure that it does what it is supposed to do.

Check the Program Output

Check the program output to see the results of the program run.

Print the Source Code

Print the source code listing.

Modify the Program Code Again

Revise the test scores average program from problem 1 to employ a *for* loop to accept the test scores instead of the *while* or *do/while* loop.

Save, Compile, and Link the Program

After you have revised the source code, you need to save the modified program. Name this program *L6-1c.cpp*. Now that you have saved the program, it is time to compile it. Once the program is successfully compiled, link it with the C++ library files needed by the program.

Run the Program

When the program is successfully compiled and linked, run it.

Check the Program Output

Check the program output to see the results of the program run.

Print the Source Code

Print the source code listing.

Close the File

When you are finished with the program file, make sure that you have saved any final changes and then close the file.

Problem 2 - Generate a Celsius Conversion Table

In this exercise you will develop a problem definition, algorithm, and user friendly C++ program that will generate a Celsius conversion table for all even temperatures from 32 degrees to 212 degrees Fahrenheit and produce a formatted printed report.

Pre-Lab

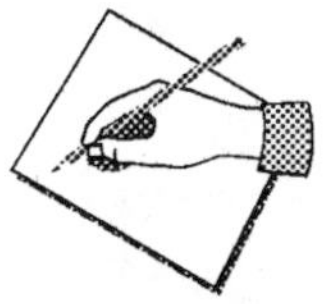

PROBLEM STATEMENT

Using the formula $C = 5/9(F - 32)$, write a program that employs a *for* statement to generate a Celsius conversion table for all even temperatures from 32 degrees to 212 degrees Fahrenheit. Produce a formatted *printed* table of the temperature range in Celsius and Fahrenheit.

Procedure & Questions:

PROBLEM DEFINITION

Output: What output is needed according to the problem statement?

____

Input: What input will be needed for processing to obtain the required output?

____

Will the program user be required to enter the input or can you hard-code the needed input as constant amounts?

____

Processing: What processing is required to convert the Fahrenheit temperature to Celsius?

____

____

Discussion:

According to the problem statement, the output will be a formatted printed report showing the temperature in Fahrenheit and the Celsius equivalent. There is not any input needed for this problem. Use the formula, $C = 5/9(F - 32)$, to convert the degrees Fahrenheit to degrees Celsius. Since there is a fixed number of even degrees between 32 and 212, this is an ideal application for the *for* statement.

Procedure:

THE ALGORITHM

Write a step-by-step algorithm using the input, output, and processing that you developed in the problem definition.

BEGIN

END.

In-the-Lab

Procedure & Discussion:

Start Your Compiler

Start your C++ program development environment.

Write the Program

Make sure that a new file is open. Using the algorithm that you developed, complete the following program shell for the converting degrees Fahrenheit to degrees Celsius program.

The following C++ code contains segments that will clear the screen for DOS based C++ compilers. There is also a segment defining "print" as an object pointing to the printer port PRN. This print segment is also for DOS based compilers. Using *print* << in the place of *cout* << will allow you to send output from your program to the printer. If your compiler is not DOS based, check with your instructor or lab supervisor for instructions on clearing the display screen and sending output to the printer.

```
// LAB 6-2 (L6-2.CPP)
// AUTHOR : type your name here
// DATE WRITTEN : type the date here

#include <iostream.h>
#include <iomanip.h>
#include <stdio.h>
#include <fstream.h>
#include <process.h>          // FOR DOS USERS ONLY
#include <conio.h>            // FOR DOS USERS ONLY

void main()
{

// DEFINE VARIABLES



// ******************************************************************************
//
//      THIS SEGMENT OF CODE DEFINES   "print"  AS AN OUTPUT FILE POINTING
//      TO YOUR PRINTER PORT  (PRN)                ***** (DOS ONLY) *****
//
//******************************************************************************

   ofstream print;                       // DEFINE print AS AN OUTPUT FILE STREAM
   print.open("PRN");                    // OPEN PRINT FILE AND POINT TO PRN
   if (!print)                           // MAKE SURE PRINTER IS READY
   {
      cout << "There is a problem with the printer.\n";
      exit(1);
   }

// DISPLAY PROGRAM DESCRIPTION MESSAGE
   clrscr();                             // CLEARS THE SCREEN IN DOS C++ COMPILERS



// PRINT HEADINGS



// PRINT CONVERSION TABLE USING A FOR LOOP





// CLOSE THE PRINT FILE


}  // END PROGRAM
```

Save, Compile, and Link the Program

After you have entered the source code, you need to save the program. Name this program *L6-2.cpp.* Now that you have saved the program, it is time to compile and link it.

Run the Program

When the program is successfully compiled and linked, run it. If you are using a DOS based C++ compiler, **make sure that the printer is ready, since the output is directed to the printer instead of the display monitor.** If you are not able to send the output directly to the printer, obtain a print out of the program results using the same method as for earlier lab exercises.

Figure 6-2 shows what the printed output should look like. If your output is not similar, edit the code so that it produces correct output.

Degrees Fahrenheit	Degrees Celsius
----------------------	-------------------
32	0
34	1.11
36	2.22
38	3.33
40	4.44
42	5.56
44	6.67
46	7.78
48	8.89
.	.
.	.
.	.
212	100

Figure 6-2 The printed output for degrees Fahrenheit converted to degrees Celsius .

Print the Source Code

Print a source code listing of your program.

Close the File

When you are finished with the program file make sure that you have saved any final changes and then close the file.

A Programming Challenge

Some programming languages, like BASIC, allow you to use a STEP command within a **for** statement like this:

FOR Counter = <initial value> TO <final value> STEP N DO

The STEP command allows the loop counter to increment by some value (N), other than the value 1, with each loop iteration.

Write a **for** loop in C++ that will emulate this STEP operation. Provide for user entry of any desired step value. To demonstrate its operation, use your step loop to display every fifth integer, from 1 to 100.

Exit C++

When you are finished with the lab exercises, exit your C++ programming environment.

LAB PROJECT #7
Functions For Top/Down Design

Lab Objectives

In this lab, you will . . .

- Design modular, well structured programs.
- Create and employ user-defined functions.
- Use actual arguments and formal parameters.
- Learn the importance of a function prototype.
- Use recursive functions.

Introduction

In this project you will be creating and employing user-defined functions to write modular, well structured, C++ programs. The programs that you have been working with so far have consisted of one main section defined by function *main()*. Functions that you create yourself are called *user-defined* functions.

Functions eliminate the need for duplicate statements within a program. If you have a task that needs to be performed more than once, the statements can be written just once in a function. Then, the function is *called* each time the task must be performed. Using functions adds to the clarity and readability of your program code. And most importantly, the use of functions allows you to solve very large complex problems using a top/down program design approach.

A function can be made to return a single value or to return a set of values to the calling program. Functions can also be written to perform specific tasks, such as input, processing, or output segments of the program.

The function is given a name and *called*, or *invoked*, using its name each time the task is to be performed within the *calling program*. All user-defined functions to be used in function *main()* are defined after the closing brace of *main()*.

A function is defined by a *function header*. The header dictates what types of data the function will accept from the calling program, and what type of data the function will return to the calling program. The header is the *interface* between the calling program and the function.

Data passed to the function, when the function is called, are *actual arguments*. *Formal parameters* are defined within the function header and take on the value(s) of the actual arguments when the function is called. Parameters can be passed between the calling program and function by *value* or *reference*. When passing parameters by value, the actual arguments in the calling program are not affected by operations on the formal parameters within the function. Thus, passing parameters by value is one-way communication of data from the calling program to the function. Passing parameters by reference is two-way communication of data from the calling program to the function and back to the calling program. In C++ reference parameters are defined using the ampersand (&) symbol prior to the parameter name in the function heading.

One way to determine if a parameter needs to be value or reference is to ask yourself if the actual arguments need to be changed by the function. If so, then the parameter should be a reference parameter. If you do not want the actual argument changed by the function, the parameter should be a value parameter.

A *function prototype*, sometimes referred to as a *function declaration*, is a model of the interface to the function that is used by the compiler to check calls to the function for the proper number of arguments and correct data types of the arguments. A function prototype is required by C++ for each function used in your program. The function prototype can simply be a copy of the function header followed by a semicolon. It must appear prior to function *main()*.

A recursive function is a function that calls itself until a primitive state is reached. There must always be a primitive state to terminate a recursive function call. Otherwise, a run-time error will occur. Recursive operations can be performed as part of an *if/else* statement. The primitive state forms the *if* clause, while the recursive call is part of the *else* clause of the statement. All recursive operations can also be performed using iteration. *Note*: since recursion eats up time and memory as compared to iteration, you should only consider recursion when a simple iterative solution is not possible, and when the execution and memory efficiency of the solution is within acceptable limits.

In Problem 1 you will modify the problem definition, algorithm and program, that you developed earlier in Problem 2 of Lab Project #4 for Ma and Pa's payroll to use functions.

In Problem 2 you will develop a problem definition, algorithm, and program that employs a recursive function to generate a Fibonacci sequence. You will then modify this program to use an iterative function to generate a Fibonacci sequence. And finally, you will time both programs to evaluate their efficiency.

In both problems, you will write the source code program that accepts the required input and produces an output report. You will compile, link, run, test, and print your programs.

Problem 1 - Using Functions

In this exercise you will revise the problem definition, algorithm, and program you developed for Ma and Pa's payroll in Problem 2 of Lab Project #4 to use functions.

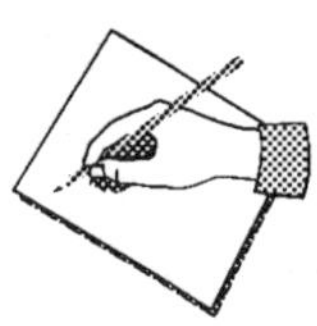

Pre-Lab

PROBLEM STATEMENT

Revise the previously written payroll program to use functions. Recall that the payroll program will calculate Herb's net pay given the following information:

Employee's Name
Number of weekly hours worked
Hourly rate of pay
FICA (7.15%)
Federal Withholding (16%)
State Withholding (4.75%)

Ma or Pa will only be required to enter the first three entries when running the program. The program must generate a *printed* report using the following format:

```
Employee Name: XXXXXXXXXXXXXXXXXXXX

Rate of Pay:                 $XXX.XX
Hours Worked:                  XX.XX
Gross Pay:                  $XXXX.XX
```

Deductions:

FICA	$XXX.XX
Fed. Withholding	$XXX.XX
State Withholding	$ XXX.XX
	________
Total Deductions	$XXX.XX

Net Pay: $XXXX.XX

Procedure & Questions:

PROBLEM DEFINITION

Output: What output is needed according to the problem statement?

____

Can a function be used to produce the output? ____________________

What arguments must be sent to the function from the program? ____________

____

What arguments must be sent back to the program from the function? __________

____

Which arguments must be value parameters and which ones should be reference parameters?

____

Input: What input will be needed for processing to obtain the required output?

____

Will the program user be required to enter the input or can you hard-code the needed input as constant amounts?

____

Can you create a function to accept the needed input from the user? __________

What arguments must be sent to the function from the program? ____________

____

What arguments must be sent back to the program from the function? __________

____

Which arguments must be value parameters and which ones should be reference parameters?

____

Processing: What processing is required to calculate the gross pay?

____

What processing is required to calculate the FICA?

____

What processing is required to calculate the federal withholdings?

____

What processing is required to calculate the state withholdings?

____

What processing is required to calculate the total deductions?

____

What processing is required to calculate the net pay?

____

What data must a function accept to perform the payroll calculations?

____

What data must a payroll function return, if any?

____

Can a function be used for processing? ______________________________

What arguments must be sent to the function from the program? ______________

____

What arguments must be sent back to the program from the function? ______________

____

Which arguments must be value parameters and which ones should be reference parameters?

____

Discussion:

According to the problem statement, the output will be a *printed* formatted report showing the employee's name, rate of pay, hours worked, gross pay, itemized deductions, and net pay. The employee's name, pay rate, and hours worked are needed as input. These items can not be hard-coded into the program as constants and must be accepted as variable input from the keyboard.
The FICA, Federal Withholding percentages, and State Withholdings can be declared as constants. To calculate the gross pay, you need to multiply the pay rate by the hours worked. The FICA, Federal, and State Withholdings each need to be multiplied by the gross pay. Add the itemized deductions together to calculate the total deductions. The net pay is simply the gross pay minus the total deductions. The input, processing, and output can be programmed using functions that are called by the payroll program.

Procedure:

THE ALGORITHM

Write an algorithm to perform each of the three tasks listed in the following initial algorithm:

```
BEGIN
   GET INPUT FROM MA OR PA.
   CALCULATE PAYROLL.
   PRINT PAYROLL REPORT.
END.

GET INPUT FUNCTION
   BEGIN



   END.
```

Complete the following questions to determine the function interface. (This function interface section has been completed for you. Complete the remaining function interface sections in a similar manner.)

What will you name this function? *Get_Input()*

What does this function do? *Prompts and accepts the payroll input.*

What types of data must the function accept from the calling program?

Accepts: *A character string for Name, a floating point value for Hours, a floating point value for Rate.*

What types of data must the function return to the calling program?

Returns: *A character string for Name, a floating point value for Hours, a floating point value for Rate.*

Do you need the function to change any of the parameters passed? *yes*

Which parameters must be passed by value and which by reference? *Name, Hours, and Rate must be passed by reference.*

Write a prototype/header for this function.

void Get_Input(char Name[MAX], float &Hours, float &Rate);

CALCULATE PAYROLL FUNCTION

BEGIN

END.

Complete the following questions to determine the function interface.

What will you name this function? ______________________________

What does this function do? ______________________________

What types of data must the function accept from the calling program?

Accepts: ______________________________

What types of data must the function return to the calling program?

Returns: ______________________________

Do you need the function to change any of the parameters passed? ______________

Which parameters must be passed by value and which by reference? ______________

____

Write a prototype/header for this function.

____

PRINT PAYROLL REPORT FUNCTION

BEGIN

END.

Complete the following questions to determine the function interface.

What will you name this function? ______________________________

What does this function do? ______________________________

What types of data must the function accept from the calling program?

Accepts: ______________________________

What types of data must the function return to the calling program?

Returns: ______________________________

Do you need the function to change any of the parameters passed? ______________

Which parameters must be passed by value and which by reference? ______________

____

Write a prototype/header for this function.

____

In-the-Lab

Procedure & Discussion:

Start Your Compiler

Start your C++ program development environment.

Write the Program

Open the *L4-2.cpp* payroll program written for Ma and Pa in Project #4. Using the algorithms that you developed, revise the program and complete the following program shell.

```
// LAB 7-1 (L7-1.CPP)
// AUTHOR : type your name here
// DATE WRITTEN : type the date here

#include <iostream.h>
#include <stdio.h>
#include <iomanip.h>
#include <fstream.h>
#include <process.h>          // FOR USERS OF DOS BASED C++ COMPILERS
#include <conio.h>            // FOR USERS OF DOS BASED C++ COMPILERS
```

```
// DECLARE GLOBAL CONSTANTS



// FUNCTION PROTOTYPES



void main()
{

// DEFINE VARIABLES



// DISPLAY PROGRAM DESCRIPTION MESSAGE
   clrscr();                              // FOR USERS OF DOS BASED C++ COMPILERS



// CALL FUNCTION TO GET VALUES FROM MA OR PA

// CALL FUNCTION TO CALCULATE PAYROLL

// CALL FUNCTION TO PRINT PAYROLL

} // END main()

// THIS FUNCTION WILL GET THE EMPLOYEE DATA FROM MA OR PA

{


} // END INPUT FUNCTION

// THIS FUNCTION WILL MAKE THE PAYROLL CALCULATIONS

{


} // END CALCULATE PAYROLL FUNCTION
```

```
// THIS FUNCTION WILL PRINT THE PAYROLL DATA

{
        Display a message to the user that the printer must be on to print the report and that the
        payroll report is being printed.

// *****************************************************************************************
//
//      THIS SEGMENT OF CODE DEFINES   "print"   AS AN OUTPUT FILE POINTING
//      TO YOUR PRINTER PORT  (PRN)
//      (DOS ONLY)
//
//*****************************************************************************************

    ofstream print;                         // DEFINE print AS AN OUTPUT FILE STREAM
    print.open("PRN");                      // OPEN PRINT FILE AND POINT TO PRN
    if (!print)                             // MAKE SURE PRINTER IS READY
    {
        cout << "There is a problem with the printer.\n";
        exit(1);
    }

        Write the print statements to send a formatted payroll report to the printer.

// CLOSE PRINT FILE

} // END PRINT FUNCTION
```

Save, Compile, and Link the Program

After you have revised the payroll source code, you need to save the modified program with a new name. Give this program the name *L7-1.cpp.* Now that you have saved the program, compile and link it.

Run the Program

When the program is successfully compiled and linked, run it.

Check the Program Output

A sample of the input screen from the payroll program is shown in Figure 7-1 and a sample printed output from the revised payroll program is shown in Figure 7-2. Your input and printed output should look similar to these. If not, edit your program code so that you obtain the correct output. If you are not able to send the output directly to the printer, obtain a print out of the program results using the same method as described in earlier labs.

```
Dear Ma or Pa

This is a payroll program that will calculate an employee's
gross pay, deductions, and net pay.


Please enter the employee's name:  Herb

Please enter the number of hours that Herb worked:  38

Please enter the rate of pay for Herb:  $9.35
```

Figure 7-1 Sample input screen for the revised payroll program.

```
Employee Name :  Herb

      Rate of Pay :                          $9.35
      Hours Worked :                            38
      Gross Pay :                          $355.30
      Deductions :
                FICA                        $25.40
                Fed. Withholding            $56.85
                State Withholding           $16.88
                                            ----------
                Total Deductions            $99.13

      Net Pay                              $256.17
```

Figure 7-2 Sample printed output for Ma and Pa's revised payroll program.

Observe the Program Execution with the Debugger

Use a debugger to single step the program execution and observe the operation of the functions in your program. If you are using TURBO C++, refer to Problem 2 in Project #2 for specific instructions for single stepping the program execution.

Check the Importance of Prototyping

To observe the importance of the function prototypes in C++, hide them from the compiler and try to compile the payroll program. Place // in front of the function prototype statements in your payroll program so that the compiler bypasses them as comments. After you have commented out the prototype statements, compile the program. Observe the error message generated. Correct the error situation by removing the // from the prototype statements. Recompile the program to see that the error is now removed. C++ uses the prototype to check the type of data and arguments sent to the function.

It would also be a good idea to change the number of and/or data types in the function prototypes. Recompile the program and observe the error messages generated.

What can you conclude about C++ prototypes?

____

Print the Source Code

Print a source code listing of your program.

Close the File

When you are finished with the program file, make sure that you have saved any final changes and then close the file.

Problem 2 - Recursion

In this exercise you will develop a problem definition, algorithm, and C++ program that will use a recursive function to generate a Fibonacci sequence. You will also develop an algorithm and program that employs an iterative function to generate a Fibonacci sequence. And finally, you will time both programs to evaluate their execution efficiency.

Pre-Lab

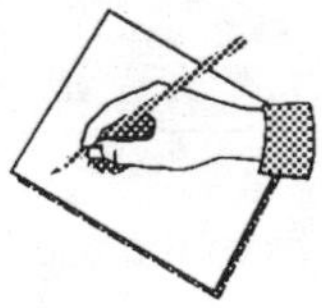

PROBLEM STATEMENT

A Fibonacci sequence of numbers is defined as follows:

$$F_0 = 0$$
$$F_1 = 1$$
$$F_n = F_{n-1} + F_{n-2}, \text{ for } n > 1$$

This says that the first two numbers in the sequence are 0 and 1. Then, each additional Fibonacci number is the sum of the two previous numbers in the sequence. Thus, the first ten Fibonacci numbers are:

0, 1, 1, 2, 3, 5, 8, 13, 21, 34

Here, we say that the first number occupies position 0 in the sequence, the second number position 1 in the sequence, and so on. Thus, the last position in a ten number sequence is position 9.

Develop a problem definition, algorithm, and program that employs a *recursive* function to generate a Fibonacci sequence of all numbers up to some position, *n*, entered by the user.

Procedure & Questions:

PROBLEM DEFINITION

Output: What output is needed according to the problem statement?

____

Can a function be used to produce the output? ________________________________

What arguments must be sent to the function from the program? ______________

____

What arguments must be sent back to the program from the function? ___________

____

Which arguments must be value parameters and which ones should be reference parameters?

____

Input: What input will be needed for processing to obtain the required output?

____

Will the program user be required to enter the input or can you hard-code the needed input as constant amounts?

____

Can you create a function to accept the needed input from the user? ____________

What arguments must be sent to the function from the program? ______________

____

What arguments must be sent back to the program from the function? ___________

____

Which arguments must be value parameters and which ones should be reference parameters?

____

Processing: The processing for a Fibonacci sequence can be divided into three cases depending on the position, *n*.

CASE 1: What processing is required if *n* is 0?

____

CASE 2: What processing is required if *n* is 1?

____

CASE 3: What processing is required for *n* greater than 1?

____

What arguments must be sent to the function from the program? ______________

____

What arguments must be sent back to the program from the function? ______________

____

Which arguments must be value parameters and which ones should be reference parameters?

____

____

Discussion:

According to the problem statement, the output will be a display showing the generated Fibonacci sequence. The final position, *n*, is needed as input from the user. A recursive function that uses the definition of a Fibonacci sequence given in the problem statement will be used to generate the sequence. If *n* is 0, the sequence is 0. If *n* is 1, the sequence is 0, 1. If *n* is greater than 1, the sequence is 0, 1, (the sum of the two previous numbers in the sequence up to position *n*).

Procedure:

THE ALGORITHM

Write an algorithm to perform each of the three tasks listed in the following initial algorithm:

```
BEGIN
   GET LAST SEQUENCE POSITION.
   CALCULATE SEQUENCE.
   DISPLAY RESULTS.
END.
```

```
GET LAST SEQUENCE POSITION FUNCTION
   BEGIN



   END.
```

What will you name this function? ______________________________

What does this function do? ______________________________

What types of data must the function accept from the calling program?

Accepts: ______________________________

What types of data must the function return to the calling program?

Returns: ______________________________

Do you need the function to change any of the parameters passed? ______________

Which parameters must be passed by value and which by reference? ______________

____

Write a prototype/header for this function.

____

CALCULATE SEQUENCE FUNCTION
BEGIN

END.

What will you name this function? ______________________________

What does this function do? ______________________________

What types of data must the function accept from the calling program?

Accepts: ______________________________

What types of data must the function return to the calling program?

Returns: ______________________________

Do you need the function to change any of the parameters passed? ______________

Which parameters must be passed by value and which by reference? ______________

____

Write a prototype/header for this function.

____

DISPLAY RESULTS FUNCTION

BEGIN

END.

What will you name this function? ______________________________

What does this function do? ______________________________

What types of data must the function accept from the calling program?

Accepts: ______________________________

What types of data must the function return to the calling program?

Returns: ______________________________

Do you need the function to change any of the parameters passed? ______________________________

Which parameters must be passed by value and which by reference? ______________________________

____

Write a prototype/header for this function.

____

In-the-Lab

Procedure & Discussion:

Start Your Compiler

Start your C++ program development environment.

Write the Program

Make sure that a new file is open. Using the algorithms that you developed, complete the following program shell for the Fibonacci sequence program. *Hint:* Use *unsigned long int* as the data type for the variables that will hold the sequence values. This will decrease the possibility that a given value will cause an overflow error.

```
// LAB 7-2 (L7-2.CPP)
// AUTHOR : type your name here
// DATE WRITTEN : type the date here

#include <iostream.h>
#include <conio.h>              // FOR DOS USERS ONLY

// FUNCTION PROTOTYPES



void main()
{

// DEFINE VARIABLES



// CALL FUNCTION TO GET LAST SEQUENCE POSITION FROM USER



// CALL FUNCTION TO DISPLAY FIBONACCI SEQUENCE



}  // END MAIN

// THIS FUNCTION WILL GET THE LAST SEQUENCE POSITION FROM THE USER

{


} // END FUNCTION

// THIS FUNCTION WILL RETURN THE FIBONACCI NUMBER FOR THE POSITION IT RECEIVES

{


} // END FUNCTION

// THIS FUNCTION WILL DISPLAY THE FIBONACCI SEQUENCE

{


} // END FUNCTION
```

Save, Compile and Link the Program

After you have entered the source code, you need to save the program. Name this program *L7-2.cpp.* Now that you have saved the program, compile and link it.

Run and Test the Program

When the program is successfully compiled and linked, run and test it.

Figure 7-3 shows a sample Fibonacci sequence generated by the program for $n = 100$. If your output is not similar, edit the program code so that it produces correct results.

```
Please enter the last desired Fibonacci sequence position:  100

The Fibonacci sequence up to position 100 is:

0, 1, 1, 2, 3, 5, 8, 13, 21, 34, 55, 89, 144, 233, 377, 610, 987, 1597, 2584, 41
81, 6765, 10946, 17711, 28657, 46368, 75025, 121393, 196418, 317811, 514229, 832
040, 1346269, 2178309, 3524578, 5702887, 9227465, 14930352, 24157817, 39088169,
63245986, 102334155, 165580141, 267914296, 433494437, 701408733, 1134903170, 183
6311903, 2971215073, 512559680, 3483774753, 3996334433, 3185141890, 2886509027,
1776683621, 368225352, 2144908973, 2513134325, 363076002, 2876210327, 3239286329
, 1820529360, 764848393, 2585377753, 3350226146, 1640636603, 695895453, 23365320
56, 3032427509, 1073992269, 4106419778, 885444751, 696897233, 1582341984, 227923
9217, 3861581201, 1845853122, 1412467027, 3258320149, 375819880, 3634140029, 400
9959909, 3349132642, 3064125255, 2118290601, 887448560, 3005739161, 3893187721,
2603959586, 2202180011, 511172301, 2713352312, 3224524613, 1642909629, 572466946
, 2215376575, 2787843521, 708252800, 3496096321, 4204349121, 3405478146, 3314859
971,
```

Figure 7-3 Output generated by the Fibonacci sequence with 100 as the last sequence position.

Print the Source Code and Sample Runs of the Program

Print a source code listing of your program. Get a print-out of the program results.

Close the File

When you are finished with the program file make sure that you have saved any final changes and then close the file.

A Programming Challenge

Develop an algorithm and program that employs an *iterative* function to generate a Fibonacci sequence of all numbers up to some position, *n*, entered by the user. Enter, compile, link, run, test, and print this program.

Measure the amount of time it takes the recursive program developed earlier in this lab exercise and the iterative program developed here to generate a Fibonacci sequence of 100 elements.

What do you conclude about the efficiency of recursion versus iteration?

____

____

Why does the recursive program take so long?

____

____

Exit C++

Exit your C++ compiler when you are finished.

LAB PROJECT #8
Using Arrays

Lab Objectives

In this lab, you will . . .

- Define, fill, manipulate, and display one-dimensional arrays.
- Pass arrays to user-defined functions for manipulation.
- Sort array elements.
- Search an array for given elements.

Introduction

In this project you will be working with the array data structure. Arrays provide an organized means for locating and storing data, just as the post office boxes in the post office lobby provide an organized means of locating and storing mail. The array data structure can be used to store just about any type of data including integers, floats, characters, arrays, pointers, and records (structures). Arrays are so versatile that they can be used to implement other data structures such as stacks, queues, linked lists, and binary trees. The array provides a convenient means of storing large amounts of data in primary, or user, memory.

There are both one-dimensional and multi-dimensional arrays. In this lab project you will be using the one-dimensional array and in the next lab project you will expand into multi-dimensional arrays.

The two major components of any array are the *elements* stored in the array and the *indices* which locate the stored elements. The elements of an array are the data stored in the array. The elements can be any data type that you have studied so far. There is one major restriction to the array elements: *The elements in a given array must all be of the same data type*. The array indices locate the array elements. The C++ compiler automatically assigns integer indices to the array element list beginning with the index 0. The last element in an array is some integer N. Since the indices begin with 0 and go to N, there are $N + 1$ elements in the array.

All arrays in C++ must be defined. You must specify the data type of the data elements, the name of the array, and the size of the array in the definition. Refer to your text for more information on defining arrays.

To access the array elements, you must use direct assignment statements, read/write statements, or loops. The *for* loop structure is the most common way of accessing multiple array elements.

You can pass an entire array to a function, or pass single array elements to a function. The important thing to remember is that to pass the entire array, you must pass the address of the array. In C++, the *array name* is the address of the first element of the array.

Searching and sorting are common operations performed on arrays. You will be using a *binary search* and a *bubble sort* in these lab exercises.

In Problem 1 you will develop a problem definition, algorithm and program that defines a set of arrays to store the user's name, street address, city, state, zip code, and telephone number. You will use functions to fill and display the arrays.

In Problem 2 you will develop a problem definition, algorithm, and program that sorts and searches an array of integers.

In both problems, you will write the source code program that accepts the required input and produces an output report. You will compile, link, run, test, and print your programs.

Problem 1 - Filling and Displaying Character Arrays

In this exercise you will use arrays to store the name, street address, city, state, zip code, and telephone number of the program user. You will develop functions to fill and display the arrays.

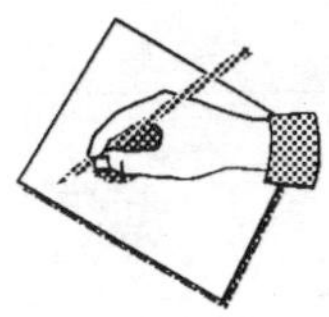

Pre-Lab

PROBLEM STATEMENT

Write a program that uses six character arrays to store the user's name, street address, city, state, zip code, and telephone number. Provide one function to fill the arrays and another to display the array contents using proper addressing format.

Procedure & Questions:

PROBLEM DEFINITION

Output: What output is needed according to the problem statement?

____

Can a function be used to produce the output? ______________________

What arguments must be sent to the output function from the program?

____

What arguments must be sent back to the program from the function?

____

Which arguments must be value parameters and which ones should be reference parameters?

____

Input: What input will be needed for processing to obtain the required output?

____

Will the program user be required to enter the input or can you hard-code the needed input as constant amounts?

____

Can a function be used to accept the input? ______________________________

What arguments must be sent to the input function from the program?

____

What arguments must be sent back to the program from the function?

____

Which arguments must be value parameters and which ones should be reference parameters?

____

How can you pass the arrays to a function?

____

What built-in C++ input function can you use to accept the string data into the arrays?

____

Processing: What processing is required to obtain the output?

____

Discussion:

According to the problem statement, the output will be a properly formatted display showing the user's name, street address, city, state, zip code, and telephone number. The name, street address, city, state, zip code, and telephone number are needed as input. These items can not be hard-coded into the program as constants and must be accepted as variable input from the keyboard. There is no processing required after the input data is accepted from the user. The input and output can be programmed using functions that are called by *main()*.

Procedure:

The Algorithm

Here is an initial algorithm for function *main()*. Write an algorithm for the input and output functions that you developed in the problem definition.

```
BEGIN
   CALL FUNCTION TO FILL ADDRESS ARRAYS.
   CALL FUNCTION TO DISPLAY ADDRESS ARRAYS.
END.
```

INPUT FUNCTION

BEGIN

END.

What will you name this function? ______________________________

What does this function do? ______________________________

What types of data must the function accept from the calling program?

Accepts: ______________________________

What types of data must the function return to the calling program?

Returns: ______________________________

Do you need the function to change any of the parameters passed? ______________

Which parameters must be passed by value and which by reference? ______________

____

Write a prototype/header for this function.

____

OUTPUT FUNCTION

BEGIN

END.

What will you name this function? ______________________________

What does this function do? ______________________________

What types of data must the function accept from the calling program?

Accepts: ______________________________

What types of data must the function return to the calling program?

Returns: ____

Do you need the function to change any of the parameters passed? ____________________

Which parameters must be passed by value and which by reference? ____________________

____

Write a prototype/header for this function.

____

In-the-Lab

Procedure & Discussion:

Start Your Compiler

Start your C++ program development environment.

Write the Program

Using the algorithms and prototypes that you developed, complete the following program shell.

```
// LAB 8-1 (L8-1.CPP)
// AUTHOR : type your name here
// DATE WRITTEN : type the date here

#include <iostream.h>
#include <stdio.h>
#include <iomanip.h>
#include <fstream.h>
#include <conio.h>                    // FOR DOS BASED C++ COMPILERS ONLY

// DECLARE GLOBAL CONSTANT FOR ARRAY SIZE



// FUNCTION PROTOTYPES



void main()
{
```

```
// DEFINE ADDRESS ARRAYS



//CALL FUNCTION TO FILL ADDRESS ARRAYS FROM USER ENTRIES



// CALL FUNCTION TO DISPLAY ADDRESS ARRAYS



} // END main()

// THIS FUNCTION WILL FILL THE ARRAYS FROM USER ENTRIES
{





} // END INPUT FUNCTION

// THIS FUNCTION WILL DISPLAY THE CONTENTS OF THE ADDRESS ARRAYS
{





} // END DISPLAY FUNCTION
```

Save, Compile, and Link the Program

After you have entered the source code, you need to save the program. Give this program the name *L8-1.cpp.* Now that you have saved the program, compile it. Once the program is successfully compiled, link it.

Run and Test the Program

When the program is successfully compiled and linked, run and test it.

Check the Program Results

A sample of the input screen from the address program is shown in Figure 8-1 and a sample output screen is shown in Figure 8-2. Your input and output should look similar to these. If not, edit your program code so that you obtain the correct output.

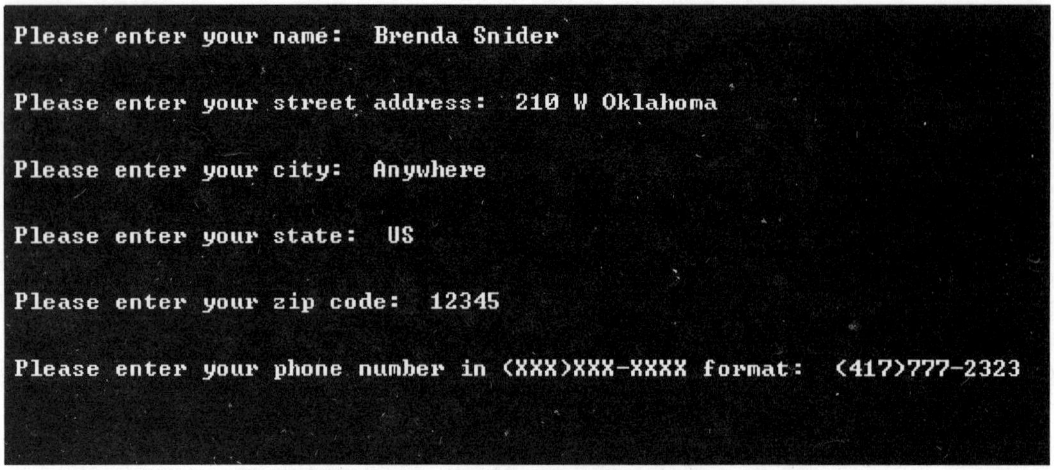

Figure 8-1 Sample input screen for the address program.

Figure 8-2 Sample output screen for the address program.

Observe the Program Execution with the Debugger

Use a debugger to single step the program execution and observe how the address arrays are filled during the execution of your program. Use a watch window to set a watch on the arrays so that you can observe them. If you are using TURBO C++, refer to Problem 2 in Project #2 for specific instructions for single stepping the program execution and using a watch window.

Print the Source Code and Sample Runs of the Program

Print a source code listing of your program. Get sample print-outs of the program runs for documentation.

Close the File

When you are finished with the program file, make sure that you have saved any final changes and then close the file.

Problem 2 - Sort and Search

In this exercise you will develop a problem definition, algorithm, and C++ program that will randomly fill an integer array. You will then sort and search the array to find a value specified by the user.

Pre-Lab

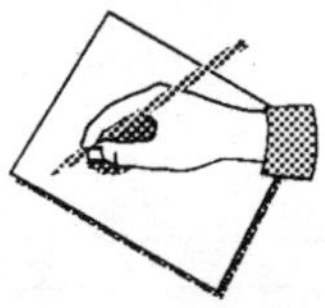

PROBLEM STATEMENT

Write a program that uses functions to randomly fill an integer array, sort the array using the bubble sort algorithm, prompt the user for an element to find in the search (an integer element between 0 and 99). And finally, search for the specified element in the sorted array using a binary search algorithm. Display the following:

Appropriate messages to the user.
The unsorted array.
The sorted array.
The element and its index position, if it was found with the search.
A message to the user which indicates if the element was not found in the search.

Procedure & Questions:

PROBLEM DEFINITION

Output: What output is needed according to the problem statement?

____

____

Can a function be used to produce the output? __________________________

What arguments must be sent to the output function from the program?

____

What arguments must be sent back to the program from the function?

____

Which arguments must be value parameters and which ones should be reference parameters?

____

____

Input: What input will be needed for processing to obtain the required output?

____

Will the program user be required to enter the input or can you hard-code the needed input as constant amounts?

____

Can a function be used to accept the input? _______________________

What arguments must be sent to the input function from the program?

____

What arguments must be sent back to the program from the function?

____

Which arguments must be value parameters and which ones should be reference parameters?

____

____

How can you pass the arrays to a function?

____

Processing: What processing is required to obtain the specified output?

____

____

____

Discussion:

According to the problem statement, the output will be a display showing the unsorted integer array, the sorted array, the specified element and its index position in the array. If you are using a DOS-based compiler, the array can be filled with a function that uses the standard *random()* and *randomize()* functions. You must use *srand()* and *rand()* with non-DOS compilers. You will employ a function that uses the bubble sort algorithm for sorting the array and employ a function that uses the iterative binary search algorithm for searching for the specified element.

The bubble sort algorithm makes several passes through the array, comparing adjacent values during each pass. The adjacent values are exchanged if the first value is larger than the second value (ascending sort). The process terminates when $N - 1$ passes have been made (where N is the number of elements in the array) or when no more exchanges are possible. This gives the effect of the smaller values "bubbling" to the top, or front, of the array.

The binary search requires that the array is sorted prior to the search. It keeps dividing the array in half, directing itself to the half where the value is likely to be found.

Procedure:

THE ALGORITHM

Here is an initial algorithm for function *main()* using the input, output, and processing developed in the problem definition. Write an algorithm for the array fill and display functions. Use the algorithms provided for the bubble sort and iterative binary search.

BEGIN
  CALL FUNCTION TO FILL THE ARRAY WITH RANDOM VALUES.
  CALL FUNCTION TO DISPLAY THE UNSORTED ARRAY.
  CALL FUNCTION TO SORT THE ARRAY.
  CALL FUNCTION TO DISPLAY THE SORTED ARRAY.
  GET SEARCH ELEMENT FROM THE USER.
  CALL FUNCTION TO SEARCH THE ARRAY FOR ELEMENT AND DISPLAY THE ELEMENT
    AND ITS POSITION.
END.

FILL ARRAY FUNCTION
  BEGIN

  END.

What will you name this function? ______________________________

What does this function do? ______________________________

What types of data must the function accept from the calling program?

Accepts: ______________________________

What types of data must the function return to the calling program?

Returns: ______________________________

Do you need the function to change any of the parameters passed? ______________

Which parameters must be passed by value and which by reference? ______________

____

Write a prototype/header for this function.

____

DISPLAY ARRAY FUNCTION
BEGIN

END.

What will you name this function? ______________________________

What does this function do? ______________________________

What types of data must the function accept from the calling program?

Accepts: ______________________________

What types of data must the function return to the calling program?

Returns: ______________________________

Do you need the function to change any of the parameters passed? ______________________________

Which parameters must be passed by value and which by reference? ______________________________

____

Write a prototype/header for this function.

____

Here is the algorithm for the bubble sort in pseudocode form:

```
BubbleSort( )
BEGIN
    Set Passes = 1.
    Set Exchange = TRUE.
    While (Passes < Number of Array Elements) AND (Exchange = = TRUE)
        Set Exchange = FALSE.
        For Index = (First Array Index) To (Last Array Index - Passes)
            If A[Index] > A[Index + 1])
                Swap (A[Index], A[Index +1]).
                Set Exchange = TRUE.
        Set Passes = Passes + 1.
END.
```

What will you name this function? ______________________________

What does this function do? ______________________________

What types of data must the function accept from the calling program?

Accepts: ______________________________

What types of data must the function return to the calling program?

Returns: ______________________________

Do you need the function to change any of the parameters passed? ______________

Which parameters must be passed by value and which by reference? ______________

____

Write a prototype/header for this function.

____

Your job will be to code the above algorithm as a C++ function. In addition, you will have to code a *Swap()* function that can be called by the bubble sort function to exchange two array elements as shown in the algorithm.

Write an algorithm for the swap function needed by the bubble sort function.

SWAP FUNCTION
BEGIN

END.

What is this function's name? ______________________________

What does this function do? ______________________________

What types of data must the function accept from the calling program?

Accepts: ______________________________

What types of data must the function return to the calling program?

Returns: ______________________________

Do you need the function to change any of the parameters passed? ______________

Which parameters must be passed by value and which by reference? ____________________

____

Write a prototype/header for this function.

____

Here is the iterative solution for the binary search in pseudocode form:

```
BinarySearch( )
BEGIN
    Set Found = FALSE.
    While ( !Found AND First <= Last ) Do
        Set Mid = (First + Last) / 2.
        If (Element = = A[Mid] ) Then
            Set Found = TRUE.
        Else
            If (Element < A[Mid] ) Then
                Set Last = Mid – 1.
            Else
                Set First = Mid + 1.
    If (Found) Then
        Return (Mid).
    Else
        Return (–1).
END.
```

What will you name this function? ____________________________________

What does this function do? ____________________________________

What types of data must the function accept from the calling program?

Accepts: ____________________________________

What types of data must the function return to the calling program?

Returns: ____________________________________

Do you need the function to change any of the parameters passed? ____________________

Which parameters must be passed by value and which by reference? ____________________

____

Write a prototype/header for this function.

____

Your job will be to code the above algorithm as a C++ function.

In-the-Lab

Procedure & Discussion:

Start Your Compiler

Start your C++ program development environment.

Write the Program

Make sure that a new file is open. Using the above algorithms, complete the following program shell for filling, sorting, searching, and displaying the array. Make sure that you report whether or not the element being searched for was found in the array. If it is found, report the array index of the element.

```
// LAB 8-2 (L8-2.CPP)
// AUTHOR : type your name here
// DATE WRITTEN : type the date here

#include <iostream.h>
#include <stdlib.h>
#include <conio.h>              // FOR DOS USERS ONLY

// GLOBAL CONSTANT FOR ARRAY SIZE


// FUNCTION PROTOTYPES



void main()
{
// DEFINE ARRAY AND VARIABLES


    clrscr();                   // CLEAR THE SCREEN FOR DOS BASED C++ COMPILERS
// CALL FUNCTION TO FILL THE ARRAY WITH RANDOM INTEGERS


// CALL FUNCTION TO DISPLAY RANDOM ARRAY


// CALL FUNCTION TO SORT THE ARRAY


// CALL FUNCTION TO DISPLAY SORTED ARRAY


// GET ELEMENT TO SEARCH FOR FROM THE USER
```

```
// CALL SEARCH FUNCTION AND DISPLAY ELEMENT POSITION

} // END MAIN

// THIS FUNCTION WILL FILL THE ARRAY WITH RANDOM NUMBERS
{

} // END ARRAY FILL FUNCTION

// THIS FUNCTION WILL SWAP THE VALUES FOR THE SORT FUNCTION
{

} // END SWAP FUNCTION

// THIS FUNCTION WILL SORT THE ARRAY
{

} // END SORT FUNCTION

// THIS FUNCTION WILL SEARCH FOR THE ELEMENT
{

} // END SEARCH FUNCTION

// THIS FUNCTION WILL DISPLAY THE ARRAY CONTENTS
{

} // END DISPLAY FUNCTION
```

Save, Compile, and Link the Program

After you have entered the source code, you need to save the program. Give this program the name *L8-2.cpp*. Now that you have saved the program, compile it. Once the program is successfully compiled, you need to link it.

Run and Test the Program

When the program is successfully compiled and linked, run and test it.

Figure 8-3 shows sample output from the sort and search program. If your output is not similar, edit the program code so that it produces correct results.

```
The elements of the unsorted array are:
 25 72 48 25 92 65 68 62 17 43 52 65 94 64 22 97 60 53 65 41 36 69 54 43 84

The elements of the sorted array are:
 17 22 25 25 36 41 43 43 48 52 53 54 60 62 64 65 65 65 68 69 72 84 92 94 97

What element do you want to search for? 62

The element 62 was found at index [13] of the sorted array.
```

Figure 8-3 Array Search and Sort output.

Print the Source Code Sample Runs of the Program

Print a source code listing of your program. Get print-outs of the program runs.

Close the File

When you are finished with the program file make sure that you have saved any final changes and then close the file.

Exit C++

Exit your C++ compiler when you are finished.

LAB PROJECT #9
Multidimensional Arrays

Lab Objectives

In this lab, you will . . .

- Define, fill, manipulate, and display multidimensional arrays.
- Pass multidimensional arrays to user-defined functions for manipulation.

Introduction

A multidimensional array is an extension of a one-dimensional array, which stores multiple lists of elements. For example, a two-dimensional array stores lists in a two-dimensional table format of rows and columns, where each row is a list. The rows provide the vertical dimension of the array and the columns provide the horizontal array dimension. A three-dimensional array stores lists in a three dimensional format of rows, columns, and planes, where each plane is a two-dimensional array. The rows provide the vertical dimension, the columns provide the horizontal dimension, and the planes provide the depth dimension of the array.

You will be using the most common multidimensional array, the *two-dimensional* array shown in Figure 9-1, in this lab project. You can see that a two-dimensional array contains multiple rows combined to form a single rectangular structure of data. You can think of this rectangular data structure as a *table* of elements.

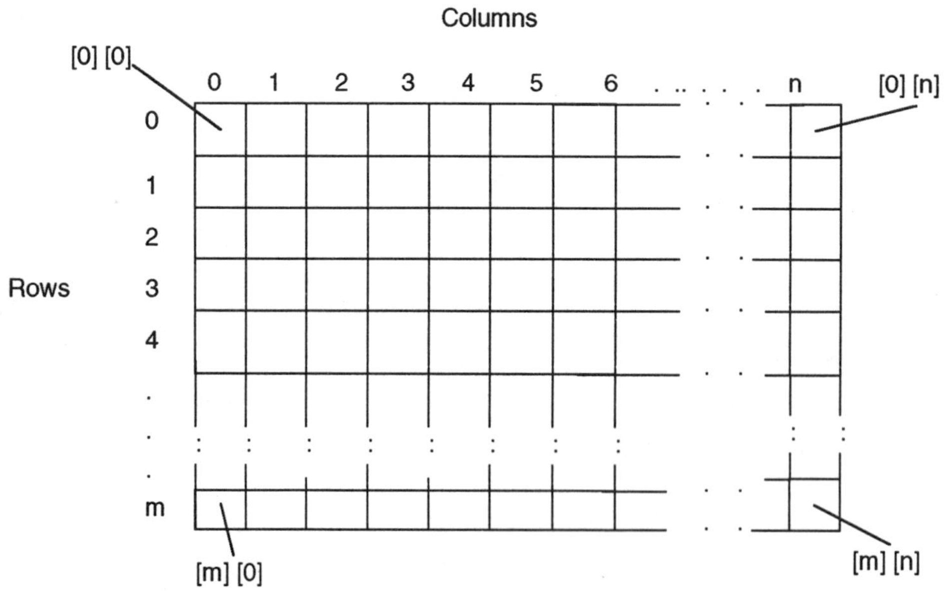

Figure 9-1 The structure of a two-dimensional array.

The elements in a two-dimensional array are located by their row and column indices. The rows are labeled on the vertical axis and range from 0 to *m*. The columns are labeled on the horizontal axis and range from 0 to *n*.

The size of a two-dimensional array is determined by how many rows and columns it contains. Each dimension starts with 0, the last row position is *m*, and the last column position is *n*.

In general, if the last row index is *m*, how many rows does a two-dimensional array contain?

___

In general, if the last column index in *n*, how many columns does a two-dimensional array contain?

___

Since a two-dimensional array has $m + 1$ rows and $n + 1$ columns, its dimension, or size, is $m + 1$ rows by $n + 1$ columns. The dimension can be written as $(m+1) \times (n+1)$.

The elements stored in the array are located by their row and column index values. For example, the element in the upper left corner is located at index [0][0], as shown in Figure 9-1. The element in the lower right corner is located at index [*m*][*n*]. The row index is listed before the column index when accessing a two-dimensional array.

Remember that all arrays in C++ must be defined. Just as with one-dimensional arrays, you must specify the data type of the data elements, the name of the array, and the size of the array in the definition. The only difference when defining a two-dimensional array is in the size specification. You must specify both the row and column sizes. Refer to your text for more information on defining arrays.

Recall that there is a major restriction to the array elements: *The elements in a given array must all be of the same data type*.

Accessing the array elements in a two-dimensional array is done in much the same way as for a one-dimensional array. You can use direct assignment statements, read/write statements, or loops. The difference is that to locate the elements in a two-dimensional array you must specify a row index and column index. The *for* loop structure is the most common way of accessing multiple array elements. When you use a loop to access a multidimensional array, you *must* use a separate loop for each dimension of the array and the loops must be nested.

In Problem 1 you will develop a problem definition, algorithm and program that defines a 3 x 5 two-dimensional array to accept 15 integer elements and display the elements in a 5 x 3 table format. You will use functions to fill and display the array.

In Problem 2 you will develop a problem definition, algorithm, and program that uses a two-dimensional array to store the monthly rental price for resort cabins over a five-year period. You will develop functions to fill the array, compute and store the total rental income for each cabin by year, compute and store the percentage of increase/decrease in price between adjacent years for each cabin, and produce a printed report.

In both problems, you will write the source code program that accepts the required input and produces an output report. You will compile, link, run, test, and print your programs.

Problem 1 - Fill and Flip a Two-dimensional Array

In this exercise you will accept elements from the keyboard and will use a two-dimensional array to store them. Once the elements have been read, you will display the array with the rows and columns reversed, or flipped. You will develop functions to fill and display the array.

Pre-Lab

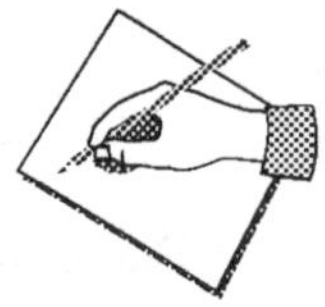

PROBLEM STATEMENT

Write a program that will accept 15 integer elements from the keyboard and use a two-dimensional array to store them. Once the elements have been read, display them as a 3×5 array and then as a 5×3 array. *Hint:* Reverse the rows and columns to display the flipped array. Develop functions to fill and display the array.

Procedure & Questions:

PROBLEM DEFINITION

Output: What output is needed according to the problem statement?

Can a function be used to produce the output?

What arguments must be sent to the output function from the program?

What arguments must be sent back to the program from the function?

Which arguments must be value parameters and which ones should be reference parameters?

Input: What input will be needed for processing to obtain the required output?

Will the program user be required to enter the input or can you hard-code the needed input as constant amounts?

Can a function be used to accept the input?

What arguments must be sent to the input function from the program?

What arguments must be sent back to the program from the function?

Which arguments must be value parameters and which ones should be reference parameters?

How can you pass the arrays to a function?

___

Processing: What processing is required to obtain the output?

___

Discussion:

According to the problem statement, the output will be the original 3×5 array and a 5×3 array which results from reversing the rows and columns of the original array. The array elements are needed as input from the program user. These items can not be hard-coded into the program as constants and must be accepted as variable input from the keyboard. To flip the array simply reverse the row and column indices. The input and output can be programmed using functions that are called by *main()*.

Procedure:

THE ALGORITHM

Here is an initial algorithm for function *main()*. Write an algorithm for the input and output functions that you developed in the problem definition.

```
BEGIN
   CALL FUNCTION TO FILL THE ORIGINAL ARRAY.
   CALL FUNCTION TO DISPLAY THE ARRAY.
   CALL FUNCTION TO DISPLAY THE FLIPPED ARRAY.
END.
```

```
INPUT FUNCTION
   BEGIN



   END.
```

What will you name this function? ___

What does this function do? ___

What types of data must the function accept from the calling program?

Accepts: ___

What types of data must the function return to the calling program?

Returns: ___

Do you need the function to change any of the parameters passed? ___

Which parameters must be passed by value and which by reference? ___

___

Write a prototype/header for this function.

____

DISPLAY ARRAY FUNCTION

BEGIN

END.

What will you name this function? ____

What does this function do? ____

What types of data must the function accept from the calling program?

Accepts: ____

What types of data must the function return to the calling program?

Returns: ____

Do you need the function to change any of the parameters passed? ____________________

Which parameters must be passed by value and which by reference? ____________________

____

Write a prototype/header for this function.

____

In-the-Lab

Procedure & Discussion:

Start Your Compiler

Start your C++ program development environment.

Write the Program

Using the algorithms and prototypes that you developed, complete the following program shell.

```
// LAB 9-1 (L9-1.CPP)
// AUTHOR : type your name here
// DATE WRITTEN : type the date here

#include <iostream.h>
```

```
#include <conio.h>                      // FOR USERS OF DOS BASED C++ COMPILERS

// FUNCTION PROTOTYPES




// DECLARE GLOBAL CONSTANTS FOR ARRAY SIZE


void main()
{
// DEFINE INTEGER ARRAY


//CALL FUNCTION TO FILL ARRAY FROM USER ENTRIES


// CALL FUNCTION TO DISPLAY ARRAY
```

Hint: If you pass the row and column arguments carefully, you can use the same display function to display the original array and the flipped array. Think about it.

```
// CALL FUNCTION TO DISPLAY FLIPPED ARRAY


} // END main()

// THIS FUNCTION WILL FILL THE ARRAY FROM USER ENTRIES

{




} // END INPUT FUNCTION

// THIS FUNCTION WILL DISPLAY THE CONTENTS OF THE ARRAY

{




} // END DISPLAY FUNCTION
```

Save, Compile, and Link the Program

After you have entered the source code, you need to save the program. Give this program the name *L9-1.cpp.* Now that you have saved the program, compile it. Once the program is successfully compiled, link it.

Run and Test the Program

When the program is successfully compiled and linked, run and test it.

Check the Program Results

Check the results of the program run.

A sample of the input screen from the program is shown in Figure 9-2 and a sample output screen is shown in Figure 9-3. Your input and output should look similar to these.

```
This program will form a 3 x 5 array of integers
and display them as a 5 x 3 array.

Enter five elements for row 0 press the ENTER key after each element entry.
6
5
6
8
3

Enter five elements for row 1 press the ENTER key after each element entry.
1
2
3
4
5

Enter five elements for row 2 press the ENTER key after each element entry.
```

Figure 9-2 Sample input screen.

```
Here is the original array

65683
12345
67845

Here is the array with its rows and columns reversed

616
527
638
844
355
```

Figure 9-3 Sample output screen.

Print the Source Code and Sample Runs of the Program

Print a source code listing of your program. Get sample print-outs of the program runs for documentation.

Close the File

When you are finished with the program file, make sure that you have saved any final changes and then close the file.

Problem 2 - Resort Cabin Rental Report

In this exercise you will develop a problem definition, algorithm, and C++ program that will employ functions and two-dimensional arrays to do the following: fill and store the monthly rental price of six resort cabins over a five-year period; compute the total rental income for each cabin by year; compute the percentage increase/decrease in price between adjacent years for each cabin; and print a formatted report.

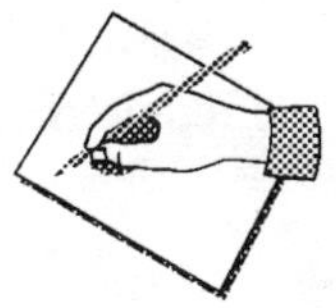

Pre-Lab

PROBLEM STATEMENT

Assume the following table represents the monthly rental price of six resort cabins over a five year period.

		YEAR				
		FIRST	**SECOND**	**THIRD**	**FOURTH**	**FIFTH**
	1	200	210	225	300	235
	2	250	275	300	350	400
CABIN	3	300	325	375	400	450
	4	215	225	250	250	275
	5	355	380	400	404	415
	6	375	400	425	440	500

Write a program that uses functions to perform the following tasks:

- Fill a two-dimensional array with the above table.
- Compute the total rental income for each cabin by year and store the yearly totals in a second array.
- Compute the percentage increase/decrease in price between adjacent years for each cabin and store the percentages in a third array.
- Print a report showing all three arrays in table form with appropriate row/column headings.

Procedure & Questions:

PROBLEM DEFINITION

Output: What output is needed according to the problem statement?

____

Can a function be used to produce the output? ____________________

What arguments must be sent to the output function from the program?

____

What arguments must be sent back to the program from the function?

____

Which arguments must be value parameters and which ones should be reference parameters?

____

Input: What input will be needed for processing to obtain the required output?

____

Will the program user be required to enter the input or can you hard-code the needed input as constant amounts?

____

Can a function be used to accept the input? ____________________

What arguments must be sent to the input function from the program?

____

What arguments must be sent back to the program from the function?

____

Which arguments must be value parameters and which ones should be reference parameters?

____

Processing: What processing is required to compute the total rental income for each cabin by year?

____

What processing is required to compute the percentage increase/decrease in price between adjacent years for each cabin?

____

Discussion:

According to the problem statement, the output will be a printed report showing the monthly cabin rental price, total yearly income per cabin, and price increase/decrease in table form with appropriate row/column headings. The rental price array must be filled by the program user via the keyboard. You must use nested *for* loops to fill the monthly rental price array. To compute the total yearly income per cabin, simply multiply the monthly price by 12 months. To compute the percentage increase/decrease in price between adjacent years, subtract year *a* from year *b* and divide by year *a*, then multiply this quotient by 100 to place the answer in percent form.

Procedure:

THE ALGORITHM

Here is an initial algorithm for function *main()*. Using the input, output, and processing developed in the problem definition, write algorithms for the functions required by the program.

BEGIN
    CALL FUNCTION TO FILL CABINS ARRAY WITH RENTAL PRICES.
    CALL FUNCTION TO CALCULATE YEARLY TOTALS AND PLACE IN ARRAY.
    CALL FUNCTION TO CALCULATE % INCREASE/DECREASE AND PLACE IN ARRAY.
    CALL FUNCTION TO PRINT CABIN RENTAL REPORT.
END.

FILL CABINS ARRAY FUNCTION
    BEGIN

    END.

What will you name this function? ______________________________

What does this function do? ______________________________

What types of data must the function accept from the calling program?

Accepts: ______________________________

What types of data must the function return to the calling program?

Returns: ______________________________

Do you need the function to change any of the parameters passed? ______________

Which parameters must be passed by value and which by reference? ______________

____

Write a prototype/header for this function.

____

COMPUTE YEARLY TOTALS FUNCTION
BEGIN

END.

What will you name this function? ____________________

What does this function do? ____________________

What types of data must the function accept from the calling program?

Accepts: ____________________

What types of data must the function return to the calling program?

Returns: ____________________

Do you need the function to change any of the parameters passed? ____________________

Which parameters must be passed by value and which by reference? ____________________

____

Write a prototype/header for this function.

____

CALCULATE % INCREASE/DECREASE FUNCTION
BEGIN

END.

What will you name this function? ____________________

What does this function do? ____________________

What types of data must the function accept from the calling program?

Accepts: ____

What types of data must the function return to the calling program?

Returns: ____

Do you need the function to change any of the parameters passed? ____________________

Which parameters must be passed by value and which by reference? ____________________

____

Write a prototype/header for this function.

____

PRINT CABIN REPORT FUNCTION
BEGIN

END.

What will you name this function? ______________________________________

What does this function do? ______________________________________

What types of data must the function accept from the calling program?

Accepts: ____

What types of data must the function return to the calling program?

Returns: ____

Do you need the function to change any of the parameters passed? ____________________

Which parameters must be passed by value and which by reference? ____________________

____

Write a prototype/header for this function.

____

In-the-Lab 

Procedure & Discussion:

Start Your Compiler

Start your C++ program development environment.

Write the Program

Make sure that a new file is open. Using the above algorithms, complete the following program shell for the rental cabin input, calculations, and report.

```
// LAB 9-2 (L9-2.CPP)
// AUTHOR : type your name here
// DATE WRITTEN : type the date here

#include <iostream.h>
#include <iomanip.h>
#include <process.h>
#include <fstream.h>          // FOR DOS USERS ONLY
#include <conio.h>            // FOR DOS USERS ONLY

// GLOBAL CONSTANT FOR ARRAY SIZE



// FUNCTION PROTOTYPES




void main()
{
// DEFINE ARRAYS



// CALL FUNCTION TO FILL CABINS ARRAY WITH RENTAL PRICES


// CALL FUNCTION TO CALCULATE YEARLY TOTALS AND PLACE IN TOTALS ARRAY


// CALL FUNCTION TO CALCULATE % INCREASE/DECREASE AND PLACE IN PERCENTS ARRAY


// CALL FUNCTION TO PRINT CABIN RENTAL REPORT


} // END MAIN
```

```
// THIS FUNCTION WILL FILL THE CABINS ARRAY WITH
// THE AVERAGE MONTHLY RENTAL INCOME FROM USER ENTRIES

{



} // END FILL FUNCTION

// THIS FUNCTION WILL CALCULATE THE YEARLY TOTALS
// AND PLACE THEM IN THE TOTALS ARRAY

{



} // END YEARLY TOTALS FUNCTION

// THIS FUNCTION WILL CALCULATE % INCREASE/DECREASE
// AND PLACE IN PERCENTS ARRAY

{




} // END % FUNCTION

// THIS FUNCTION WILL PRINT THE CABIN RENTAL REPORT


{
// DEFINE LOCAL LOOP COUNTER VARIABLES


//***************************************************************************************************
//      THIS SEGMENT OF CODE DEFINES "print" AS AN OUTPUT FILE POINTING
//       TO YOUR PRINTER PORT (PRN) FOR DOS BASED COMPILERS
//***************************************************************************************************
  ofstream print;          // DEFINE PRINTER AS AN OUTPUT FILE STREAM
  print.open("PRN");       // OPEN PRINTER FILE AND POINT TO PRN
  if (!print)              // MAKE SURE PRINTER IS READY
  {
    cout << "There is a problem with the printer.\n";
    exit(1);
  }
//***************************************************************************************************
// PRINT MONTHLY RENTAL INCOME REPORT
{



} // END CABIN LOOP
// PRINT YEARLY RENTAL INCOME REPORT
{



} // END CABIN LOOP
```

```
// PRINT % INCREASE/DECREASE REPORT
{



} // END CABIN LOOP
// CLOSE PRINTER FILE

} // END PRINT FUNCTION
```

Save, Compile, and Link the Program

After you have entered the source code, you need to save the program. Give this program the name *L9-2.cpp.* Now that you have saved the program, compile it. Once the program is successfully compiled, link it.

Run and Test the Program

When the program is successfully compiled and linked, run and test it.

Figure 9-4 shows sample input from the rental cabin program. If your output is not similar, edit the program code so that it produces correct results.

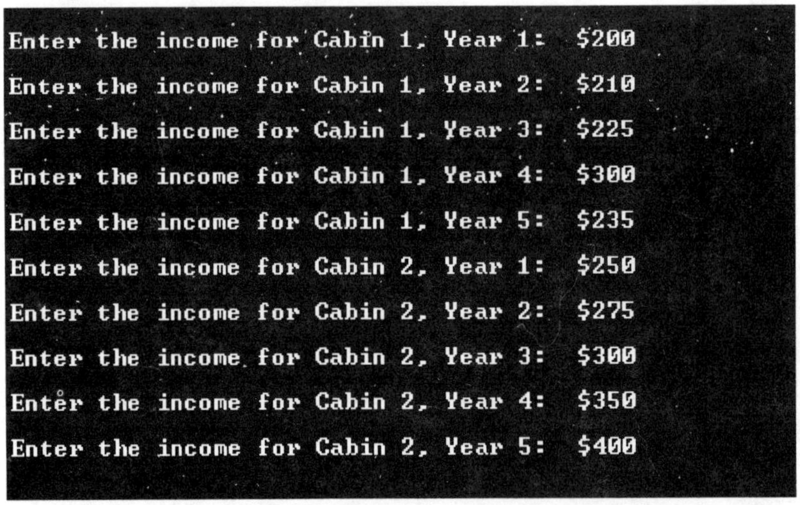

Figure 9-4 Sample cabin rental price input screen.

Figure 9-5 shows the printed reports. Your output should be the same as Figure 9-5, if you entered the numbers shown in the table in the problem definition.

MONTHLY RENTAL INCOME REPORT FOR RESORT CABINS

CABIN			YEAR		
	FIRST	SECOND	THIRD	FOURTH	FIFTH
1	$200	$210	$225	$300	$235
2	$250	$275	$300	$350	$400
3	$300	$325	$375	$400	$450
4	$215	$225	$250	$250	$275
5	$355	$380	$400	$404	$415
6	$375	$400	$425	$440	$500

TOTAL YEARLY INCOME REPORT FOR RESORT CABINS

CABIN	YEAR				
	FIRST	SECOND	THIRD	FOURTH	FIFTH
1	$2400	$2520	$2700	$3600	$2820
2	$3000	$3300	$3600	$4200	$4800
3	$3600	$3900	$4500	$4800	$5400
4	$2580	$2700	$3000	$3000	$3300
5	$4260	$4560	$4800	$4848	$4980
6	$4500	$4800	$5100	$5280	$6000

% INCREASE/DECREASE FROM YEAR TO YEAR

CABIN	YEAR			
	FIRST-SECOND	SECOND-THIRD	THIRD-FOURTH	FOURTH-FIFTH
1	5%	7.1%	33.3%	-21.7%
2	10%	9.1%	16.7%	14.3%
3	8.3%	15.4%	6.7%	12.5%
4	4.7%	11.1%	0%	10%
5	7%	5.3%	1%	2.7%
6	6.7%	6.3	3.5%	13.6%

Figure 9-5 The printed reports from the cabin rental program.

Print the Source Code and Sample Runs of the Program

Print a source code listing of your program. Get print-outs of the program runs.

Close the File

When you are finished with the program file make sure that you have saved any final changes and then close the file.

Exit C++

Exit your C++ compiler when you are finished.

LAB PROJECT #10
Using Pointers

Lab Objectives

In this lab, you will . . .

- Define pointers and use them to access and manipulate data.
- Determine if a word is a palindrome using pointers.
- Initialize and sort an array using pointers.

Introduction

What is a pointer? A pointer represents an actual memory address. Pointers provide a powerful and efficient means of accessing data, especially when that data is part of a data structure, such as an array. The array names that you have been working with are *constant pointers*, since the address they point to can never be changed by the program. A *variable pointer*, on the other hand, is a pointer that can be altered to point to any data of the same type by the program.

To define a pointer, you must tell the compiler what type of data the pointer is pointing to. For example *int *Integer_Pointer;* would be used to point to integer data. The star, *, in front of a pointer variable denotes "the contents of." In other words **p1* is read as "the contents of the memory location where *p1* is pointing."

When you assign a value to pointer, you must be careful not to "mix apples and oranges." Remember, a pointer points to an address in memory. You can assign a pointer to an address such as an array name or the address reference of a variable, *&Value* for example. You can *not* assign a pointer to an element of the array or the variable itself. For example, *p1 = Names*, if *Names* has been defined as an array, and *p2 = &Value*, if *Value* has been defined as a variable, are legal pointer assignments. However, **p1 = &Value* is not a legal assignment, since **p1* refers to data and *&Value* refers to an address. If you get the data and address assignments mixed up in your program, it will produce a data type mismatch error.

You can add or subtract integer values to or from a pointer. The result will be a pointer which is displaced from the original pointer value by the number added or subtracted. If you subtract two pointers pointing to the same array, you get the number of elements between the two pointer locations. You should not add, multiply, or divide pointers, since the results can often be unpredictable.

In Problem 1 you will develop a problem definition, algorithm and program that uses pointers to determine whether or not a word is a palindrome.

In Problem 2 you will develop a problem definition, algorithm, and program that uses an array to store a list of names. You will develop functions to sort and display the array.

In both problems, you will write the source code program that accepts the required input and produces an output report. You will compile, link, run, test, and print your programs.

Problem 1 - Palindromes

In this exercise you will write a program that will determine whether or not a word is a palindrome. You will accept a word from the keyboard and place it into an array. Once the word has been read, you will use pointers to compare the character elements to determine if the word is a palindrome. *Note:* A palindrome is a word that is spelled the same way both forward and backward. For example, "MOM" is a palindrome.

Pre-Lab

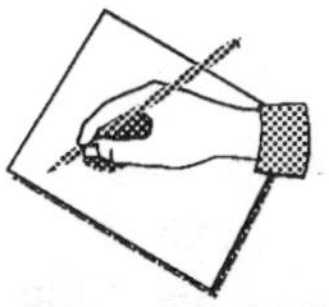

PROBLEM STATEMENT

Write a program that will determine whether or not a word is a palindrome. Place a word entered by the program user into an array and use pointers to compare the character elements for the palindrome determination. Notify the program user whether or not the word is a palindrome.

Procedure & Questions:

PROBLEM DEFINITION

Output: What output is needed according to the problem statement?

____

Input: What input will be needed for processing to obtain the required output?

____

Will the program user be required to enter the input or can you hard-code the needed input as constant amounts?

____

Processing: What processing is required to determine if the word is a palindrome?

____

____

Discussion:

According to the problem statement, the output will be a message to the user as to whether or not the word entered is a palindrome. The word is needed as input from the program user. The word can not be hard-coded into the program as a constant and must be accepted as variable input from the keyboard. To determine if the word is a palindrome, you will compare the first and last characters of the word, then continue comparing the other characters in the word, moving to the center of the word for each comparison, until you reach the center of the word. If each set of characters match, the word is a palindrome and can be spelled the same both forward and backward. If any of the comparisons do not match, the word is not a palindrome.

Procedure:

THE ALGORITHM

Here is an initial algorithm for function *main()*. Write a more detailed algorithm for the input, output, and processing.

BEGIN
  GET THE WORD FROM THE PROGRAM USER.
  TEST THE WORD TO DETERMINE IF IT IS A PALINDROME.
  DISPLAY RESULTS.
END.

BEGIN
  GET THE WORD FROM THE PROGRAM USER.

  TEST THE WORD TO DETERMINE IF IT IS A PALINDROME.

  DISPLAY RESULTS.

END.

In-the-Lab 

Procedure & Discussion:

Start Your Compiler

Start your C++ program development environment.

Write the Program

Using the algorithm that you developed, complete the following program shell. *Hint:* You can use the *strlen()* function to find the last character of the array.

```
// LAB 10-1 (L10-1.CPP)
// AUTHOR : type your name here
// DATE WRITTEN : type the date here

#include <iostream.h>
#include <stdio.h>
#include <string.h>
#include <conio.h>                    // FOR DOS BASED C++ COMPILERS ONLY

void main()
{
// DECLARE ARRAY SIZE CONSTANT

//DECLARE BOOLEAN DATA TYPE


// DEFINE CHARACTER ARRAY AND TWO CHARACTER POINTERS


// FILL ARRAY FROM USER ENTRIES USING POINTERS



// MAKE p1 POINT TO FIRST ARRAY CHARACTER

// MAKE p2 POINT TO LAST ARRAY CHARACTER

// ASSUME WORD IS A PALINDROME

// TEST ARRAY FOR PALINDROME BY COMPARING CHARACTERS USING POINTERS

```

```
// DISPLAY PALINDROME RESULTS ACCORDING TO BOOLEAN FLAG



} // END main()
```

Save, Compile, and Link the Program

After you have entered the source code, save the program. Name this program *L10-1.cpp*. Now that you have saved the program, compile and link it.

Run and Test the Program

When the program is successfully compiled and linked, run and test it.

Check the Program Results

Check the results of the program run. Sample results from the program are shown in Figure 10-1 and Figure 10-2. Your results should look similar to these.

```
Enter a word no longer than 25 characters
All characters must be the same case:  hello


Your word is not a palindrome.
```

Figure 10-1 Sample program results where the word entered is not a palindrome.

```
Enter a word no longer than 25 characters
All characters must be the same case:  radar


Your word is a palindrome.
```

Figure 10-2 Sample results where the word entered is a palindrome.

Print the Source Code and Sample Runs of the Program

Print a source code listing of your program and get sample print-outs of the program runs for documentation.

Close the File

When you are finished with the program file, make sure that you have saved any final changes and then close the file.

Problem 2 - Sort an Array Using Pointers (Indirection)

In this exercise you will develop a problem definition, algorithm, and C++ program that will employ pointers and functions to initialize an array with names, sort the names, and display the names. This problem requires that you use indirection to access an array of pointers to strings. Consult your text and/or instructor to make sure that you understand the concept of indirection before attempting this problem.

Pre-Lab

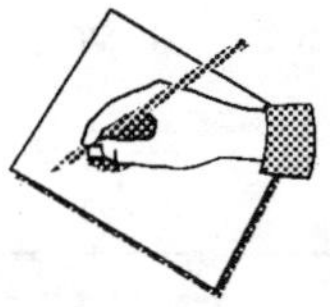

PROBLEM STATEMENT

Suppose that you have the following strings in an array:

"Athena"
"Andy"
"Jason"
"Brenda"
"Larry"
"Zane"
"Lori"
"Elaine"
"Michael"

Write a program using pointers to initialize an array with the above names in the order given. Develop a function that uses pointers to display the names in the array. Employ another function in the program to sort the names within the array using the following sort algorithm:

```
For i = 0 to Array Size
    For j = i + 1 to Array Size
        If Array[i] > Array[j]
            Swap Array [i] and Array[j]
```

Display the sorted names using a display function to verify the sorting operation.

Procedure & Questions:

PROBLEM DEFINITION

Output: What output is needed according to the problem statement?

____

A function will be used to produce the output.

What arguments must be sent to the output function from the program?

____

What arguments must be sent back to the program from the function?

____

Input: What input will be needed for processing to obtain the required output?

____

Will the program user be required to enter the input or can you hard-code the needed input as constant amounts?

____

Processing: What processing is required to sort the names?

____

____

Discussion:

According to the problem statement, the output will be the names in the order they have been initialized in the array and the sorted names. The names will be hard-coded by initializing them into the array at the time that you declare the array. The processing will employ the given sort algorithm to sort the names in the array. *Hint:* Use the standard *strcmp()* function to compare the names during the sorting operation.

Procedure:

THE ALGORITHM

Here is an initial algorithm for function *main()*. Using the input, output, and processing developed in the problem definition, write algorithms for the functions required by the program.

```
BEGIN
   FILL THE ARRAY WITH THE GIVEN NAMES.
   CALL FUNCTION TO DISPLAY THE NAME ARRAY.
   CALL FUNCTION TO SORT THE NAME ARRAY.
   CALL FUNCTION TO DISPLAY THE SORTED NAME ARRAY.
END.
```

```
SORT ARRAY FUNCTION
   BEGIN



   END.
```

What will you name this function? ______________________________

What does this function do? ______________________________

What types of data must the function accept from the calling program?

Accepts: ______________________________

What types of data must the function return to the calling program?

Returns: ______________________________

Do you need the function to change any of the parameters passed? ______________

Which parameters must be passed by value and which by reference? ______________

____

(Remember, array names and pointers are always passed by reference, since they are memory addresses.)

Write a prototype/header for this function.

____

DISPLAY ARRAY FUNCTION

BEGIN

END.

What will you name this function? ______________________________

What does this function do? ______________________________

What types of data must the function accept from the calling program?

Accepts: ______________________________

What types of data must the function return to the calling program?

Returns: ______________________________

Do you need the function to change any of the parameters passed? ______________

Which parameters must be passed by value and which by reference? ______________

____

(Remember, array names and pointers are always passed by reference, since they are memory addresses.)

Write a prototype/header for this function.

____

In-the-Lab 

Procedure & Discussion:

Start Your Compiler

Start your C++ program development environment.

Write the Program

Make sure that a new file is open. Using the above algorithms, complete the following program shell for initializing, sorting, and displaying the array.

```
// LAB 10-2 (L10-2.CPP)
// AUTHOR : type your name here
// DATE WRITTEN : type the date here

#include <iostream.h>
#include <string.h>
#include <conio.h>              // FOR DOS USERS ONLY

// FUNCTION PROTOTYPES


void main()
{
// DEFINE ARRAY AND INITIALIZE WITH THE NAMES

// CALL FUNCTION TO DISPLAY THE NAMES

// CALL FUNCTION TO SORT THE NAMES

// CALL FUNCTION TO DISPLAY THE SORTED NAMES

} // END MAIN

// THIS FUNCTION WILL SORT THE NAMES ARRAY

{
```

Remember that that you are using indirection. To access the individual characters you must use $**$*Names* , if your array's name is *Names*, and to access the entire string at a given pointer address you use $*$*Names*. Thus, $**$*Names* points to the first character of the name and $*$*Names* points to the whole name.

```
} // END SORT FUNCTION
```

```
// THIS FUNCTION WILL DISPLAY THE ARRAY
{



} // END DISPLAY FUNCTION
```

Save, Compile, and Link the Program

After you have entered the source code, you need to save the program. Give this program the name *L10-2.cpp.* Now that you have saved the program, compile and link it.

Run and Test the Program

When the program is successfully compiled and linked, run and test it.

Figure 10-3 shows sample output from the program. If your output is not similar, edit the program code so that it produces correct results.

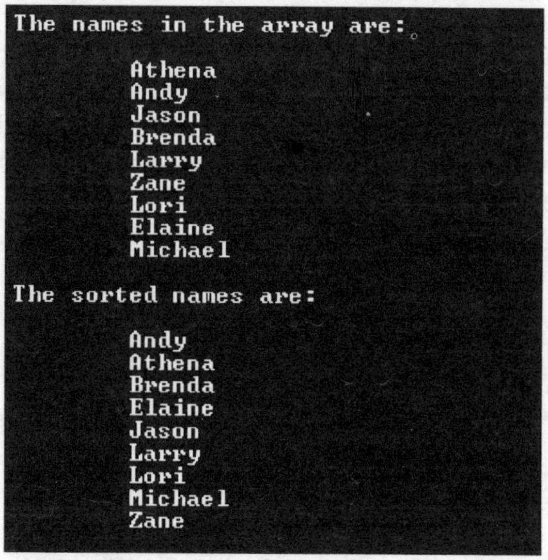

Figure 10-3 Sample program output screen.

Print the Source Code and Sample Runs of the Program

Print a source code listing of your program and get print-outs of the program runs.

Close the File

When you are finished with the program file make sure that you have saved any final changes and then close the file.

Exit C++

Exit your C++ compiler when you are finished.

LAB PROJECT #11
Structures

Lab Objectives

In this lab, you will . . .

- Declare, define, fill, and display structures.
- Pass structures to user-defined functions for manipulation.
- Create complex data structures by building nested structures.

Introduction

A *structure*, like an array, is a structured data type that provides a well-organized means of storing data. Recall that when you define an array, you must specify the number of elements it contains and the data type of the elements. The restriction of only one data type per array is a serious limitation of the array data structure. The structure data type, on the other hand, permits information of different data types to be conveniently stored, accessed, and manipulated.

The structure *members* give the structure the ability to contain data of different types. A structure consists of a collection of related members. Each member is an item of meaningful data. A structure can contain any number of members, with each member having a unique name and data type.

Like enumerated data, a structure is a user-defined data structure that must be declared before it can be used. The format of a structure declaration is shown below.

```
struct <structure name>
{
    <member 1 data type>  <member 1 name>;
    <member 2 data type>  <member 2 name>;
                          •
                          •
    <member n data type>  <member n name>;
};
```

You must define a variable after declaring the structure to access it. Remember that a declaration simply specifies the name and format of the data structure, but does not reserve storage, while a definition reserves storage. Therefore, each variable definition for a given structure creates an area in memory where data will be stored according to the declared structure format. Structure variables can be defined by listing them immediately after the closing brace of the structure declaration, or by listing the structure name followed by the corresponding variables any place in the program prior to their use.

When accessing a structure, you are actually accessing the members that make up the structure. You can access the structure members by using the dot, •, operator, or by using the pointer, →, operator. To use the dot operator for structure access, list the structure variable, the dot, and the member name. To use the pointer operator for structure access, you must define a pointer variable to point to the structure, then use the pointer variable, a pointer symbol –>, and the member name.

In addition to the standard data types that you have used so far, the structure can contain other structures. This is called a *nested structure*. The structure to be used in the nested structure must be declared previous to its use in the nested structure.

In Problem 1 you will develop a problem definition, algorithm and program that fills and displays a given declaration for a baseball pitcher stats structure. You will use functions to fill and display the structure data.

In Problem 2 you will develop a problem definition, algorithm, and program that will declare, fill, and display a nested structure that stores a person's name and address.

In both problems, you will write the source code program that accepts the required input and produces an output report. You will compile, link, run, test, and print your programs.

Problem 1 - Filling and Displaying Structures

In this exercise you will use structures to store the name, team, year, pitching and hitting stats for a baseball pitcher. You will use the given structure declaration and develop functions to fill and display the structures.

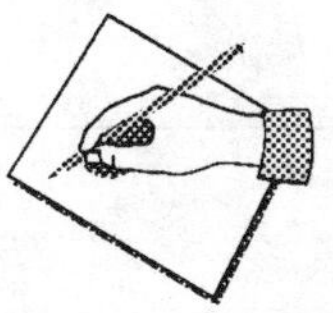

Pre-Lab

PROBLEM STATEMENT

Use the following *Baseball_Pitcher* structure declaration for this problem. Analyze the given declaration and observe how the structures are nested. In addition, notice how a pointer variable is defined to point to the structure.

```
// PITCHING STATS STRUCTURE DECLARATION
 struct Pitching
 {
  int Wins;                    // NUMBER OF PITCHER'S WINS
  int Losses;                  // NUMBER OF PITCHER'S LOSSES
  float ERA;                   // PITCHER'S EARNED RUN AVERAGE
 };

// HITTING STATS STRUCTURE DECLARATION
 struct Batting
 {
  int At_Bat;                  // NUMBER OF PITCHER'S TIMES AT BAT
  int Home_Runs;               // NUMBER OF PITCHER'S HOME RUNS
  int RBIs;                    // PITCHER'S RUNS BATTED IN
  float Average;               // PITCHER'S BATTING AVERAGE
 };

// BASEBALL PITCHER STRUCTURE DECLARATION
 struct Baseball_Pitcher
 {
  char  Name[30];              // PITCHER'S NAME
  char  Team[30];              // PITCHER'S TEAM
  int Year;                    // EFFECTIVE YEAR OF STATS
  Pitching Pitch;              // VARIABLE FOR PITCHING STRUCTURE
  Batting Bat;                 // VARIABLE FOR BATTING STRUCTURE
 };

void main()
{
```

```
// DEFINE VARIABLES
  Baseball_Pitcher Pitch, *Pitcher_Ptr;            // DEFINE POINTER VARIABLE TO STRUCTURE
  Pitcher_Ptr = &Pitch;
```

Write functions that uses the given structure pointer variable to fill and display the structure members of the foregoing *Baseball_Pitcher* structure and incorporate them into a program to fill and display a baseball pitcher's stats, including his name, team, the year, wins, losses, ERA, at bats, home runs, RBIs, and average.

Procedure & Questions:

PROBLEM DEFINITION

Output: What output is needed according to the problem statement?

____

A function will be used to produce the output.

What arguments must be sent to the output function from the program?

____

What arguments must be sent back to the program from the function?

____

Input: What input will be needed for processing to obtain the required output?

____

Will the program user be required to enter the input or can you hard-code the needed input as constant amounts?

____

A function will be used to accept the input.

What arguments must be sent to the input function from the program?

____

What arguments must be sent back to the program from the function?

____

Processing: What processing is required to obtain the output?

____

Discussion:

According to the problem statement, the output will be a display showing a pitcher's stats, including his name, team, the year, wins, losses, ERA, at bats, home runs, RBIs, and average. The pitcher's stats are needed as input. These items can not be hard-coded into the program as constants and must be accepted as variable input from the keyboard. There is no processing required after the input data is accepted from the user. The input and output can be programmed using functions that are called by *main()*.

Procedure:

THE ALGORITHM

Here is an initial algorithm for function *main()*. Write an algorithm for the input and output functions that you developed in the problem definition.

BEGIN
    CALL FUNCTION TO FILL THE Baseball_Pitcher STRUCTURE.
    CALL FUNCTION TO DISPLAY THE Baseball_Pitcher STRUCTURE.
END.

FILL Baseball_Pitcher STRUCTURE FUNCTION
    BEGIN

    END.

What will you name this function? ______________________________

What does this function do? ______________________________

What types of data must the function accept from the calling program?

Accepts: ______________________________

What types of data must the function return to the calling program?

Returns: ______________________________

Do you need the function to change any of the parameters passed? ______________________________

Which parameters must be passed by value and which by reference? ____________________

____

(Remember, array names and pointers are always passed by reference, since they are memory addresses.)

Write a prototype/header for this function.

____

DISPLAY Baseball_Pitcher STRUCTURE FUNCTION
BEGIN

END.

What will you name this function? ____________________

What does this function do? ____________________

What types of data must the function accept from the calling program?

Accepts: ____________________

What types of data must the function return to the calling program?

Returns: ____________________

Do you need the function to change any of the parameters passed? ____________________

Which parameters must be passed by value and which by reference? ____________________

____

Write a prototype/header for this function.

____

In-the-Lab

Procedure & Discussion:

<u>**Start Your Compiler**</u>

Start your C++ program development environment.

<u>**Write the Program**</u>

Using the algorithms and prototypes that you developed, complete the following program shell. *Note:* You must use the *strcpy()* function to make a direct assignment to a string pointer.

```
// LAB 11-1 (L11-1.CPP)
// AUTHOR : type your name here
// DATE WRITTEN : type the date here

#include <iostream.h>
#include <stdio.h>
#include <iomanip.h>
#include <conio.h>           // FOR DOS BASED C++ COMPILERS ONLY

// PITCHING STATS STRUCTURE DECLARATION
 struct Pitching
 {
  int Wins;                  // NUMBER OF PITCHER'S WINS
  int Losses;                // NUMBER OF PITCHER'S LOSSES
  float ERA;                 // PITCHER'S EARNED RUN AVERAGE
 };

// HITTING STATS STRUCTURE DECLARATION
 struct Batting
 {
  int At_Bat;                // NUMBER OF PITCHER'S TIMES AT BAT
  int Home_Runs;             // NUMBER OF PITCHER'S HOME RUNS
  int RBIs;                  // PITCHER'S RUNS BATTED IN
  float Average;             // PITCHER'S BATTING AVERAGE
 };

// BASEBALL PITCHER STRUCTURE DECLARATION
 struct Baseball_Pitcher
 {
  char  Name[30];            // PITCHER'S NAME
  char  Team[30];            // PITCHER'S TEAM
  int Year;                  // EFFECTIVE YEAR OF STATS
  Pitching Pitch;            // VARIABLE FOR PITCHING STRUCTURE
  Batting Bat;               // VARIABLE FOR BATTING STRUCTURE
 };

// FUNCTION PROTOTYPES
```

```
void main()
{
// DEFINE VARIABLES
 Baseball_Pitcher Pitch, *Pitcher_Ptr;              // DEFINE POINTER VARIABLE TO STRUCTURE
 Pitcher_Ptr = &Pitch;

// CALL FUNCTION TO FILL THE Baseball_Pitcher STRUCTURE FROM THE KEYBOARD


// CALL FUNCTION TO DISPLAY THE Baseball_Pitcher STRUCTURE


} // END main()

// THIS FUNCTION WILL FILL THE Baseball_Pitcher STRUCTURE FROM THE KEYBOARD

{



} // END FILL FUNCTION

// THIS FUNCTION WILL DISPLAY THE Baseball_Pitcher STRUCTURE

{



} // END DISPLAY FUNCTION
```

Save, Compile, and Link the Program

After you have entered the source code, you need to save the program. Give this program the name *L11-1.cpp.* Now that you have entered and saved the program, compile and link it.

Run and Test the Program

When the program is successfully compiled and linked, run and test it using the following data.

Name:	John Smoltz
Team:	Atlanta Braves
Year:	1989
Wins:	12
Losses:	11
ERA:	2.94
At Bats:	20
Home Runs:	0
RBIs:	11
Average:	0.190

Check the Program Results

A sample of the input screen from the pitcher stats program is shown in Figure 11-1 and a sample output screen is shown in Figure 11-2. Your input and output should look similar to these.

```
Please enter the name of the pitcher:  John Smoltz

Please enter the name of the pitcher's team:  Atlanta Braves

Please enter the year:  1989

Please enter the pitcher's number of wins:  12

Please enter the pitcher's number of losses:  11

Please enter the pitcher's ERA:  2.94

Please enter the pitcher's number of at bats:  20

Please enter the pitcher's number of home runs:  0

Please enter the pitcher's number of RBIs:  11

Please enter the pitcher's batting average:  .190
```

Figure 11-1 Sample input screen for the pitcher stats program.

```
The stats for John Smoltz are:

        Name:  John Smoltz
        Team:  Atlanta Braves
        Year:  1989
        Wins:  12
        Losses:  11
        ERA:  2.94
        At Bats:  20
        Home Runs:  0
        RBI's:  11
        Bat Average:  0.19
```

Figure 11-2 Sample output screen for the pitcher stats program.

Print the Source Code and Sample Runs of the Program

Print a source code listing of your program. Get sample print-outs of the program runs for documentation using the stats of your favorite pitcher.

Close the File

When you are finished with the program file, make sure that you have saved any final changes and then close the file.

Problem 2 - Declare and Access a Nested Structure

In this exercise you will develop a problem definition, algorithm, and C++ program to declare and define a nested structure for storing a person's name and address. You will develop functions to fill and display the structure members.

Pre-Lab

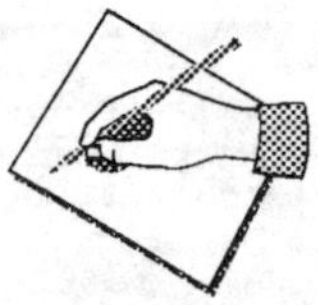

PROBLEM STATEMENT

Write a program that uses functions to fill from the keyboard and display in proper address format the members of a nested structure for a persons name and address.

Procedure & Questions:

PROBLEM DEFINITION

Output: What output is needed according to the problem statement?

A function will be used to produce the output.

What arguments must be sent to the output function from the program?

What arguments must be sent back to the program from the function?

Input: What input will be needed for processing to obtain the required output?

Will the program user be required to enter the input or can you hard-code the needed input as constant amounts?

A function will be used to accept the input from the keyboard.

What arguments must be sent to the input function from the program?

What arguments must be sent back to the program from the function?

Processing: What processing is required to obtain the specified output?

Discussion:

According to the problem statement, the output will be a display showing a person's name and address, in proper address format. The name and address items are needed as input. These items can not be hard-coded into the program as constants and must be accepted as variable input from the keyboard. There is no processing required after the input data is accepted from the user. The input and output can be programmed using functions that are called by *main()*.

Procedure:

THE ALGORITHM

Here is an initial algorithm for function *main()* using the input and output developed in the problem definition. Develop the nested structure format and write an algorithm to fill and display the structure.

BEGIN
  CALL FUNCTION TO FILL THE Person STRUCTURE.
  CALL FUNCTION TO DISPLAY THE Person STRUCTURE.
END.

Declare a structure consisting of a person's last name, first name, and middle initial.

What will the name of the structure be? ______________________________

What members does this structure need? ______________________________

____

What are the data types of each member? ______________________________

____

Write the necessary structure members in the correct structure format.

Declare a structure consisting of a person's street number, street address, city, state, and zip code.

What will the name of the structure be? ______________________________

What members does this structure need? ______________________________

____

What are the data types of each member? ______________________________

____

Write the necessary structure members in the correct structure format.

Declare a nested structure consisting of a person's name and address.

What will the name of the structure be? ______________________________

What members does this structure need? ______________________________

____

What are the data types of each member? (Think about it.) ______________________

____

Write the necessary structure members in the correct structure format.

Define a pointer variable for the above structure. ______________________________

Write the algorithm to fill the person structure.

FILL PERSON STRUCTURE FUNCTION
BEGIN

END.

What will you name this function? ______________________________

What does this function do? ______________________________

What types of data must the function accept from the calling program?

Accepts: ______________________________

What types of data must the function return to the calling program?

Returns: ______________________________

Do you need the function to change any of the parameters passed? ______________

Which parameters must be passed by value and which by reference? ______________

____

Write a prototype/header for this function.

____

Write the algorithm to display the person structure.

DISPLAY PERSON STRUCTURE FUNCTION
BEGIN

END.

What will you name this function? ______________________________

What does this function do? ______________________________

What types of data must the function accept from the calling program?

Accepts: ______________________________

What types of data must the function return to the calling program?

Returns: ______________________________

Do you need the function to change any of the parameters passed? ______________________

Which parameters must be passed by value and which by reference? ____________________

____

Write a prototype/header for this function.

____

In-the-Lab

Procedure & Discussion:

Start Your Compiler

Start your C++ program development environment.

Write the Program

Make sure that a new file is open. Using the above algorithms, complete the following program shell for filling and displaying the nested structure.

```
// LAB 11-2 (L11-2.CPP)
// AUTHOR : type your name here
// DATE WRITTEN : type the date here

#include <iostream.h>
#include <iomanip.h>
#include <stdlib.h>
#include <conio.h>            // FOR DOS USERS ONLY

// Name STRUCTURE DECLARATION



// Address STRUCTURE DECLARATION



// Person STRUCTURE DECLARATION


```

```
// POINTER VARIABLE TO ACCESS Person STRUCTURE


// FUNCTION PROTOTYPES



void main()
{
//CALL FUNCTION TO FILL THE Person STRUCTURE FROM THE KEYBOARD


//CALL FUNCTION TO DISPLAY THE Person STRUCTURE


} //END Main

// FUNCTION TO FILL Person STRUCTURE
{




} //END FILL STRUCTURE FUNCTION

// FUNCTION TO DISPLAY Person STRUCTURE
{




} //END DISPLAY STRUCTURE FUNCTION
```

Save, Compile, and Link the Program

After you have entered the source code, save this program with the name *L11-2.cpp.* Now that you have saved the program, compile and link it.

Run and Test the Program

When the program is successfully compiled and linked, run and test it. Enter the required information when prompted.

Figure 11-3 shows a sample input screen from the person's address information program. Figure 11-4 shows a sample output. If your input and output are not similar, edit the program code so that it produces correct results.

```
Enter the last name:  Snider

Enter the first name:  Brenda

Enter the Middle Initial:  F

Enter the Street Number:  210

Enter the Street Name:  W. Oklahoma

Enter the City:  Somewhere

Enter the State(XX):  MO

Enter the Zip code(XXXXX):  12345
```

Figure 11-3 Sample input screen.

```
Brenda F Snider
210 W. Oklahoma
Somewhere MO 12345
```

Figure 11-4 Sample output screen.

Print the Source Code and Sample Runs of the Program

Print a source code listing of your program and get print-outs of the program runs.

Close the File

When you are finished with the program file make sure that you have saved any final changes and then close the file.

Exit C++

Exit your C++ compiler when you are finished.

LAB PROJECT #12
Object-Oriented Programming

Lab Objectives

In this lab, you will . . .

- Declare classes and define objects for the classes.
- Implement class member functions to manipulate class data members.
- Create projects to handle multi-file programs.

Introduction

Object-oriented programs are developed from the inside out by expanding on simple classes. The fundamental components of any object-oriented program are the *class* and its *objects*. A given class provides the foundation for creating specific objects, each of which share the general characteristics and behavior of the class.

At the abstract level, a class can be described as an interface, since it defines the behavior common to all of its objects. At the implementation level, a class is a construct that describes a set of data and related operations that are common to its objects. The abstract level provides an outside view of a class, while the implementation level provides the inside view of the class, disclosing its behavioral secrets.

At the implementation level, a class is comprised of a private section and a public section each with members. Any item declared in a class is called a class *member*. To implement a class you create public members and private members. Each of the public and private sections can consist of member functions and/or member data. The public member functions and data can be accessed anywhere within the scope of a given class. Public member data can be changed and member functions can be called from outside the class, as long as the class is visible at the time of access. The private member data and functions are only accessible by the public member functions defined for the class. This means that the private member data can only be changed by the public member functions in the class and that private member functions can only be called by the public member functions. The private class members are hidden from the outside, since they can only be accessed using the public member functions. This provides for *information hiding* within the class.

Encapsulation is the idea of packaging things together in a well-defined programming unit. A class in C++ is encapsulated, since it consists of a collection of data fields and related functions. The class provides information hiding through its private member declarations.

An object is an instance of a class that can be manipulated in a program. Objects defined for a class share the fundamental framework of the class. Thus, an object of a given class has the structure and behavior defined by the class. You define an object for a class just like you define a variable for a structure. When the object is defined, memory is allocated to store the class for which the object is defined.

The format for declaring a class is shown below.

```
class <class name>
{
public:
<return type> <function 1 name> (<function 1 parameter listing>);
<return type> <function 2 name> (<function 2 parameter listing>);
            •
            •
<return type> <function n name> (<function n parameter listing>);
<data type> <variable name 1>;
<data type> <variable name 2>;
            •
            •
<data type> <variable name n>;

private:
<data type> <variable name 1>;
<data type> <variable name 2>;
            •
            •
<data type> <variable name n>;
<return type> <function 1 name> (<function 1 parameter listing>);
<return type> <function 2 name> (<function 2 parameter listing>);
            •
            •
<return type> <function n name> (<function n parameter listing>);
};
```

Object-oriented programs are normally constructed using a multi-file approach. Class declarations are placed in separate header files. All the member function implementations for a given class are placed in a separate file that includes the class header file. Finally, the application program is placed in a separate file that includes all the class header files. The individual files are edited and compiled separately then linked together to form an executable file. Most C++ compilers include a project manager that facilitates the multi-file approach to building programs.

In Problem 1 you will create an employee class and object. In Problem 2 you will create an invoice class and object. In both problems, you will declare the class in a header file, create an implementation file for the member functions, develop an application program that defines an object for the class and tests the function implementations. You will then build a project file, linking the files that you have developed. You will compile, debug, run, test, and print the project files.

Problem 1 - Create an Employee Class, Object, and Project File

In this exercise, you will declare an employee class in a header file, create an implementation file for the member functions, develop an application program that defines an object for the employee class and tests the function implementations. Finally, you will build a project file linking the files that you have developed. You will compile, debug, run, test, and print the project files.

Pre-Lab

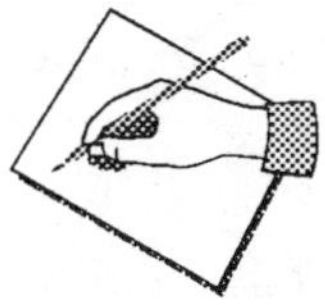

PROBLEM STATEMENT

Write an application program that defines an object for an employee class and tests the required functions to produce an employee's payroll report including the employee's name, hourly rate, hours worked, and weekly pay.

Procedure & Questions:

PROBLEM DEFINITION

The following problem definition will be used when creating the functions for this problem.

Output: What output will be produced according to the problem statement?

____

Input: What input will be needed for processing to obtain the required output?

____

Processing: What processing is required to calculate the weekly pay including the option for overtime?

____

Discussion:

According to the problem statement, the output will be a display showing the employee's name, hourly rate, hours worked, and weekly pay. The employee's name, hourly rate, and hours worked are needed as input. To process the weekly pay, you will test the hours to determine if they are less than, equal to, or greater than 40. If the hours are less than or equal to 40, the weekly pay will simply be hours worked multiplied by the hourly rate. If the hours worked are greater than 40, the weekly pay will be 40 multiplied by the hourly rate for regular pay and any hours over 40 multiplied by 1.5 of the hourly rate for overtime pay.

Procedure:

Before you can develop an application program, you need to declare an employee class in a header file and develop the implementations for the required functions in an implementation file. Finally, you can create a project to combine the separate files into a working application.

PROBLEM STATEMENT FOR THE CLASS

Declare an employee class as part of a header file. The class is to have data members to store the employee's name, hourly rate, and hours worked. The class is to have member functions to perform the following tasks:

- A constructor function to initialize the hourly rate to a minimum wage of $4.25 per hour and the hours worked to 0 (zero).
- Three separate functions to get the employee's name, hourly rate, and hours worked from the user.
- A function to return weekly pay, including overtime pay where overtime is paid at a rate of time-and-a-half for any hours worked over 40.
- Three separate access functions to display each of the data members.
- A function to display the employee's total weekly pay.

Procedure & Questions:

PROBLEM DEFINITION FOR THE CLASS

What will you name this class? ____

List the function members that need to be declared public. ______________________________

____

List the data members that need to be declared private. ________________________________

____

PROBLEM STATEMENT FOR THE FUNCTIONS

Here is a list of functions required for implementing the members of the employee class. Write algorithms for these functions from the information you developed in the problem definition. Remember, if class function members are operating directly on class data members, the data members are not passed or returned by the functions.

- Constructor function to define the employee object and initialize the data members.
- Function to get the employee name.
- Function to get the hourly rate.
- Function to get the hours worked.
- Function to calculate the weekly pay.
- Function to display the employee name.
- Function to display the hourly rate.
- Function to display the hours worked.
- Function to display the weekly pay.

THE ALGORITHMS

CONSTRUCTOR FUNCTION TO INITIALIZE THE DATA MEMBERS.

BEGIN

END.

What will you name this function? ______________________________

What does this function do? ______________________________

Which class data members are operated on by this function? ______________________________

____

Write a function header using the scoping operator, ::, to make the connection between the class and function.

____

FUNCTION TO GET THE EMPLOYEE NAME

BEGIN

END.

What will you name this function? ______________________________

What does this function do? ______________________________

Which class data members are operated on by this function? ______________________________

____

Write a function header using the scoping operator, ::, to make the connection between the class and function.

____

FUNCTION TO GET THE HOURLY RATE

BEGIN

END.

What will you name this function? ______________________________

What does this function do? ______________________________

Which class data members are operated on by this function? ______________________________

____

Write a function header using the scoping operator, ::, to make the connection between the class and function.

____

FUNCTION TO GET THE HOURS WORKED
BEGIN

END.

What will you name this function? ______________________________

What does this function do? ______________________________

Which class data members are operated on by this function? ______________________________

____

Write a function header using the scoping operator, ::, to make the connection between the class and function.

____

FUNCTION TO CALCULATE THE WEEKLY PAY
BEGIN

END.

What will you name this function? ______________________________

What does this function do? ______________________________

Which class data members are operated on by this function? ______________________________

____

Write a function header using the scoping operator, ::, to make the connection between the class and function.

____

FUNCTION TO DISPLAY THE EMPLOYEE NAME

BEGIN

END.

What will you name this function? ____

What does this function do? ____

Which class data members are operated on by this function? __________________________

____

Write a function header using the scoping operator, ::, to make the connection between the class and function.

____

FUNCTION TO DISPLAY THE HOURLY RATE

BEGIN

END.

What will you name this function? ____

What does this function do? ____

Which class data members are operated on by this function? __________________________

____

Write a function header using the scoping operator, ::, to make the connection between the class and function.

____

FUNCTION TO DISPLAY THE HOURS WORKED

BEGIN

END.

What will you name this function? ______________________________

What does this function do? ______________________________

Which class data members are operated on by this function? ______________________________

____

Write a function header using the scoping operator, ::, to make the connection between the class and function.

____

FUNCTION TO DISPLAY THE WEEKLY PAY

BEGIN

END.

What will you name this function? ______________________________

What does this function do? ______________________________

Which class data members are operated on by this function? ______________________________

____

Write a function header using the scoping operator, ::, to make the connection between the class and function.

____

Write the algorithm for the steps to be carried out by function *main()* in the application program.

BEGIN

END.

In-the-Lab

Procedure & Discussion:

Start Your Compiler

Start your C++ program development environment.

Write the Header File

Make sure that a new file is open. Using the class description that you developed, complete the following header file shell.

```
// LAB 12-1 (EMPLOYEE.H)
// AUTHOR : type your name here
// DATE WRITTEN : type the date here
```

```
// DECLARE EMPLOYEE CLASS
class
{
public:



private:



};
```

__Save and Compile the Header File__

After you have entered the source code for the class declaration, save the header file with the name *employee.h*. Compile the header file. Debug the file if there are errors. Be sure to recompile and save the file if you make any modifications to the source code.

__Write the Implementation File__

Open a new file for the function implementation file. Using the algorithms that you developed, complete the following implementation file shell.

```
// LAB 12-1 (EMPLOYEE.CPP)
// AUTHOR : type your name here
// DATE WRITTEN : type the date here

#include <iostream.h>
#include <iomanip.h>
#include <stdio.h>
#include "employee.h"     // USE THE " " TO INCLUDE THE EMPLOYEE HEADER FILE
                          // SINCE IT IS LOCATED IN THE WORKING DIRECTORY.

// CONSTRUCTOR IMPLEMENTATION



// IMPLEMENTATION OF FUNCTION TO GET NAME



// IMPLEMENTATION OF FUNCTION TO GET HOURLY RATE



// IMPLEMENTATION OF FUNCTION TO GET HOURS WORKED


```

```
// IMPLEMENTATION OF FUNCTION TO CALCULATE PAY
```

```
// IMPLEMENTATION OF FUNCTION TO DISPLAY EMPLOYEE NAME
```

```
// IMPLEMENTATION OF FUNCTION TO DISPLAY HOURLY RATE
```

```
// IMPLEMENTATION OF FUNCTION TO DISPLAY HOURS WORKED
```

```
// IMPLEMENTATION OF FUNCTION TO DISPLAY WEEKLY PAY
```

Save and Compile the Implementation File

After you have entered the source code for the function implementation, save the file with the name *employee.cpp*. Compile the file. If your compiler gives an error of not being able to find or open the *employee.h* header file, check your working directory to be sure it is where your header file is located. If you are using TURBO C++, the directory can be changed by selecting the **Change dir ...** command in the **File** menu.

Write the Application Program

Open a new file for the application program. Using the problem definition and algorithms that you developed, complete the following application program shell to define an object for the employee class and test the implementation functions that you have written.

```
// LAB 12-1 (PAY.CPP)
// AUTHOR : type your name here
// DATE WRITTEN : type the date here

#include <iostream.h>
#include <conio.h>          // FOR DOS USERS ONLY
#include <stdio.h>
#include "employee.h"       // USE THE " " TO INCLUDE THE EMPLOYEE HEADER FILE
                            // SINCE IT IS LOCATED IN THE WORKING DIRECTORY.

void main ()
{
```

```
// DEFINE Employee OBJECT


    clrscr();                  // FOR DOS USERS ONLY


    Call functions to get information from user, using the dot operator to access the members.


    clrscr();                  // FOR DOS USERS ONLY


    Call functions to display employee payroll information, using the dot operator to access the members.


} // END main()
```

Save the and Compile Application Program

After you have entered the source code for the application program, save the file with the name *pay.cpp*. Now that you have entered and saved the program, compile it to be sure that there are no syntax errors. If your compiler gives an error of not being able to find or open the *employee.h* header file, check your working directory to be sure it is where your header file is located.

Build a Project File

Most C++ compilers allow you to build multi-file programs called projects. When you build a project, you specify all the files required to build an application program. When working with program files in a project, the project manager automatically updates the information kept in the project file and identifies those files that need to be recompiled and linked to produce an executable program. Another advantage to using a project manager for your files is that you can develop, debug, and compile each file separately.

Build a project named *employee.prj*. Add the *employee.cpp* and *pay.cpp* files to the project. Do not add the *employee.h* header file to the project, since you have included it in the preprocessor directives of the other files.

If you are not using TURBO C++, consult your instructor, lab supervisor, or reference manuals for details on building a project file in your programming environment.

If you are using TURBO C++, select the **Project** option from the menu bar. Select the **Open project ...** command from the pull-down menu. Name the project *employee.prj*. Add the necessary files to the project by selecting the **Add item ...** from the **Project** menu, or by pressing the [INS] (insert) key on the keyboard. Select the *employee.cpp* and *pay.cpp* files. Select the **Done** button when you have finished adding the files required to run the application.

Compile and Link the Project File

Once all the program files have been added to the project file, compile and link it. If you are using TURBO C++, select the **Make** command from the **Compile** menu. When the project file is compiled, the project manager automatically compiles and links all the individual program files to produce an executable file.

Run and Test the Program

When the project is successfully compiled and linked, run and test it.

Check the Program Results

A sample of the input screen from the employee payroll project is shown in Figure 12-1 and a sample output screen is shown in Figure 12-2. Your input and output should look similar to these.

```
Enter the Employee Name:  Lori
Enter the Hourly Rate:  6.35
Enter the Hours Worked:  43
```

Figure 12-1 Sample input screen for the employee payroll project.

```
Employee Pay Report

Employee Name:   Lori
Hourly Rate:     $6.35
Hours Worked:    43
Weekly Pay:      $282.57
```

Figure 12-2 Sample output screen for the employee payroll project.

Print the Source Code and Sample Runs of the Program

Print a source code listings of your program files including the header file, function implementation file and application program file. Get sample print-outs of the program runs for documentation.

Close the File

Close the project file when you are finished.

Problem 2 - Create an Invoice Class, Object, and Project File

In this exercise, you will declare an invoice class in a header file, create an implementation file for the member functions, develop an application program that defines an object for the invoice class and tests the function implementations. Finally, you will build a project file linking the files that you have developed. You will compile, debug, run, test, and print the project file.

Pre-Lab

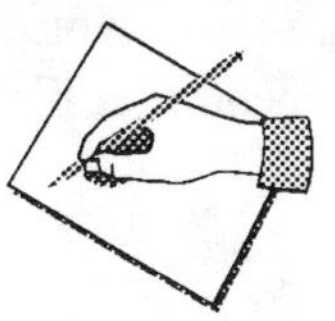

PROBLEM STATEMENT

Write an application program that defines an object for an invoice class and tests the required functions to produce an invoice report that includes an item number, item description, quantity ordered, unit price, subtotal price, sales tax amount, cost of shipping, and invoice total.

Procedure & Questions:

PROBLEM DEFINITION

The following problem definition will be used when creating the functions for this problem.

Output: What output will be produced according to the problem statement?

____

Input: What input will be needed for processing to obtain the required output?

____

Processing: What processing is required to calculate the subtotal amount of the invoice?

____

What processing is required to calculate the sales tax amount?

____

What processing is required to calculate the total amount on the invoice?

____

Discussion:

According to the problem statement, the output will be a display of the invoice data in a business-like format. The item number, description, unit price, and amount of shipping are needed as input. To process the subtotal amount, the quantity ordered will be multiplied by the unit price. To process the amount of sales tax on the order, multiply the subtotal by the sales tax rate. The invoice total is simply the sum of the subtotal, the sales tax amount, and the amount of shipping.

Procedure:

Before you can develop an application program, you need to declare an invoice class in a header file and develop the implementations for the required functions in an implementation file. Finally, you can create a project to combine the separate files into a working application.

PROBLEM STATEMENT FOR THE CLASS

Declare an invoice class as part of a header file. The class is to have data members to store the following:

Item Number
Item Description
Quantity Ordered
Unit Price
Subtotal Price

Sales Tax Rate
Sales Tax Amount
Cost of Shipping
Invoice Total

The class is to have member functions to perform the following tasks:

- A constructor function to initialize all the data items to 0 (zero), except the sales tax rate which should be initialized to 5%.
- A function to allow the user to enter all the invoice data items, except sales tax rate, from the keyboard.
- A function to calculate the subtotal price of the item.
- A function to calculate the sales tax amount of the item.
- A function to calculate the total amount of the invoice.
- A function to display the invoice data with header information in a business-like format.

Procedure & Questions:

PROBLEM DEFINITION FOR THE CLASS

What will you name this class? ______________________________

List the function members that need to be declared public. ______________________________

____

List the data members that need to be declared private. ______________________________

____

PROBLEM STATEMENT FOR THE FUNCTIONS

Here is a list of functions required for the invoice class. Write algorithms for these functions from the information you developed in the problem definition. Remember, if class function members are operating on class data members, the data members are not passed or returned by the functions.

- Constructor function to initialize the data members.
- Function to get the invoice order information from the user.
- Function to calculate the invoice subtotal.
- Function to calculate the sales tax amount.
- Function to calculate the total invoice amount.
- Function to display the complete invoice.

THE ALGORITHMS

CONSTRUCTOR FUNCTION TO INITIALIZE THE DATA MEMBERS.
BEGIN

END.

What will you name this function? ______________________________

What does this function do? ______________________________

Which class data members are operated on by this function? ______________________________

____

Write a function header using the scoping operator, ::, to make the connection between the class and function.

____

FUNCTION TO GET THE INVOICE INFORMATION
BEGIN

END.

What will you name this function? ______________________________

What does this function do? ______________________________

Which class data members are operated on by this function? ______________________________

____

Write a function header using the scoping operator, ::, to make the connection between the class and function.

____

FUNCTION TO CALCULATE THE INVOICE SUBTOTAL
BEGIN

END.

What will you name this function? ______________________________

What does this function do? ______________________________

Which class data members are operated on by this function? ______________________

____

Write a function header using the scoping operator, ::, to make the connection between the class and function.

____

FUNCTION TO CALCULATE THE SALE TAX AMOUNT

BEGIN

END.

What will you name this function? ______________________________

What does this function do? ______________________________

Which class data members are operated on by this function? ______________________

____

Write a function header using the scoping operator, ::, to make the connection between the class and function.

____

FUNCTION TO CALCULATE TOTAL INVOICE AMOUNT

BEGIN

END.

What will you name this function? ______________________________

What does this function do? ______________________________

Which class data members are operated on by this function? ______________________

____

Write a function header using the scoping operator, ::, to make the connection between the class and function.

____

FUNCTION TO DISPLAY THE INVOICE INFORMATION
BEGIN

END.

What will you name this function? ______________________________

What does this function do? ______________________________

Which class data members are operated on by this function? ______________________________

____

Write a function header using the scoping operator, ::, to make the connection between the class and function.

____

Write the algorithm for the steps to be carried out by function *main()* in the application program.

BEGIN

END.

In-the-Lab 

Procedure & Discussion:

Start Your Compiler

Start your C++ program development environment.

Write the Header File

Make sure that a new file is open. Using the class description that you developed, complete the following header file shell.

```
// LAB 12-2 (INVOICE.H)
// AUTHOR : type your name here
// DATE WRITTEN : type the date here

// DECLARE INVOICE CLASS
class
{
public:



private:



};
```

Save and Compile the Header File

After you have entered the source code for the class declaration, save the header file with the name *invoice.h*. Now that you have entered and saved the header file, compile it to be sure there are no syntax errors. Debug the file if there are errors. Be sure to recompile and save the file if you make any modifications to the source code.

Write the Implementation File

Open a new file for the function implementation file. Using the algorithms that you developed, complete the following implementation file shell.

```
// LAB 12-2 (INVOICE.CPP)
// AUTHOR : type your name here
// DATE WRITTEN : type the date here

#include <iostream.h>
#include <iomanip.h>
```

```
#include <stdio.h>
#include <conio.h>          // FOR DOS USERS ONLY
#include "invoice.h"        // USE THE " " TO INCLUDE THE EMPLOYEE HEADER FILE
                            // SINCE IT IS LOCATED IN THE WORKING DIRECTORY.

// CONSTRUCTOR IMPLEMENTATION



// IMPLEMENTATION OF FUNCTION TO GET INVOICE INFORMATION



// IMPLEMENTATION OF FUNCTION TO CALCULATE INVOICE SUB TOTAL



// IMPLEMENTATION OF FUNCTION TO CALCULATE SALES TAX AMOUNT



// IMPLEMENTATION OF FUNCTION TO CALCULATE INVOICE TOTAL AMOUNT



// IMPLEMENTATION OF FUNCTION TO DISPLAY INVOICE INFORMATION
```

Save and Compile the Implementation File

After you have entered the source code for the function implementation, save the file with the name *invoice.cpp.* Compile the file to be sure that there are no syntax errors. If your compiler gives an error of not being able to find or open the *invoice.h* header file, check your working directory to be sure it is where your header file is located.

Write the Application Program

Open a new file for the application program. Using the problem definition and algorithms that you developed, complete the following application program shell to define an object for the invoice class and test the implementation functions that you have written.

```
// LAB 12-2 (STATMENT.CPP)
// AUTHOR : type your name here
// DATE WRITTEN : type the date here

#include <iostream.h>
#include <conio.h>              // FOR DOS USERS ONLY
#include <stdio.h>
#include "invoice.h"            // USE THE " " TO INCLUDE THE INVOICE HEADER FILE
                                // SINCE IT IS LOCATED IN THE WORKING DIRECTORY.

void main ()
{
// DEFINE Invoice OBJECT



   clrscr();              // FOR DOS USERS ONLY

   Call functions to get information from user, using the dot operator to access the members.

   clrscr();              // FOR DOS USERS ONLY


   Call functions to display invoice  information, using the dot operator to access the members.


} // END main ()
```

Save the and Compile Application Program

After you have entered the source code for the application program, save the file with the name *statment.cpp.* Compile the file. If your compiler gives an error of not being able to find or open the *invoice.h* header file, check your working directory to be sure it is where your header file is located.

Build a Project File

Build a project named *invoice.prj*. Add the *invoice.cpp* and *statment.cpp* files to the project. Remember, do not add the *invoice.h* header file to the project, since you have included it in the preprocessor directives of the other files.

Compile and Link the Project File

Once all the program files have been added to the project file, compile and link the project. When the project file is compiled, the project manager automatically compiles and links all the individual program files to produce an executable file.

Run and Test the Program

When the project is successfully compiled and linked, run and test it.

Check the Program Results

A sample of the input screen from the invoice project is shown in Figure 12-3 and a sample output screen is shown in Figure 12-4. Your input and output should look similar to these.

```
Enter the Item Number <5 digits>:  54321

Enter the Item Description <30 characters max>:  Printer Ribbon

Enter the Quantity Ordered:  12

Enter the Unit Price:  $6.72

Enter the cost of Shipping:  $4.52
```

Figure 12-3 Sample input screen for the invoice project.

```
                         ***  INVOICE  ***

Item Number        Description         Unit Price     Quantity     Sub Total
-----------        -----------         ----------     --------     ---------
54321              Printer Ribbon           $6.72           12        $80.64
                                                     Sales Tax: $       4.03
                                                      Shipping: $       4.52
                                                         Total: $      89.19
```

Figure 12-4 Sample output screen for the invoice project.

Print the Source Code and Sample Runs of the Program

Print source code listings of your program files. Get sample print-outs of the program runs for documentation.

Close the File

Close the project file and any other open files when you are finished.

Exit C++

Exit your C++ compiler when you are finished.

LAB PROJECT #13
Class Inheritance

Lab Objectives

In this lab, you will . . .

- Declare base classes and pass inherited members to derived classes.
- Implement class member functions to manipulate class data members.
- Define objects for the classes in application programs.
- Create projects to handle multi-file programs.

Introduction

One of the most important properties of object-oriented programming is *inheritance*. Inheritance allows newly created classes to inherit members from existing classes. These new *derived classes* will include their own members and members inherited from the *base class*. A collection of classes with common, inherited members are related to each other through inheritance. Such inheritance creates a class hierarchy. The classes that include those things that are most commonly inherited are at the top of the hierarchy. The derived class should always be related to its base class via the IS-A relationship.

A derived class is declared using the following format:

```
class <derived class> : public <base class>
{
public:
  <Public derived class member functions>
  <Public derived class member data>

protected: (OR) private:
  < Protected/private derived class member functions>
  < Protected/private derived class member data>
};
```

Notice that the base class is declared public in the derived class declaration. This allows the inherited members of the public base class to maintain their access level in the derived class. The members declared as protected have accessibility that is somewhere between that of a private member and a public member. If a member is a private member of a base class, it is not accessible to a derived class. However, a protected member of a base class is accessible to any derived classes. On the other hand, a protected member is "protected" from being accessed outside of the class family, thereby preserving data hiding within the family. You control the amount of data member inheritance by designating the members as private, protected, or public in the base class declaration.

A base class is declared using the following format:

```
class <class name>
{
public:
  <Public base class member functions>
  <Public base class member data>

protected: (OR) private:
  < Protected/private base class member functions>
  < Protected/private base class member data>
};
```

In Problem 1 you will declare a bank account base class and a credit card derived class. In Problem 2 you will declare a resistor circuit base class. You will declare series and parallel circuit derived classes. In both problems, you will declare the classes in header files, create implementation files for the member functions, develop application programs that define objects for the classes and tests the function implementations. You will then build a project file, linking the files that you have developed. You will compile, debug, run, test, and print the project files.

Problem 1 - Create a Bank Account Class Family

In this exercise, you will declare a bank account base class and a credit card account derived class in header files. You will create an implementation file for the member functions. Then you will develop an application program that defines an object for the credit card class and tests the function implementations. Finally, you will build a project linking the files that you have developed. You will compile, debug, run, test, and print the files.

Pre-Lab

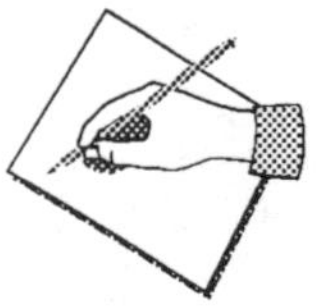

PROBLEM STATEMENT

Write an application program that defines an object for a credit card class that is derived from a general bank account class. The program should test the required functions to debit monthly charges and interest from the card holder's bank account balance and to deposit monthly credit card payments to the bank account balance. Produce a credit card statement, reporting the name of the card holder, the account number, the beginning bank account balance, the monthly credit card charges, the monthly payments, the interest charged at a 15% annual rate of the unpaid credit card charges, the ending bank account balance, and the balance due.

Procedure & Questions:

PROBLEM DEFINITION

The following problem definition will be used when creating the functions for this problem.

Output: What output will be produced according to the problem statement?

____

Input: What input will be needed for processing to obtain the required output?

____

Processing: What processing is required to calculate the interest on the monthly charges?

____

What processing is required to calculate the credit card balance due?

____

What processing is required to calculate the ending bank account balance?

____

Discussion:

According to the problem statement, the output will be a display reporting the name of the card holder, the account number, the beginning bank account balance, the monthly credit card charges, the interest charged and the charge balance due. The name of the card holder, the account number, the beginning bank account balance, the monthly payments, and the monthly credit card charges are needed as input from the user. To calculate the interest on the monthly charges, you will subtract the monthly payments from the monthly charges and multiply the unpaid monthly charges by 0.15/12. To calculate the ending account balance, you will deduct the monthly credit card charges and interest from the bank account balance and add the monthly payments to the bank account balance.

Procedure:

Before you can develop an application program, you need to declare a bank account base class and a derived credit card class in header files, and develop the implementations for the required functions in an implementation file. Finally, you can create a project to combine the separate files into a working application.

Problem Statement for the Classes

Declare a bank account base class as part of a header file. The class is to have data members to store an account number and account balance. The class is to have member functions to perform the following tasks:

- A function to make deposits.
- A function to get the account number from the user.
- A function to get the beginning account balance from the user.
- A function to access the account balance.
- A function to access the account number.

Declare a derived credit card class to inherit the bank account class members. In addition it will contain data members to store the card holder's name, monthly credit card charges, monthly payments, interest rate, interest due, beginning account balance, ending account balance, charge balance due and the following function members:

- A constructor function to initialize the account data members.
- A function to get the card holder's account information.
- A function to debit the monthly credit card charges.
- A function to calculate and debit the monthly interest.
- A function to display the credit card statement.

Procedure & Questions:

Problem Definition for the Bank Account Base Class

What will you name this class? ____

List the members that need to be declared public? ________________________________

____

List the members that need to be declared private? ________________________________

____

Problem Definition for the Credit Card Derived Class

What will you name this class? ____

Which members will this derived class inherit from its base class? ____________________

List the members that need to be declared public in this derived class. ________________

____

List the members that need to be declared private in this derived class. _______________

____

Construct a Venn diagram for the class family.

PROBLEM STATEMENT FOR THE FUNCTIONS

Write algorithms for the implementation of the functions listed in the class problem statements using the information you developed in the problem definitions.

THE BANK ACCOUNT ALGORITHMS

FUNCTION TO MAKE A DEPOSIT
BEGIN

END.

What will you name this function? ____________________

Which class data members are operated on by this function? ____________________

____

Write a function header using the scoping operator, ::, to make the connection between the class and function.

____

FUNCTION TO GET THE ACCOUNT NUMBER
BEGIN

END.

What will you name this function? ____________________

Which class data members are operated on by this function? ____________________

____

Write a function header using the scoping operator, ::, to make the connection between the class and function.

____

FUNCTION TO GET THE ACCOUNT BEGINNING BALANCE
BEGIN

END.

What will you name this function? ____________________

Which class data members are operated on by this function? ____________________

____

Write a function header using the scoping operator, ::, to make the connection between the class and function.

____

FUNCTION TO ACCESS THE ACCOUNT NUMBER
BEGIN

END.

What will you name this function? ____________________

Which class data members are operated on by this function? ____________________

____

Write a function header using the scoping operator, ::, to make the connection between the class and function.

____

FUNCTION TO ACCESS THE ACCOUNT BALANCE

BEGIN

END.

What will you name this function? ______________________________

Which class data members are operated on by this function? ______________________________

____

Write a function header using the scoping operator, ::, to make the connection between the class and function.

____

THE CREDIT CARD ALGORITHMS

CONSTRUCTOR FUNCTION TO INITIALIZE THE DATA MEMBERS.

BEGIN

END.

What will you name this function? ______________________________

Which class data members are operated on by this function? ______________________________

____

Write a function header using the scoping operator, ::, to make the connection between the class and function.

____

FUNCTION TO GET THE CARD HOLDER ACCOUNT INFORMATION
BEGIN

END.

What will you name this function? ______________________________

Which class data members are operated on by this function? ______________________________

____

Write a function header using the scoping operator, ::, to make the connection between the class and function.

____

FUNCTION TO CALCULATE AND DEBIT MONTHLY INTEREST
BEGIN

END.

What will you name this function? ______________________________

Which class data members are operated on by this function? ______________________________

____

Write a function header using the scoping operator, ::, to make the connection between the class and function.

____

FUNCTION TO DISPLAY CREDIT CARD STATEMENT

BEGIN

END.

What will you name this function? ______________________________

Which class data members are operated on by this function? ______________________________

____

Write a function header using the scoping operator, ::, to make the connection between the class and function.

____

Write the algorithm for the steps to be carried out by function *main()* in the application program.

BEGIN

END.

In-the-Lab

Procedure & Discussion:

Start Your Compiler

Start your C++ program development environment.

Write the Bank Account Base Class Header File

Make sure that a new file is open. Using the class description that you developed, complete the following header file shell.

```
// LAB 13-1 (ACCOUNT.H)
// AUTHOR : type your name here
// DATE WRITTEN : type the date here

#ifndef ACCOUNT_H
#define ACCOUNT_H

// DECLARE BANK ACCOUNT  BASE CLASS

#endif
```

Save and Compile the Header File

After you have entered the source code for the class declaration, save the header file with the name *account.h*, then compile the file. Debug the file if there are errors. Be sure to recompile and save the file if you make any modifications to the source code.

Write the Credit Card Derived Class Header File

Make sure that a new file is open. Using the class description that you developed, complete the following header file shell.

```
// LAB 13-1 (CARD.H)
// AUTHOR : type your name here
// DATE WRITTEN : type the date here

#include "account.h"          // USE THE " " TO INCLUDE THE HEADER FILE
                              // SINCE IT IS LOCATED IN THE WORKING DIRECTORY.
```

```
// DECLARE CREDIT CARD DERIVED CLASS
```

Save and Compile the Header File

After you have entered the source code for the class declaration, save the header file with the name *card.h*. Compile the file. If your compiler gives an error of not being able to find or open the *account.h* header file, check your working directory to be sure it is where your header file is located.

Write the Bank Account Implementation File

Open a new file for the bank account function implementation file. Using the algorithms that you developed, complete the following implementation file shell.

```
// LAB 13-1 (ACCOUNT.CPP)
// AUTHOR : type your name here
// DATE WRITTEN : type the date here

#include "account.h"          // USE THE " " TO INCLUDE THE HEADER FILE
                              // SINCE IT IS LOCATED IN THE WORKING DIRECTORY.

// IMPLEMENTATION OF FUNCTION TO CREDIT A DEPOSIT



// IMPLEMENTATION OF FUNCTION TO GET THE ACCOUNT NUMBER



// IMPLEMENTATION OF FUNCTION TO GET THE BEGINNING BALANCE



// IMPLEMENTATION OF FUNCTION TO ACCESS THE ACCOUNT BALANCE



// IMPLEMENTATION OF FUNCTION TO ACCESS THE ACCOUNT NUMBER
```

Save and Compile the Implementation File

After you have entered the source code for the function implementations, save the file with the name *account.cpp.* Now that you have entered and saved the file, compile it to be sure that there are no syntax errors. If your compiler gives an error of not being able to find or open the *account.h* header file, check your working directory to be sure it is where your header file is located.

Write the Credit Card Implementation File

Open a new file for the credit card function implementation file. Using the algorithms that you developed, complete the following implementation file shell.

```
// LAB 13-1 (CARD.CPP)
// AUTHOR : type your name here
// DATE WRITTEN : type the date here

#include "card.h"                // USE THE " " TO INCLUDE THE HEADER FILE
                                 // SINCE IT IS LOCATED IN THE WORKING DIRECTORY.

// IMPLEMENTATION OF CONSTRUCTOR FUNCTION




// IMPLEMENTATION OF FUNCTION TO GET CARD HOLDER ACCOUNT INFORMATION




// IMPLEMENTATION OF FUNCTION TO DEBIT THE MONTHLY CREDIT CARD CHARGES




// IMPLEMENTATION OF FUNCTION TO CALCULATE AND DEBIT MONTHLY INTEREST




// IMPLEMENTATION OF FUNCTION TO DISPLAY CREDIT CARD STATEMENT
```

Save and Compile the Implementation File

After you have entered the source code for the function implementations, save the file with the name *card.cpp*. Compile and debug the file.

Write the Application Program

Open a new file for the application program. Using the problem definition and algorithms that you developed, complete the following application program shell to define an object for the credit card class and test the implementation functions that you have written.

```
// LAB 13-1 (CHARGE.CPP)
// AUTHOR : type your name here
// DATE WRITTEN : type the date here

#include <iostream.h>
#include <conio.h>              // FOR DOS USERS ONLY
#include <stdio.h>
#include "account.h"            // USE THE " " TO INCLUDE THE HEADER FILES
#include "card.h"               // SINCE THEY ARE LOCATED IN THE WORKING DIRECTORY.

void main ()
{
// DEFINE CREDIT CARD OBJECT


// CALL FUNCTIONS FOR MONTHLY CREDIT CARD TRANSACTIONS


// CALL FUNCTION FOR MONTHLY CREDIT CARD STATEMENT


} END main ()
```

Save and Compile the Application Program

After you have entered the source code for the application program, save the file with the name *charge.cpp*, then compile the file. If your compiler gives an error of not being able to find or open the *account.h* or *card.h* header files, check your working directory to be sure it is where your header files are located.

Build a Project File

Build a project named *charge.prj*. Add the *charge.cpp*, *credit.cpp* and *account.cpp* files to the project. Do not add the *account.h* or *card.h* header files to the project, since you have included them in the preprocessor directives of the other files.

Compile and Link the Project File

Once the necessary program files have been added to the project, compile and link it. When the project file is compiled, the project manager automatically compiles and links all the individual program files to produce an executable file.

Run and Test the Program

When the project is successfully compiled and linked, run and test it.

Check the Program Results

Samples of the input and report screens for no balance due are shown in Figure 13-1 and 13-2.

```
Enter the Card Holder's Name : Brenda

Enter the Account Number : 12345

Enter the Beginning Balance for this month : 200

Enter the amount of charges for this month : 355

Enter the amount of payment for this month : 225
```

Figure 13-1 Sample input screen for no balance due.

```
                        CREDIT CARD STATEMENT
                        ------ ---- ---------

                Card Holder : Brenda
                Account Number :  12345

        Account Beginning Balance . . . . . . $      200
        Payments Credited   . . . . . . . . . $      225
        Card Charges Deducted . . . . . . . . $      355
        Interest Deducted. . . . . . . . . .  $        0
        Current Balance Due . . . . . . . . . $        0
        Account Ending Balance   . . . . . .  $       70

PRESS ENTER TO CONTINUE . . .
```

Figure 13-2 Sample report screen for no balance due.

Samples of the input and report screens for a balance due are shown in Figure 13-3 and 13-4.

```
Enter the Card Holder's Name : Brenda

Enter the Account Number : 12345

Enter the Beginning Balance for this month : 0

Enter the amount of charges for this month : 175

Enter the amount of payment for this month : 30
```

Figure 13-3 Sample input screen for a charge balance due.

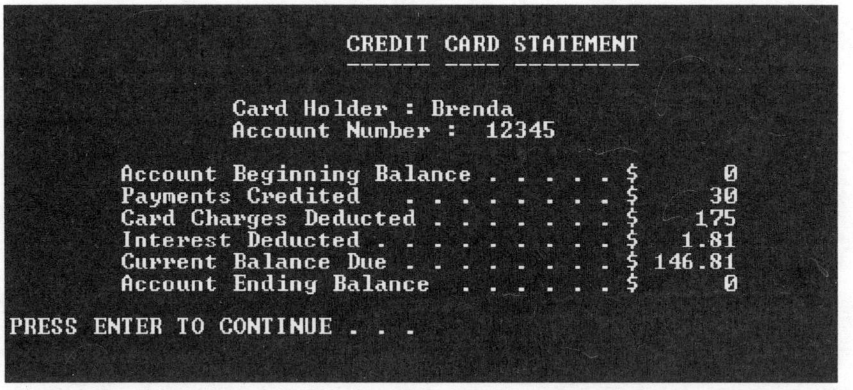

Figure 13-4 Sample output report for a charge balance due.

Your input and output should look similar to these.

Print the Source Code and Sample Runs of the Program

Print source code listings of your program files including the class header files, function implementation files and application program file. Get sample print-outs of the program runs for documentation.

Close the File

Close the project file and any other open file when you are finished.

Problem 2 - Create a Resistor Circuit Class Family

In this exercise, you will declare a resistor circuit base class in a header file and two derived classes for a series circuit and a parallel circuit that inherit the resistor circuit base class members. You will create implementation files for the member functions, develop an application program that defines an object for the classes and tests the function implementations. Finally, you will build a project file linking the files that you have developed. You will compile, debug, run, test, and print the project file.

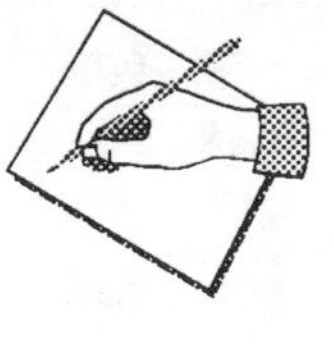

Pre-Lab

PROBLEM STATEMENT

Write an application program that defines a series resistance object and a parallel resistance object from a resistor circuit base class. Include statements in the program that test the required functions allowing the user to enter the number of resistors in the circuit and the resistor values. The program must display the resistor values along with the equivalent resistance of both a series circuit and a parallel circuit.

Procedure & Questions:

PROBLEM DEFINITION

The following problem definition will be used when creating the functions for this problem.

Output: What output will be produced according to the problem statement?

____

Input: What input will be needed for processing to obtain the required output?

____

Processing: What processing is required to calculate the equivalent resistance of a series circuit?

____

What processing is required to calculate the equivalent resistance of a parallel circuit?

____

Discussion:

According to the problem statement, the output will be a display reporting the resistor values along with the equivalent resistance of a series circuit and a parallel circuit. The number of resistors and the resistor values are needed as input from the user. The formula to calculate the equivalent resistance of a series circuit is $\mathbf{R_s = R_1 + R_2 + \ldots + R_n}$. This is simply the sum of the resistor values. The formula to calculate the equivalent resistance of a parallel circuit is $\mathbf{R_p = 1/(1/R_1 + 1/R_2 + \ldots + 1/R_n)}$. This is the inverse of the sum of the inverses of the resistor values.

Procedure:

Before you can develop an application program, you need to declare a resistor circuit base class and derived classes for the series circuit and the parallel circuit in header files, and develop the implementations for the required functions in an implementation file. Finally, you can create a project to combine the separate files into a working application.

PROBLEM STATEMENT FOR THE CLASSES

Declare a resistor circuit base class as part of a header file. The class is to have the following members:

Function Members:

- A constructor function initializing the resistors to 0.
- A function that will allow the user to enter the number of resistors in the circuit and the resistor values.
- A function that will display the resistor values along with the equivalent resistance of the circuit.

Data Members:

- The resistor values stored in an array.
- The number of resistors in the circuit.
- The equivalent resistance of the circuit.

Declare two derived classes to inherit the resistor circuit base class members. Provide the following function members in the derived classes:

Series Circuit:

- A function to calculate the equivalent resistance of a series circuit.

Parallel Circuit:

- A function to calculate the equivalent resistance of a parallel circuit.

Procedure & Questions:

PROBLEM DEFINITION FOR THE RESISTOR CIRCUIT BASE CLASS

What will you name this class? ____

List the members that need to be declared public in this base class. ______________________

____

List the members that need to be declared protected/private in this base class. _______________

____

PROBLEM DEFINITION FOR THE SERIES CIRCUIT DERIVED CLASS

What will you name this class? ____

Which members of this derived class will be inherited form its base class? __________________

____

List the members that need to be declared public in this derived class. ____________________

____

List the members that need to be declared protected/private in this derived class. _____________

____

PROBLEM DEFINITION FOR THE PARALLEL CIRCUIT DERIVED CLASS

What will you name this class? ______________________________

Which members of this derived class will be inherited from its base class? ______________________________

____

List the members that need to be declared public in this derived class. ______________________________

____

List the members that need to be declared protected/private in this derived class. ______________________________

____

Construct a Venn Diagram for the class family.

PROBLEM STATEMENT FOR THE FUNCTIONS

Write algorithms for the implementation of the functions listed in the class problem statement using the information you developed in the problem definition.

THE RESISTOR CIRCUIT ALGORITHMS

CONSTRUCTOR FUNCTION TO INITIALIZE THE CIRCUIT VALUES TO ZERO
BEGIN

END.

What will you name this function? ______________________________

Which class data members are operated on by this function? ________________________________

____

Write a function header using the scoping operator, ::, to make the connection between the class and function.

____

FUNCTION TO GET THE NUMBER OF RESISTORS AND THEIR VALUES
BEGIN

END.

What will you name this function? ____

Which class data members are operated on by this function? ________________________________

____

Write a function header using the scoping operator, ::, to make the connection between the class and function.

____

FUNCTION TO DISPLAY THE RESISTER VALUES AND EQUIVALENT RESISTANCE
BEGIN

END.

What will you name this function? ____

Which class data members are operated on by this function? ________________________________

____

Write a function header using the scoping operator, ::, to make the connection between the class and function.

____

The Series Circuit Algorithms

FUNCTION TO CALCULATE THE EQUIVALENT RESISTANCE OF A SERIES CIRCUIT

BEGIN

END.

What will you name this function? ____

Which class data members are operated on by this function? _______________________

____

Write a function header using the scoping operator, ::, to make the connection between the class and function.

____

The Parallel Circuit Algorithms

FUNCTION TO CALCULATE EQUIVALENT RESISTANCE OF A PARALLEL CIRCUIT

BEGIN

END.

What will you name this function? ____

Which class data members are operated on by this function? _______________________

____

Write a function header using the scoping operator, ::, to make the connection between the class and function.

____

Write the algorithm for the steps to be carried out by function *main()* in the application program.

BEGIN

END.

In-the-Lab

Procedure & Discussion:

Start Your Compiler

Start your C++ program development environment.

Write the Resistor Circuit Base Class Header File

Make sure that a new file is open. Using the class description that you developed, complete the following header file shell.

```
// LAB 13-2 (RESISTOR.H)
// AUTHOR : type your name here
// DATE WRITTEN : type the date here

#ifndef RESISTOR_H
#define RESISTOR_H

// DECLARE RESISTOR  BASE CLASS



#endif
```

Save and Compile the Header File

After you have entered the source code for the class declaration, save the header file with the name *resistor.h* then compile the file.

Write the Series Circuit Derived Class Header File

Make sure that a new file is open. Using the class description that you developed, complete the following header file shell.

```
// LAB 13-2 (SERIES.H)
// AUTHOR : type your name here
// DATE WRITTEN : type the date here

#include "resistor.h"

// DECLARE SERIES CIRCUIT DERIVED CLASS
```

Save and Compile the Header File

After you have entered the source code for the class declaration, save the header file with the name *series.h*. Compile the file.

Write the Parallel Circuit Derived Class Header File

Make sure that a new file is open. Using the class description that you developed, complete the following header file shell.

```
// LAB 13-2 (PARALLEL.H)
// AUTHOR : type your name here
// DATE WRITTEN : type the date here

#include "resistor.h"

// DECLARE PARALLEL CIRCUIT DERIVED CLASS
```

Save and Compile the Header File

After you have entered the source code for the class declaration, save the header file with the name *parallel.h*. Compile the file.

Write the Resistor Circuit Base Class Implementation File

Open a new file for the resistor circuit function implementation file. Using the algorithms that you developed, complete the following implementation file shell.

```
// LAB 13-2 (RESISTOR.CPP)
// AUTHOR : type your name here
// DATE WRITTEN : type the date here

#include "resistor.h"

// IMPLEMENTATION OF CONSTRUCTOR FUNCTION




// IMPLEMENTATION OF FUNCTION TO GET NUMBER OF RESISTORS AND VALUES




// IMPLEMENTATION OF FUNCTION TO DISPLAY THE RESISTOR VALUES
// AND EQUIVALENT RESISTANCE
```

Save and Compile the Implementation File

After you have entered the source code for the function implementation, save the file with the name *resistor.cpp.* Compile the file.

Write the Series Circuit Derived Class Implementation File

Open a new file for the series circuit function implementation file. Using the algorithms that you developed, complete the following implementation file shell.

```
// LAB 13-2 (SERIES.CPP)
// AUTHOR : type your name here
// DATE WRITTEN : type the date here

#include "series.h"

// IMPLEMENTATION OF FUNCTION TO CALCULATE THE EQUIVALENT SERIES RESISTANCE
```

Save and Compile the Implementation File

After you have entered the source code for the function implementation, save the file with the name *series.cpp.* Compile the file.

Write the Parallel Circuit Derived Class Implementation File

Open a new file for the parallel circuit function implementation file. Using the algorithms that you developed, complete the following implementation file shell.

```
// LAB 13-2 (PARALLEL.CPP)
// AUTHOR : type your name here
// DATE WRITTEN : type the date here

#include "parallel.h"

// IMPLEMENTATION OF FUNCTION TO CALCULATE THE EQUIVALENT PARALLEL RESISTANCE
```

Save and Compile the Implementation File

After you have entered the source code for the function implementation, save the file with the name *parallel.cpp.* Compile the file.

Write the Application Program

Open a new file for the application program. Using the problem definition and algorithms that you developed, complete the following application program shell to define an object for the resistor class and test the implementation functions that you have written.

```
// LAB 13-1 (CIRCUIT.CPP)
// AUTHOR : type your name here
// DATE WRITTEN : type the date here

#include <iostream.h>
#include <conio.h>          // FOR DOS USERS ONLY
#include <stdio.h>
#include "series.h"
#include "parallel.h"

void main ()
{
// DEFINE VARIABLES


// DEFINE SERIES RESISTANCE AND PARALLEL RESISTANCE OBJECTS
```

```
// GET NUMBER OF RESISTORS AND THEIR VALUES



// CALCULATE EQUIVALENT RESISTANCE OF THE SERIES CIRCUIT



// DISPLAY SERIES RESISTOR REPORT



// CALCULATE EQUIVALENT RESISTANCE OF THE PARALLEL CIRCUIT



// DISPLAY PARALLEL RESISTOR REPORT



} END main ()
```

Save and Compile the Application Program

After you have entered the source code for the application program, save the file with the name *circuit.cpp*. Compile the application program file.

Build a Project File

Build a project named *circuit.prj*. Add the *circuit.cpp*, *series.cpp*, and *parallel.cpp* files to the project. Do not add the *resistor.h*, *series.h*, or *parallel.h* header files to the project, since you have included them in the preprocessor directives of the other files.

Compile and Link the Project File

Once the necessary program files have been added to the project, compile and link it. When the project file is compiled, the project manager automatically compiles and links all the individual program files to produce an executable file.

Run and Test the Program

When the project is successfully compiled and linked, run and test it.

Check the Program Results

A sample input/output screen for the circuit program is shown in Figure 13-5. Your input and output should look similar to this.

```
Enter Number of resistors in this circuit:  3

Enter the value of resistor number 1:  2

Enter the value of resistor number 2:  4

Enter the value of resistor number 3:  6

This circuit is composed of 3 resistors.
The following are the values assigned to the resistors in this circuit.
Resistor 1:  2
Resistor 2:  4
Resistor 3:  6

The equivalent resistance of this series circuit is 12.00

The equivalent resistance of this parallel circuit is 1.09
```

Figure 13-5 Sample input and output.

Print the Source Code and Sample Runs of the Program

Print source code listings of your program files including the class header files, function implementation files, and application program file. Get sample print-outs of the program runs for documentation.

Close the File

Close the project file and any other open files when you are finished.

Exit C++

Exit your C++ compiler when you are finished.

LAB PROJECT #14
Abstract Data Types : Stacks, Queues, and Linked Lists

Lab Objectives

In this lab, you will . . .

- Declare classes to implement ADTs.
- Define objects for the ADT classes in application programs.
- Use stacks and queues to determine if a word is a palindrome.
- Use an ordered linked list to manipulate character data.

Introduction

Abstract data types, or ADTs, provide for data abstraction. The idea behind data abstraction is to combine data with a set of operations that are defined for that data in an encapsulated package called an ADT. The ADT can then be used by simply knowing what the operations do, without needing to know the details of how the computer implements the data or its operations.

An ADT is not the same thing as a data structure. A data structure provides a way of structuring, or organizing, data within a programming language. You will be concerned about data structures when you implement an ADT, since you will have to decide how to organize and store the ADT data.

The data in an ADT must be private, which means that it is hidden from any operations that are not defined for the ADT. The ADT includes operations, or functions, that manipulate the ADT data. These operations are public, which means that they are used by outside applications to access and manipulate the private ADT data. Since the data must be private and the functions are public, the class in C++ provides an ideal implementation for an ADT.

You will be using three ADTs in this lab project. They are the stack, queue, and linked list. The difference in these ADTs is in the way that you have access to the data elements.

The *stack* is a collection of data elements and related operations where all the insertions and deletions of elements to and from the stack are made at one end of the stack called the *top*. A stack operates on the last-in, first-out, or LIFO principle. In general, a stack is used to reverse the order of data placed in it.

The *queue* is a collection of data elements where all insertions of elements into the queue are made at one end of the queue, called the *rear* of the queue; and all deletions of elements from the queue are made at the other end of the queue, called the *front* of the queue. A queue operates on the first-in, first-out, or FIFO principle. The queue preserves the order of the elements from input to output.

A *list* is a sequence of data elements whose basic operations are insertion and deletion of elements to and from the list. A *linked list* is a sequential collection of data elements such that, given any element in the list, the location of its successor element is specified by an explicit link, rather than by its natural position in the collection. An *ordered linked list* is a linked list where all the data elements are in some natural order from the first node to the last node in the list. An alphabetized list of elements is an example of an ordered linked list. To create an ordered linked list, the algorithm to insert a node must search the list for the correct insertion point prior to adding the node to the list.

A linked list consists of a sequence of nodes. A node contains two things: an *element* and a *locator*, or *link*. The element is the information that is stored in the node, and the locator is the link that locates the next node in the list. A struct is used to declare a node in C++.

In Problem 1 you will code the class declarations for a stack and queue, enter the code for the implementation files and develop an application program that uses a stack and a queue to determine if a word is a palindrome. You will then modify the program to use only stacks to solve the problem.

In Problem 2 you will code the class declaration for a linked list, enter the code for the implementation file and develop an application program to use an ordered linked list to store character data in ascending order.

In both problems, you will declare the classes in header files, create implementation files for the member functions, and develop application programs that define objects for the classes and test the function implementations. You will then build a project, linking the files that you have developed. You will compile, debug, run, test, and print the project files.

Problem 1 - Palindromes using ADTs

In this exercise, you will use class declarations and implementations for a stack and queue. You will develop an application program that defines an object for the stack and queue classes and tests the function implementations to determine if a word entered by the user is a palindrome. Finally, you will build a project linking the files that you have developed. You will compile, debug, run, test, and print the files.

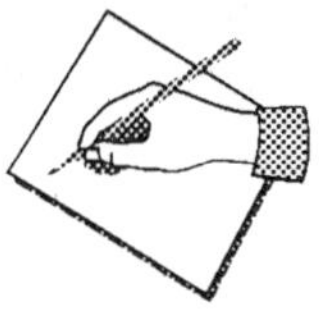

Pre-Lab

PROBLEM STATEMENT

Enter the code for the class declarations and necessary implementations for a stack and queue. Write an application program that allows the user to enter a word, and uses a stack and a queue to test the word to determine if it is a palindrome. Produce a report to the user as to whether the word is a palindrome or not. Recall that a word is a palindrome if it is spelled the same both forward and backward.

Procedure & Questions:

PROBLEM DEFINITION

Output: What output will be produced according to the problem statement?

____

Input: What input will be needed for processing to obtain the required output?

____

Processing: What processing is required to determine if the word is a palindrome?

____

Discussion:

According to the problem statement, the output will be a display reporting if the word entered is a palindrome. The word to test is needed as input from the user. To determine if the word is a palindrome you will compare the characters of the word to determine if they are the same both forward and backward. *Hint*: use character arrays as the data structures to hold the stack and queue.

Procedure & Questions:

PROBLEM DEFINITION FOR THE STACK CLASS

The stack class will need data members for the top element and an array to store the stack elements. Use the following summary of legal stack operations when defining the function members of the stack class.

CreateStack( ) - Creates an empty stack.
Push( ) - Places an element on the top of a stack.
Pop( ) - Removes an element from the top of a stack.
TopElement( ) - Inspects the top element of the stack, leaving the stack unchanged.
EmptyStack( ) - Determines if the stack is empty.
FullStack( ) - Determines if the array is full that is being used to hold the stack.

What will you name this class? ____

List the members that need to be declared public. ______________________________________

____

List the members that need to be declared private. ______________________________________

____

PROBLEM STATEMENT FOR THE STACK FUNCTIONS

Develop algorithms for the functions to implement the legal stack operations listed in the stack class problem definition.

CreateStack( ) - Creates an empty stack.

Which class data members are operated of by this function? ______________________________

Write a function header using the :: operator to make the connection between the class and function.

____

Push( ) - Places an element on the top of a stack.

Which class data members are operated of by this function? ______________________

Write a function header using the :: operator to make the connection between the class and function.

____

Pop( ) - Removes an element from the top of a stack.

Which class data members are operated of by this function? ______________________

Write a function header using the :: operator to make the connection between the class and function.

____

TopElement( ) - Inspects the top element of the stack, leaving the stack unchanged.

Which class data members are operated of by this function? ______________________

Write a function header using the :: operator to make the connection between the class and function.

____

EmptyStack( ) - Determines if the stack is empty.

Which class data members are operated of by this function? ______________________

Write a function header using the :: operator to make the connection between the class and function.

____

FullStack( ) - Determines if the array being used to hold the stack is full.

Which class data members are operated of by this function? ______________________

Write a function header using the :: operator to make the connection between the class and function.

____

PROBLEM DEFINITION FOR THE QUEUE CLASS

The queue class will need data members for the front element, rear element, element count, and an array to store the queue elements. Use the following summary of legal queue operations when defining the members of the queue class.

CreateQueue( ) - Creates an empty queue.
Insert( ) - Adds an element on the rear of a queue.
Remove( ) - Removes an element from the front of a queue.
FrontElement( ) - Copies the front element of a queue, leaving the queue unchanged.
EmptyQueue( ) - Determines if the queue is empty.
FullQueue( ) - Determines if the array is full that is used to hold the queue.

What will you name this class? ______________________

List the members that need to be declared public. ______________________

____

List the members that need to be declared private. ______________________

____

PROBLEM STATEMENT FOR THE QUEUE FUNCTIONS

Develop algorithms for the functions to implement the legal queue operations listed in the queue class problem definition.

CreateQueue( ) - Creates an empty queue.

Which class data members are operated of by this function? ______________________

Write a function header using the :: operator to make the connection between the class and function.

____

Insert( ) - Adds an element to the rear of a queue.

Which class data members are operated of by this function? ______________________

Write a function header using the :: operator to make the connection between the class and function.

____

Remove( ) - Removes an element from the front of a queue.

Which class data members are operated of by this function? ______________________

Write a function header using the :: operator to make the connection between the class and function.

____

FrontElement( ) - Copies the front element of a queue, leaving the queue unchanged.

Which class data members are operated of by this function? ______________________

Write a function header using the :: operator to make the connection between the class and function.

____

EmptyQueue( ) - Determines if the queue is empty.

Which class data members are operated of by this function? ____________________

Write a function header using the :: operator to make the connection between the class and function.

____

FullQueue( ) - Determines if the array being used to hold the queue is full.

Which class data members are operated of by this function? ____________________

Write a function header using the :: operator to make the connection between the class and function.

____

THE MAIN ALGORITHM

Write an algorithm for the steps to be carried out by function *main()* in the application program using a stack and a queue to determine if a word is a palindrome. Employ the legal stack and queue operations developed above. *Hint:* be sure to include a loop to fill the stack and queue and a loop to empty and compare the stack and queue for testing if the word is a palindrome.

BEGIN

END.

In-the-Lab 

Procedure & Discussion:

Start Your Compiler

Start your C++ program development environment.

Write the Stack Class Header File

Before you can write the application program, you need to code the class declarations and function implementations for the stack and queue. Make sure that a new file is open. Use the class description that you developed, complete the following header file shell.

```
//STACK CLASS DECLARATION HEADER FILE (STACK.H)

#ifndef STACK_H
#define STACK_H

// DECLARE CONSTANTS AND VARIABLES



// STACK CLASS DECLARATION
class
{
 public:





 private:



};
#endif
```

Save and Compile the Header File

After you have entered the source code for the stack class declaration, save it with the name *stack.h* and then compile it.

Write the Queue Class Header File

Make sure that a new file is open. Use the class description that you developed, complete the following header file shell.

```
//QUEUE CLASS DECLARATION HEADER FILE (QUEUE.H)

#ifndef QUEUE_H
#define QUEUE_H

//DEFINE CONSTANTS AND VARIABLES



// DECLARE QUEUE CLASS
class
{
public:



private:


};
#endif
```

Save and Compile the Header File

After you have entered the source code for the queue class declaration, save it with the name *queue.h* and then compile it.

Write the Stack Implementation File

Open a new file for the stack function implementation file. Using the algorithms that you developed, complete the following implementation file shell.

```
// STACK IMPLEMENTATION FILE (STACK.CPP)

#include "stack.h"
#include <iostream.h>

// CONSTRUCTOR TO IMPLEMENT CreateStack( )



//IMPLEMENTATION OF EmptyStack()



//IMPLEMENTATION OF FullStack()
```

```
//IMPLEMENTATION OF Push()
```

```
//IMPLEMENTATION OF Pop()
```

```
//IMPLEMENTATION OF TopElement()
```

Save and Compile the Stack Implementation File

After you have entered the source code for the stack function implementations, save the file with the name *stack.cpp* and then compile the file.

Write the Queue Implementation File

Open a new file for the queue function implementation file. Using the algorithms that you developed, complete the following implementation file shell.

```
//QUEUE IMPLEMENTATION FILE (QUEUE.CPP)

#include "queue.h"
#include <iostream.h>

// CONSTRUCTOR TO IMPLEMENT CreateQueue()
```

```
//IMPLEMENTATION OF EmptyQueue()
```

```
//IMPLEMENTATION OF FullQueue()
```

```
//IMPLEMENTATION OF Insert()
```

```
//IMPLEMENTATION OF Remove()
```

```
//IMPLEMENTATION OF FrontElement()
```

Save and Compile the Queue Implementation File

After you have entered the source code for the queue function implementations, save the file with the name *queue.cpp*. Now that you have saved the file, compile it.

Write the Application Program

Open a new file for the application program. Using the problem definition and algorithm that you developed, complete the following application program shell using a stack and a queue for determining if a word entered by the user is a palindrome. Define objects for the stack and queue classes and test their implementation functions.

```
// LAB 14-1 APPLICATION FILE (L14-1.CPP)
// AUTHOR : type your name here
// DATE WRITTEN : type the date here

#include "stack.h"
#include "queue.h"
#include <iostream.h>
#include <conio.h>          // FOR DOS USERS ONLY
#include <stdio.h>
#include <ctype.h>

void main()
{
// DEFINE STACK AND QUEUE OBJECTS


// DEFINE VARIABLES


// GET STRING TO BE TESTED FROM USER
```

```
// LOOP TO FILL STACK AND QUEUE




// LOOP TO EMPTY THE STACK AND QUEUE TO TEST IF THE WORD IS A PALINDROME




} //END main()
```

Save and Compile the Application Program

After you have entered the source code for the application program, save the file with the name *L14-1.cpp*, then compile it.

Build a Project File

Build a project named *LAB14-1.prj*. Add the *stack.cpp*, *queue.cpp* and *L14-1.cpp* files to the project. Do not add the header files to the project, since you have included them in the preprocessor directives of the other files.

Compile and Link the Project File

Once the necessary program files have been added to the project, compile and link it. The project manager automatically compiles and links all the individual program files to produce an executable file.

Run and Test the Program

When the project is successfully compiled and linked, run and test it.

Check the Program Results

Sample output screens from the palindrome project are shown in Figure 14-1 and Figure 14-2. Your input and output should look similar to these.

```
        TYPE THE WORD TO BE TESTED ONE CHARACTER AT A TIME,
        PRESSING ENTER AFTER EACH CHARACTER.
        ENTER AN ASTERISK (*) TO END THE WORD.

M
O
M
*

MOM IS A PALINDROME.  HURRAY!!!
Press ENTER to continue.
```

Figure 14-1 Sample output screen for a word that is a palindrome.

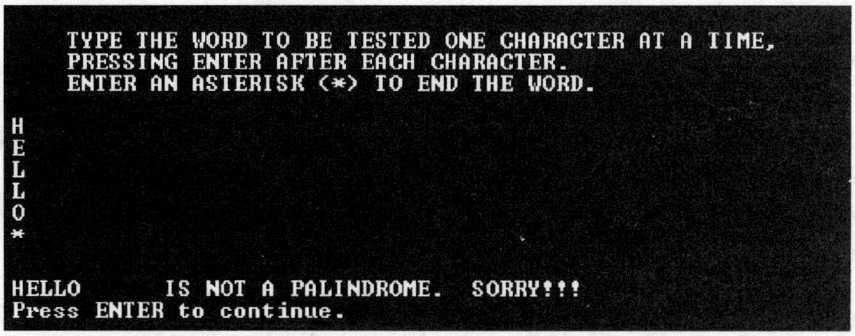

Figure 14-2 Sample output screen for a word that is not a palindrome.

Print Sample Runs and the Source Code of the Program

Get sample print-outs of the program runs for documentation. Print source code listings of your program files including the class header files, function implementation files and application program file.

Close the File

Close the project file when you are finished.

A Programming Challenge

Modify your program to use only stacks to determine if a word entered by the user is a palindrome. *Hint:* You will need to use three stacks. Why? ______________________________

____

____

Problem 2 - Ordered Linked List

In this exercise, you will develop a linked list class declaration, related function implementations, and an application program that defines an object for the linked list class. The program will test the function implementations to manipulate an ordered linked list ADT storing character data in ascending order. You will add characters to the list, delete characters from the list, and display the list. You will build a project to exercise the ordered linked list.

Pre-Lab

PROBLEM STATEMENT

An ordered linked list is one in which the information in the list is ascending or descending from the first node to the last node in the list. To develop an ordered linked list ADT, the *InsertNode()* operation needs to search for the proper insertion point of the information being added to the list prior to inserting the node into the list.

Write an application program to develop an ordered linked list ADT that will store character data in ascending order, from the beginning to the end of the list. Your program should allow the user to add characters to the list, display the list contents, allow the user to add additional characters to the ordered linked list, display the list with the new elements, delete characters from the ordered linked list, and display the list after you have deleted the characters.

Procedure & Questions:

PROBLEM DEFINITION

Output: What output will be produced according to the problem statement?

____

A function will be used to display the contents of the linked list. What arguments must be sent to the display function from the program?

____

What arguments must be sent back to the program from the function?

____

Which arguments must be value parameters and which ones should be reference parameters? ____

____

Input: What input will be needed for processing to obtain the required output?

____

A function will be used to allow the user to input characters and one to allow the user to remove characters from the list. What arguments must be sent to these functions from the program?

____

What arguments must be sent back to the program from these functions?

____

Which arguments must be value parameters and which ones should be reference parameters? ____

____

Processing: What processing is required to add and delete characters to and from the ordered linked list?

____

Discussion:

According to the problem statement, the output will be the original ordered linked list contents, the list contents after adding more characters, and the list contents after you have deleted characters. The characters are needed as input from the user. To add a character to the list, you must search for the correct insertion point and insert the character. To delete a character to the list, you must search for the character and remove its node.

Procedure & Questions:

PROBLEM DEFINITION FOR THE LINKED LIST CLASS

The linked list class will need a data member for locating the first element in the linked list. Use the following summary of legal linked list operations when defining the function members of the linked list class.

CreateList( ) - Creates an empty list.
InsertNode( ) - Adds a node to the list.
DeleteNode( ) - Removes a specified node from the list.
TraverseList( ) - Traverses the list, processing the list information as required.
EmptyList( ) - Determines if the list is empty.

What will you name this class? ____

List the members that need to be declared public. ______________________________

____

List the members that need to be declared private. ______________________________

____

PROBLEM STATEMENT FOR THE LINKED LIST FUNCTIONS

Develop algorithms for the functions to implement the legal linked list operations listed in the linked list class problem definition.

CreateList( ) - Creates an empty list.

Which class data members are operated of by this function? ______________________

Write a function header using the :: operator to make the connection between the class and function.

____

InsertNode( ) - Adds a node to the list.

Which class data members are operated of by this function? ______________________

Write a function header using the :: operator to make the connection between the class and function.

____

DeleteNode( ) - Removes a specified node from the list.

Which class data members are operated of by this function? ______________________

Write a function header using the :: operator to make the connection between the class and function.

____

TraverseList( ) - Traverses the list, processing the list information as required.

Which class data members are operated of by this function? ______________________

Write a function header using the :: operator to make the connection between the class and function.

____

EmptyList( ) - Determines if the list is empty.

Which class data members are operated of by this function? ____________________

Write a function header using the :: operator to make the connection between the class and function.

____

THE MAIN ALGORITHM

Here is an initial algorithm for the steps to be carried out by function *main()* in the application program using an ordered linked to manipulate character elements. Write algorithms for the functions to allow the user to enter characters to the linked list, to allow the user to remove a character from the linked list, and to display the contents of the linked list. Be sure to employ the legal linked list operations developed above.

BEGIN
  CALL ADD CHARACTERS FUNCTION TO ADD CHARACTERS TO THE LIST.
  CALL FUNCTION TO DISPLAY THE LIST.
  CALL ADD CHARACTERS FUNCTION TO ADD ANOTHER CHARACTER TO THE LIST.
  CALL FUNCTION TO DISPLAY THE LIST.
  CALL REMOVE CHARACTERS FUNCTION TO REMOVE A CHARACTER FROM THE LIST.
  CALL FUNCTION TO DISPLAY THE LIST.
END.

ADD CHARACTERS FUNCTION
BEGIN

END.

What will you name this function? ____________________

What does this function do? ____________________

What types of data must the function accept and return from the calling program?

Accepts: ____________________

Returns: ____________________

Which parameters must be passed by value and which by reference? ______________________________

____

Write a prototype/header for this function.

____

REMOVE CHARACTERS FUNCTION
BEGIN

END.

What will you name this function? ____

What does this function do? ____

What types of data must the function accept and return from the calling program?

Accepts: ____

Returns: ____

Which parameters must be passed by value and which by reference? ______________________________

____

Write a prototype/header for this function.

____

DISPLAY FUNCTION
BEGIN

END.

What will you name this function? ____

What does this function do? ____

What types of data must the function accept and return from the calling program?

Accepts: ____

Returns: ____

Which parameters must be passed by value and which by reference? ________________

____

Write a prototype/header for this function.

____

In-the-Lab

Procedure & Discussion:

Start Your Compiler

Start your C++ program development environment.

Write the Linked List Header File

Before you can write the application program, you need to code the class declaration and function implementations for the linked list. Make sure that a new file is open. Use the class description that you developed, complete the following header file shell.

```
//LAB 14-2 (LIST.H)          // HEADER FILE FOR LINKED LIST STORING
                             // CHARACTERS IN ASCENDING ORDER

#ifndef LIST_H
#define LIST_H

// DEFINE VARIABLES



struct Node
{
  char Character;            //CHARACTER IN THE LIST
  Node *Next;                //POINTS TO NEXT NODE IN MEMORY
};
```

```
// DEFINE LINKED LIST CLASS
class
{
public:



private:

};
#endif  // LIST.H
```

Save and Compile the Header File

After you have entered the source code for the class declaration, save it with the name *list.h.* Then, compile it and correct any errors.

Write the Linked List Implementation File

Open a new file for the linked list function implementation file. Using the algorithms that you developed, complete the following implementation file shell.

```
// LAB 14-2 (LIST.CPP)    //LINKED LIST IMPLEMENTATION FILE

#include "list.h"
#include <iostream.h>
#include <stdlib.h>
#include <string.h>

// CONSTRUCTOR TO IMPLEMENT CreateList()



// IMPLEMENTATION OF InsertNode()



//IMPLEMENTATION OF DeleteNode()
```

```
//IMPLEMENTATION OF TraverseList()
```

```
//IMPLEMENTATION OF EmptyList()
```

Save and Compile the Implementation File

After you have entered the source code for the linked list function implementations, save it with the name *list.cpp.* Now that you have saved the file, compile it and correct any errors.

Write the Application Program

Open a new file for the application program. Using the problem definition and algorithms that you developed, complete the following application program shell to define an object for the linked list class and test the implementation functions that you have written.

```
// LAB 14-2 (L14-2.CPP)
// AUTHOR : type your name here
// DATE WRITTEN : type the date here

#include <iostream.h>
#include <stdio.h>
#include <string.h>
#include <conio.h>          // FOR DOS USERS ONLY
#include "list.h"

//FUNCTION PROTOTYPES


void main()
{
//DEFINE LIST OBJECT

//CALL FUNCTION TO ADD CHARACTERS TO THE LIST

//CALL FUNCTION TO DISPLAY THE LIST CONTENTS

//CALL FUNCTION TO ADD ANOTHER CHARACTER TO THE LIST

//CALL FUNCTION TO DISPLAY THE LIST CONTENTS

// CALL FUNCTION TO REMOVE CHARACTERS FROM THE LIST

//CALL FUNCTION TO SHOW THE LIST CONTENTS

} //END main()
```

// FUNCTION TO SHOW THE CURRENT CONTENTS OF THE LIST

// FUNCTION TO ALLOW USER TO ENTER INFO FOR NEW NODE & INSERTS INTO LINKED LIST

// FUNCTION TO ALLOW USER TO REMOVE A NODE FROM THE LIST

Save and Compile the Application Program

After you have entered the source code for the application program, save the file with the name *L14-2.cpp* and compile it.

Build a Project File

Build a project named *list.prj*. Add the *list.cpp*, and *L14-2.cpp* files to the project. Do not add the header files to the project, since you have included them in the preprocessor directives of the other files.

Compile and Link the Project File

Once the necessary program files have been added to the project, compile and link it. The project manager automatically compiles and links all the individual program files to produce an executable file.

Run and Test the Program

When the project is successfully compiled and linked, run and test it.

Check the Program Results

Sample screens from the ordered linked list project are shown in Figure 14-3, 14-4, 14-5, 14-6, 14-7, and Figure 14-8. Your input and output should look similar to these.

```
Enter the characters to add to the list, pressing ENTER after each.
Enter '/' to end process of adding characters to the list.
Enter Character:  t
Enter Character:  j
Enter Character:  e
Enter Character:  b
Enter Character:  s
Enter Character:  l
Enter Character:  p
Enter Character:  /
```

Figure 14-3 Sample screen for entering characters into the ordered linked list.

```
Currently, the ordered nodes are as follows.
  b  e  j  l  p  s  t  NULL
```

Figure 14-4 Sample screen of the characters in the ordered linked list.

```
Enter the characters to delete from the list,pressing ENTER after each.
Enter '/' to end the process of deleting characters from list.
Enter Character:  p
```

Figure 14-5 Sample screen for entering characters to delete from the ordered linked list.

```
Currently, the ordered nodes are as follows.
  b  e  j  l  s  t  NULL
```

Figure 14-6 Sample screen of the characters in the ordered linked list after deleting a character.

```
Enter the characters to add to the list, pressing ENTER after each.
Enter '/' to end process of adding charachers to the list.
Enter Character:  z
```

Figure 14-7 Sample screen for entering characters to add to the ordered linked list.

```
Currently, the ordered nodes are as follows.
  b  e  j  l  s  t  z  NULL
```

Figure 14-8 Sample screen of the characters in the ordered linked list after adding a character.

<u>**Print Sample Runs and the Source Code of the Program**</u>

Get sample print-outs of the program runs for documentation. Print source code listings of your program files including the class header files, function implementation files, and application program file.

<u>**Close the File**</u>

Close the project file and any other open files when you are finished.

<u>**Exit C++**</u>

Exit your C++ compiler when you are finished.

LAB PROJECT #15
File I/O

Lab Objectives

In this lab, you will . . .

- Use classes to define and implement file input and output operations.
- Create menu driven projects to write, read, append, and change file data.

Introduction

A file is a sequential data structure that consists of components that are all of the same data type. Files provide a means for your program to communicate with the outside world. Any I/O operations performed by your program, even keyboard input and display output, are handled via files. Files in C++ can either be ASCII character files or binary files. The default type of file is the character file. If a file is to be a binary file, the binary file mode must be specified when the file stream is opened.

All file I/O in C++ is in the form of file streams that employ predefined classes. The *ifstream* class is used to create input file stream objects, the *ofstream* class is used to create output file stream objects, and the *fstream* class is used to create file stream objects that will be used for both input and output. All three of these file streams are declared in the *fstream.h* header file. File streams that you create are called *named* file streams. To create a named file stream, you must define a file stream object for one of the *fstream.h* file classes, and attach the stream object to a particular disk file using the *open( )* function. The *open( )* function can have up to three arguments: a physical disk filename, a file mode designator, and a protection mode designator. See Table 15-1 and 15-2 for a list of the predefined file mode and file protection mode designators.

TABLE 15-1 OPEN MODE DESIGNATORS DEFINED IN C++

Mode	Definition
ios :: in	Open file for reading.
ios :: out	Open file for writing.
ios :: ate	Seek to end of file upon opening.
ios :: app	Open for appending to end of file.
ios :: nocreate	Open fails if file does not exist.
ios :: noreplace	Open fails if file exists.
ios :: trunc	Open file and discard existing contents.
ios :: binary	Binary file : CRLF pairs not translated.

TABLE 15-2 FILE PROTECTION MODE DESIGNATORS DEFINED IN C++

Mode	Definition
S_IREAD	Read Only.
S_IWRITE	Write Only.
S_IREAD | S_IWRITE	Read and Write.

Once a file stream is opened, it is ready for processing. The individual components within a file are accessed via a file stream window. The window must be positioned over the component to be accessed. When a file is opened, the window, sometimes called a file stream buffer, is automatically created to access the file components. Typical tasks that are performed on disk files include writing new files, reading existing files, appending existing files, and changing the information in existing files.

The C++ language has various predefined functions to facilitate the coding of these tasks. Two of these functions are the *seekp( )* and the *seekg( )* functions that allow you to place the file window in a particular position in the file. The *seekp( )* function is used in file write operations and the *seekg( )* function is used in file read operations.

After a file stream is processed, it *must* always be closed using the *close( )* function. In fact, it is a good idea to close a file stream as soon as you are done processing the file.

In Problem 1 you will code a file class declaration, develop the necessary implementation files and develop an application program that creates a new file to store character data. You will write the data to the file and read the data from the file to the display.

In Problem 2 you will modify the program from Problem 1 so that data can be appended to the end of the file and data already in the file can be modified.

You will declare the file class definition in a header file, create an implementation file for the file manipulation functions, develop an application program that defines file objects for the class and tests the function implementations. You will then build a project, linking the files that you have developed. You will compile, debug, run, test, and print the project files.

Problem 1 - Reading and Writing Files

In this exercise, you will create a class declaration and function implementations for disk file manipulation. You will develop an application program that defines an object for the file class and tests the function implementations to create and display a parts inventory file. Finally, you will build a project linking the files that you have developed.

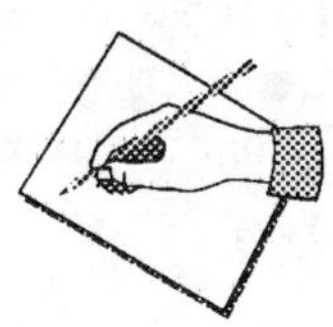

Pre-Lab

PROBLEM STATEMENT

Write a file class declaration and implementations for creating/writing a parts inventory file and reading/displaying the file. Write a menu driven application program that allows the user to make the following choices:

- Create and write a parts inventory file that contains the following information:
  Part Name
  Part Number
  Part Price
  Quantity on Hand
- Read and display a report of the parts inventory file.
- Exit the program.

Procedure & Questions:

PROBLEM DEFINITION

Output: What output will be produced according to the problem statement?

____

Input: What input will be needed for processing to obtain the required output?

____

Processing: What processing is required to create a parts inventory file?

____

____

What processing is required to read and display the parts inventory file?

____

____

Discussion:

According to the problem statement, the output will be a display reporting the parts inventory. The menu choice, filename and parts data are needed as input from the user. To create a file and write the data to the file, you will open the file for output, accept the data from the user, and write it to the file stream. To read and display the file, you will open the file for input, read the information from the file, and display the report.

Procedure:

Before you can develop an application program, you need to declare a file class in a header file, and develop the implementations for the required functions in an implementation file. Finally, you can create a project to combine the separate files into a working application program.

PROBLEM STATEMENT FOR THE FILE CLASS

Declare a file class as part of a header file. The class is to have data members to store the parts inventory information and a data member to store a filename. The class is to have member functions to perform the following tasks:

- Initialize the private filename data member with a disk filename entered by the user.
- Create and write a new file.
- Read and display an existing file.

Procedure & Questions:

PROBLEM DEFINITION FOR THE FILE CLASS

What will you name this class? ______________________________

List the members that need to be declared public. ______________________________

____

List the members that need to be declared private. ______________________________

____

PROBLEM STATEMENT FOR THE FUNCTIONS

Complete the following algorithms for the implementation of the functions listed in the class problem statement.

THE FILE MANIPULATION ALGORITHMS

FUNCTION TO GET A FILENAME FROM THE USER
    BEGIN
        PROMPT THE USER FOR A FILENAME.
        ACCEPT THE FILENAME INTO THE FILENAME DATA MEMBER.
    END.

What will you name this function? ______________________________

What does this function do? ______________________________

Which class data members are operated on by this function? ______________________________

____

Write a function header using the scoping operator, ::, to make the connection between the class and function.

____

FUNCTION TO WRITE, OR CREATE, A NEW FILE
    BEGIN
        DEFINE AN OUTPUT FILE STREAM OBJECT.
        OPEN THE FILE STREAM IN OUTPUT MODE AND ATTACH IT TO A DISK FILENAME.
        GET THE NEW FILE COMPONENTS FROM THE USER AND WRITE THEM TO THE FILE.
        CLOSE THE FILE STREAM.
    END.

What will you name this function? ______________________________

What does this function do? ____

Which class data members are operated on by this function? ______________________

____

Write a function header using the scoping operator, ::, to make the connection between the class and function.

____

FUNCTION TO READ AND DISPLAY AN EXISTING FILE
BEGIN
DEFINE AN INPUT FILE STREAM OBJECT.
OPEN THE FILE STREAM IN INPUT MODE AND ATTACH IT TO A DISK FILENAME.
READ THE FILE COMPONENTS AND DISPLAY THEM TO THE USER.
CLOSE THE FILE STREAM.
END.

What will you name this function? ____

What does this function do? ____

Which class data members are operated on by this function? ______________________

____

Write a function header using the scoping operator, ::, to make the connection between the class and function.

____

PROBLEM STATEMENT FOR THE FILE ACCESS MENU

The menu should allow the user to make the following choices:

- Create and write a parts inventory file.
- Read and display a report of the parts inventory file.
- Exit the program.

Write an algorithm for the file access menu. *Hint:* Use a switch statement and call the appropriate file manipulation function according to the user's menu choice.

THE MENU ALGORITHM

BEGIN

END.

ALGORITHM FOR FUNCTION *main( )*

Write an algorithm for the steps to be carried out by function *main()* in the application program. Make sure to include the menu algorithm that you developed above.

BEGIN

END.

In-the-Lab

Procedure & Discussion:

Start Your Compiler

Start your C++ program development environment.

Write the File Class Header File

Before you can write the application program, you need to code the class declarations and function implementations for manipulating the file. Make sure that a new file is open. Complete the following file class declaration shell to code the file class header file.

```
// FILE CLASS DECLARATION HEADER FILE (FILE.H)

#ifndef FILES_H
#define FILES_H

#include <fstream.h>

// FILE CLASS DECLARATION
class
{
public:





private:




};
#endif
```

Save and Compile the Header File

After you have entered the source code for the file class declaration, save it with the name *files.h* and then compile it.

Write the File Manipulation Implementation File

Open a new file and complete the following code for the file manipulation implementation file.

```
// FILE MANIPULATION IMPLEMENTATION FILE (FILES.CPP)

#include "files.h"
#include <stdio.h>
#include <stdlib.h>
#include <string.h>
#include <conio.h>            // FOR DOS USERS ONLY

// FUNCTION TO GET FILENAME FROM THE USER

{




} // END OF GET FILENAME FUNCTION
```

```
// FUNCTION TO WRITE, OR CREATE, A NEW FILE

{
   //DEFINE OUTPUT FILE OBJECT


   //OPEN FILE



   //GET FILE COMPONENTS AND WRITE TO FILE




   // CLOSE FILE

} //END WRITE IMPLEMENTATION FUNCTION

// FUNCTION TO READ AND DISPLAY  AN EXISTING FILE

{
   //DEFINE INPUT FILE OBJECT


   //OPEN FILE



   //READ AND DISPLAY THE FILE COMPONENTS




   // CLOSE FILE

} //END READ AND DISPLAY FUNCTION
```

Save and Compile the File Manipulation Implementation File

After you have entered the source code for the file manipulation function implementations, save the file with the name *files.cpp* and then compile it.

Write the Application Program

Open a new file for the application program. Using the problem definition and algorithm that you developed, complete the following application program shell with a menu interface to create a new disk file, write the file components, read, and display the parts inventory report.

```
// LAB 15-1 APPLICATION FILE (L15-1.CPP)
// AUTHOR : type your name here
// DATE WRITTEN : type the date here

#include "files.h"
#include <iostream.h>
#include <ctype.h>
#include <conio.h>          // FOR DOS USERS ONLY

void main()
{
// DECLARE File OBJECT AND LOCAL VARIABLES


// GET FILENAME FROM USER


// GENERATE FILE ACCESS MENU TO CALL FILE ACCESS FUNCTIONS










} //END main()
```

Save and Compile the Application Program

After you have entered the source code for the application program, save the file with the name *L15-1.cpp* and then compile it.

Build a Project File

Build a project named *LAB15-1.prj*. Add the *files.cpp*, and *L15-1.cpp* files to the project. Do not add the *files.h* header file to the project, since you have included it in the preprocessor directives of the other files.

Compile the Project File

Once the necessary program files have been added to the project, compile it. The project manager automatically compiles and links all the individual program files to produce an executable file.

Run and Test the Program

When the project is successfully compiled and linked, run and test it.

Check the Program Results

A sample menu is shown in Figure 15-1.

```
            PARTS INVENTORY MENU

Write and create a new file <W>

Read and display file <R>

Quit <Q>

            ENTER CHOICE ---> _
```

Figure 15-1 Sample menu for the file access program.

Sample input and output screens from the file manipulation project are shown in Figure 15-2 and Figure 15-3.

```
Enter file component.

Enter the part name or DONE when finished:  Bolts

Enter the part number:  11111

Enter the price of the part:  0.24

Enter the quantity of part on hand:  1500
Enter file component.

Enter the part name or DONE when finished:  Nuts

Enter the part number:  22222

Enter the price of the part:  0.42

Enter the quantity of part on hand:  1243
```

Figure 15-2 Sample input screen for the parts inventory file.

```
The current file contents are:

PART NAME          PART NUMBER       PRICE    QUANTITY ON HAND
---------          -----------       -----    ----------------
Bolts              11111             0.24           1500
Nuts               22222             0.42           1243
Washers            33333             0.15           2087
Pipes              44444             5.89           250


Press Enter to continue.
```

Figure 15-3 Sample output report for the parts inventory file.

Your menu, input, and output should look similar to these.

Print the Source Code and Sample Runs of the Program

Print source code listings of your program files including the class header file, function implementation file and application program file. Get sample print-outs of the program runs.

Close the File

Close the project file when you are finished with it, but do not close the other files at this time. You will add other file manipulation features in Problem 2 of this lab project.

Problem 2 - Append and Modify a File

In this exercise, you will modify the file class declaration, function implementations, and application program created in Problem 1. You will add function members to the *files.h* class declaration file to append a file and change a file's contents. You will add the implementations for these functions to the *files.cpp* implementation file and add these options to the menu in the application program. You will build a project linking the files that you have modified.

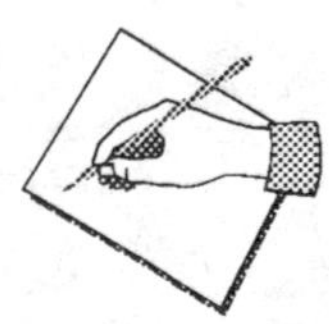

Pre-Lab

PROBLEM STATEMENT

Add the options for the user to append additional parts to the parts inventory file created in Problem 1 and to modify, or change, the parts inventory data.

Procedure & Questions:

PROBLEM DEFINITION

Output: What output will be produced according to the problem statement?

____

Input: What input will be needed for processing to obtain the required output?

____

Processing: What processing is required to append additional parts to the parts inventory file?

____

____

What processing is required to modify the data already in the parts inventory file?

____

____

Discussion:

The input and output will be the same as in Problem 1. The output will be a display reporting the parts inventory. The menu choice, filename, and parts data are needed as input from the user. To append data to a file, you will open the file for output with the append open mode designation, accept the data from the user, and write it to the file stream. To change the data already in the file, you will open the file for input and output, get the component to be changed from the user, search the file for the component, delete the old component, seek the end of the file, and write the new information to the end of the file.

Procedure:

Add two new functions to the *files.h* file manipulation class header file that will append and change the file, develop and add the implementations for the append and change functions in the *files.cpp* implementation file, and then modify the menu in the application program to give the user access to the new file operations. Finally, create a project to combine the separate files into a working application.

PROBLEM STATEMENT FOR THE CLASS

Modify the file manipulation class header file. The class is to have data members to store the parts inventory information and a data member to store a filename. In addition, the class is to have member functions to perform the following tasks:

- Initialize the private filename data member with a disk filename entered by the user.
- Create and write a new file.
- Read and display an existing file.
- Append the file.
- Change the file data.

Procedure & Questions:

PROBLEM STATEMENT FOR THE FUNCTIONS

Complete the following algorithms for the functions to append and change the file.

THE FILE MANIPULATION ALGORITHMS

```
FUNCTION TO APPEND A FILE
   BEGIN
      DEFINE AN OUTPUT FILE STREAM OBJECT.
      OPEN THE FILE STREAM IN APPEND MODE AND ATTACH IT TO A DISK FILENAME..
      GET THE ADDITIONAL FILE COMPONENTS FROM THE USER AND WRITE THEM TO
         THE FILE.
      CLOSE THE FILE STREAM.
   END.
```

What will you name this function? ______________________________

What does this function do? ______________________________

Which class data members are operated on by this function? ______________________________

____

Write a function header using the scoping operator, ::, to make the connection between the class and function.

____

FUNCTION TO CHANGE A FILE
BEGIN
DEFINE AN INPUT/OUTPUT FILE STREAM OBJECT.
OPEN THE FILE STREAM IN BOTH INPUT AND OUTPUT MODE AND ATTACH IT TO A DISK FILENAME.
GET THE COMPONENT TO BE CHANGED FROM THE USER AND SEARCH THE FILE FOR THE COMPONENT.
SEEK THE OLD COMPONENT POSITION.
ERASE THE OLD COMPONENT INFORMATION FROM THE FILE.
SEEK THE END OF FILE POSITION.
WRITE THE NEW COMPONENT INFORMATION TO THE END OF THE FILE.
CLOSE THE FILE STREAM.
END.

What will you name this function? ______________________________

What does this function do? ______________________________

Which class data members are operated on by this function? ______________________________

____

Write a function header using the scoping operator, ::, to make the connection between the class and function.

____

PROBLEM STATEMENT FOR THE MENU

The modified menu should allow the user to make the following choices:

- Create and write a parts inventory file.
- Read and display a report of the parts inventory file.
- Append the file.
- Change the file.
- Exit the program.

Write an algorithm to modify the file access menu.

THE MENU ALGORITHM

BEGIN

END.

THE MAIN ALGORITHM

Write an algorithm for the steps to be carried out by the modified function *main()* in the application program. Make sure to include your menu algorithm from above.

BEGIN

END.

In-the-Lab

Procedure & Discussion:

Start Your Compiler

Start your C++ program development environment.

Modify the File Declaration Class Header File

Open the *file.h* header file. Add the new function members to the class declaration.

Save and Compile the Header File

After you have modified the source code for the file class declaration, save it and compile it.

Modify the Files Implementation File

Open the *files.cpp* function implementation file. Add the following code to the file manipulation implementation file.

```
// FUNCTION TO APPEND A FILE

{
   //DEFINE APPEND FILE OBJECT

   //OPEN FILE

   //GET FILE COMPONENTS AND APPEND TO FILE

   // CLOSE FILE

} END APPEND IMPLEMENTATION FUNCTION

// FUNCTION TO CHANGE THE FILE

{
   //DEFINE LOCAL VARIABLES

   //DEFINE INPUT/OUTPUT FILE OBJECT

   //OPEN FILE
```

```
//GET  COMPONENT TO CHANGE FROM USER AND SEARCH FILE
//IF COMPONENT FOUND, ERASE AND PLACE NEW COMPONENT AT END OF FILE



    //SET WindowPos TO FILE WINDOW POSITION


    //READ A FILE COMPONENT


    //COMPARE FILE COMPONENT TO USER ENTRY


        //SEEK FOUND COMPONENT POSITION


        //REPLACE COMPONENT WITH *'s


        //GET NEW COMPONENT FROM USER


        //SEEK END OF FILE


        //ADD NEW COMPONENT TO END OF FILE


//WRITE MESSAGE TO USER IF COMPONENT IS NOT FOUND



// CLOSE FILE

} END CHANGE FILE FUNCTION
```

Save and Compile the Modified File Manipulation Implementation File

After you have added the source code for the new file manipulation function implementations, save the file and compile it. Fix any errors. Compile and save the file again, if you modify the code..

Modify the Application Program

Open the *L15-1.cpp* application program file. Add the menu options and function calls for appending and changing a file.

Save and Compile the Application Program

After you have modified the source code for the application program, save it with the name *L15-2.cpp* and then compile it.

Build a Project File

Build a project named *LAB15-2.prj*. Add the *files.cpp*, and *L15-2.cpp* files to the project. Do not add the *files.h* header file to the project, since you have included it in the preprocessor directives of the other files.

Compile the Project File

Once the necessary program files have been added to the project, compile it.

Run and Test the Program

When the project is successfully compiled and linked, run and test it.

Check the Program Results

A modified sample menu is shown in Figure 15-4.

```
            PARTS INVENTORY MENU
Write and create a new file <W>
Read and display file <R>
Append file <A>
Change file <C>
Quit <Q>

            ENTER CHOICE --->
```

Figure 15-4 Modified menu for the file access program.

Select the menu option for appending the file and add an item to your parts inventory file. Sample input and output screens for appending the parts inventory file are shown in Figure 15-5 and 15-6.

```
Enter new file component.
Enter the part name or DONE when finished:  Nails
Enter the part number:  66666
Enter the price of the part:  0.05
Enter the quantity of part on hand:  5000
```

Figure 15-5 Sample input screen for appending the parts inventory file.

```
The current file contents are:

PART NAME          PART NUMBER        PRICE    QUANTITY ON HAND
---------          -----------        -----    ----------------
Bolts              11111              0.24          1500
Nuts               22222              0.42          1243
Washers            33333              0.15          2087
Pipes              44444              5.89          250
Nails              66666              0.05          5000


Press Enter to continue.
```

Figure 15-6 Sample output report for the appended parts inventory file.

Select the menu option to change the file data. Change the price or quantity on hand of some of the items in your inventory file. Sample input and output screens for changing the file data are shown in Figure 15-7 and 15-8.

```
Which Component(Enter the part Name) do you wish to change? Nails

Component found, what do you wish to change it to? Enter new file component.

Enter the part name or DONE when finished:  Nails

Enter the part number:  55555

Enter the price of the part:  0.07

Enter the quantity of part on hand:  6000
```

Figure 15-7 Sample input screen for changing the data in the parts inventory file.

```
The current file contents are:

PART NAME          PART NUMBER        PRICE    QUANTITY ON HAND
---------          -----------        -----    ----------------
Bolts              11111              0.24          1500
Nuts               22222              0.42          1243
Washers            33333              0.15          2087
Pipes              44444              5.89          250
*****              *****              ****          ****
Nails              55555              0.07          6000


Press Enter to continue.
```

Figure 15-8 Sample output report for the modified parts inventory file.

Your menu, input and output should look similar to these.

<u>Print the Source Code and Sample Runs of the Program</u>

Print source code listings of your program files including the class header file, function implementation file, and application program file. Get sample print-outs of the program runs for documentation.

<u>Close the File</u>

Close the project file and any other open files when you are finished.

<u>Exit C++</u>

Exit your C++ compiler when you are finished.

APPENDIX A
Important Options To Check Before Using the TURBO C++ Compiler

There are some important options that you may need to set to prepare for the object-oriented C++ programming presented in your text and this lab manual. *If you are working with a computer system that has already been prepared for object-oriented C++ programming, check with your instructor or lab supervisor before changing any C++ options.* If your computer has not been prepared for C++ programming there are some options that you need to set. This appendix contains sections for TURBO C++ for DOS and TURBO C++ for Windows with some suggestions for setting compiler, directories, and environment options in the TURBO C++ programming environment. Refer to your TURBO C++ users manual for more information about other options that you can set to customize the TURBO C++ compiler and IDE. *If you are not using TURBO C++ check the documentation for your compiler and C++ development environment for options that may need to be set for object-oriented C++ programming.*

TURBO C++ for DOS

Here are the options that we suggest you set in TURBO C++ for DOS in order to compile and run the programs in this lab manual:

Compiler Options

Since TURBO C++ is a compiler for both C and C++ programs, there are some compiler options you need to set to prepare for C++ programming. When you select the **C++ Options** in the **Compiler** menu choice of the **Options** Menu Bar item, shown in Figure A-1, a Dialog box, shown in Figure A-2, is displayed that gives you the choice of having the compiler compile for **C++ Always**.

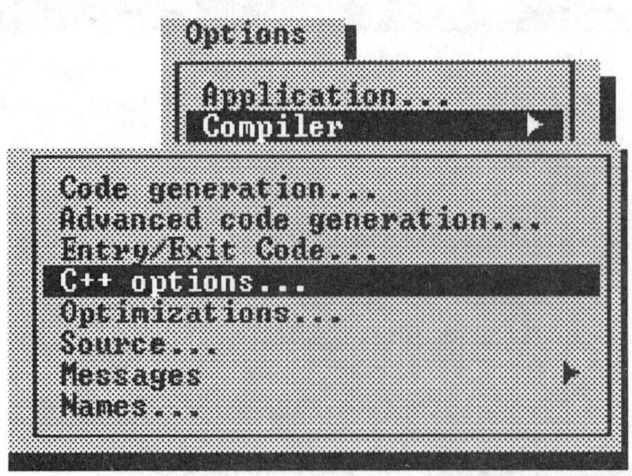

Figure A-1. The **Compiler** choice of the **Options** menus.

The **C++ Always** button should have the dot beside it, as shown in Figure A-2. This option must be on to allow you to compile and run the solutions to the C++ object-oriented programming problems presented in your text and this lab manual.

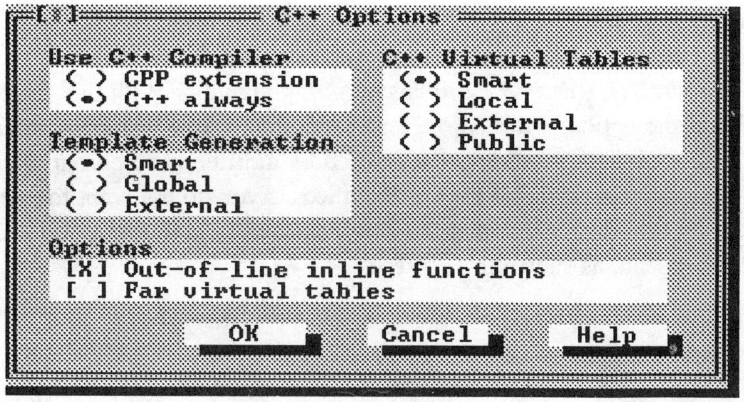

Figure A-2 The **C++ Options** Dialog box.

Directories Options

Choosing the **Directories** menu choice of the **Options** Menu Bar item, shown in Figure A-3, displays a Dialog box that will allow you to instruct the compiler which directories to use and where they are located on your computer.

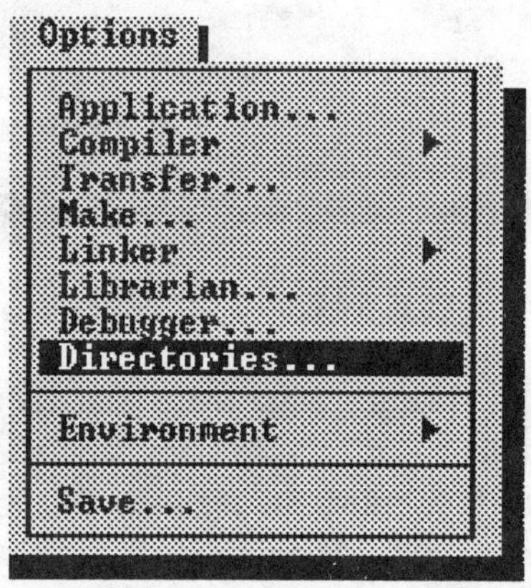

Figure A-3 The **Directories** choice of the **Options** menu.

The **Include Directories** should be where the TURBO C++ include files are located. The **Library Directories** should be where the TURBO C++ library files are located. The **Output Directories** should indicate where you want your programs to be saved. The **Source Directories** should be where your program source files are located. See Figure A-4 for example directory settings. As you can see, the **Output Directories** and **Source Directories** are the same, in this recommended configuration.

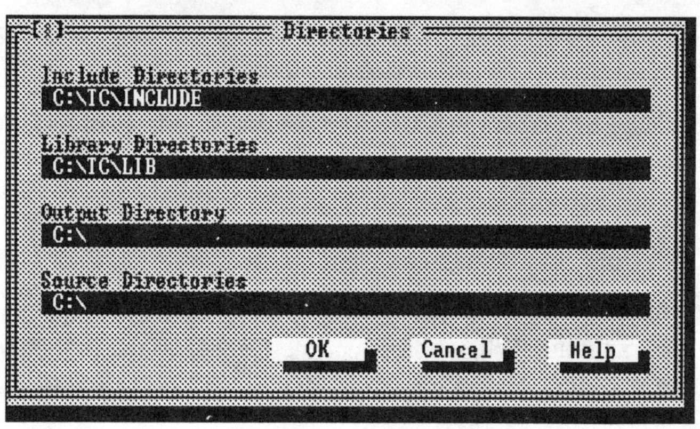

Figure A-4 TURBO C++ directory settings example.

Environment Editor Options

A new feature beginning with TURBO C++ 3.0 is syntax highlighting. With this feature, the Edit window is syntax-sensitive. When the option is turned on, keywords, identifiers, symbols, integers, comments, and any other part of the syntax of the C++ code are identified by a different foreground and background color. This feature is on by default when TURBO C++ is installed. If you do not want to use this feature you can select the **Options** item on the Menu Bar, then the **Environment** item in the pull down menu. Then, select **Editor** from the next sub- menu, as shown in Figure A-5.

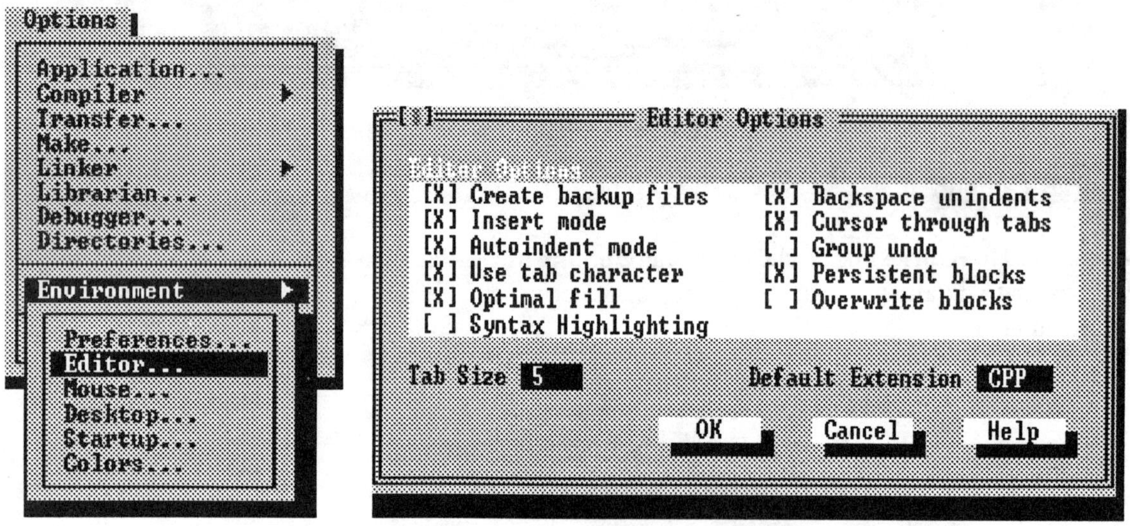

Figure A-5 Select the **Editor** option to turn off the **Syntax Highlighting** option.

To turn off the syntax highlighting feature, make sure that there is NOT a check by the **Syntax Highlighting** option in the Dialog box that is displayed when you choose the **Editor** option, as shown in Figure A-5. To remove the check in the box, move the highlight bar to **Syntax Highlighting** and press the space bar. Click **OK** or press **ENTER** to finish the operation.

Once the options are set for C++ programming you are ready to begin the lab Projects. To gain the most benefit from this manual, you need to complete each step of the problems, including the Pre-Lab and In-the-Lab sections

---

TURBO C++ for Windows

Here are the options that we suggest you set in TURBO C++ for Windows in order to compile and run the programs in this lab manual:

Compiler Options

Since TURBO C++ is a compiler for both C and C++ programs, there are some compiler options you need to set to prepare for C++ programming. When you select the **C++ Options** in the **Compiler** menu choice of the **Options** Menu Bar item a Dialog box is displayed that gives you the choice of having the compiler compile for **C++ Always**.

The **C++ Always** button should have the dot beside it. This option must be on to allow you to compile and run the solutions to the C++ object-oriented programming problems presented in your text and this lab manual.

- Set **Options | Compiler | C++ options** to **C++ always**.

Environment Options

In order to use the Hot Keys available in TURBO C++, you will need to set the **Command Set** to **Alternate** by selecting the menu choices shown below. A summary of TURBO C++ Hot Keys is available in Appendix B.

- Set **Options | Environment | Preferences | Command Set** to **Alternate**.

Directories Options

Choosing the **Directories** menu choice of the **Options** Menu Bar item displays a Dialog box, shown in Figure A-5, that will allow you to instruct the compiler which directories to use and where they are located on your computer.

- Set **Options | Directories** as shown in Figure A-5.

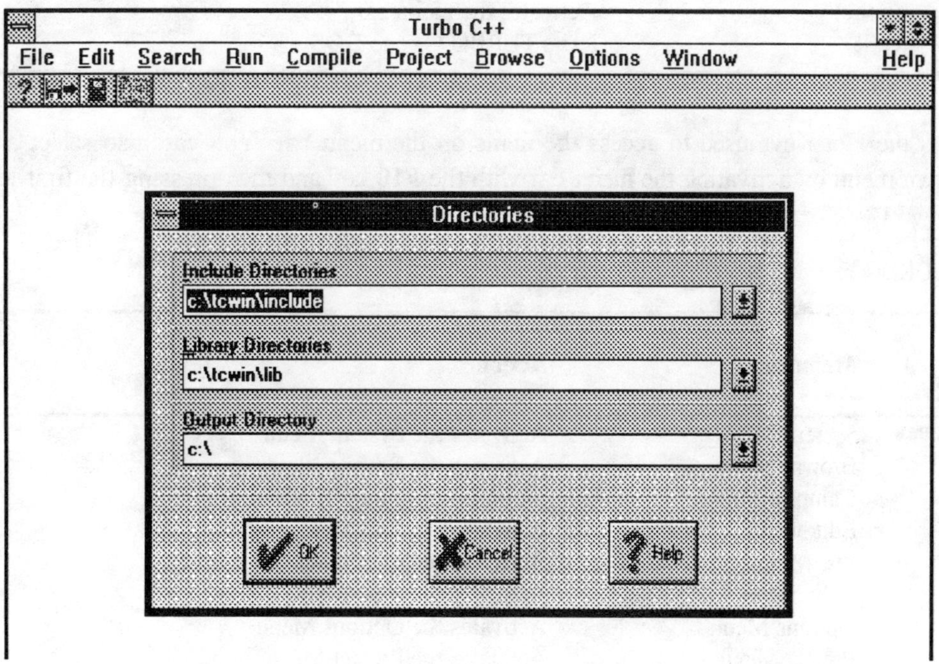

Figure A-5 Setting the directories options.

The **Include Directories** should be where the TURBO C++ include files are located. The **Library Directories** should be where the TURBO C++ library files are located. The **Output Directory** should indicate where you want your programs to be saved.

Once the options are set for C++ programming you are ready to begin the Lab Projects. To gain the most benefit from this manual, you need to complete each step of the problems, including the Pre-Lab and In-the-Lab sections.

APPENDIX B
TURBO C++ Hot Key Summary

The following tables summarize the TURBO C++ Hot Keys. To use these Hot Keys in TURBO C++ for Windows, make sure that your command set options are set to the *Alternate* command set. Select the *Alternate* command set by choosing **Options | Environment | Preferences** and clicking the **Alternate** button in the **Command Set** category. Table B-1 lists the most commonly used Hot Keys.

TABLE B-1 GENERAL PURPOSE TURBO C++ HOT KEYS

Hot Keys	**Menu Item**	**Action**
F1	Help	Displays a Help screen
F2	Save	Saves the file in the active Edit Window
F3	Open	Opens a file
F5	Zoom	Zooms to the active window
F6	Next	Cycles through the open windows
F7	Trace Into	Traces into functions in Debug mode
F8	Step Over	Steps over functions in Debug mode
F9	Make EXE	Makes an executable (.EXE) file
F10	(none)	Activates the menu bar
ALT + X	Quit	Exits TURBO C++ to DOS

Table B-2 lists the Hot Keys used to access the items on the menu bar. You can also select a menu bar item's pull down menu by activating the menu bar with the **F10** key and then pressing the first letter of the needed item.

TABLE B-2 TURBO C++ MENU BAR HOT KEYS

Hot Keys	**Menu Item**	**Action**
ALT + SPACEBAR	System Menu	Activates the System Menu
ALT + B	Browse Menu	Activates the Browse Menu
ALT + C	Compile Menu	Activates the Compile Menu
ALT + E	Edit Menu	Activates the Edit Menu
ALT + F	File Menu	Activates the File Menu
ALT + H	Help Menu	Activates the Help Menu
ALT + O	Options Menu	Activates the Options Menu
ALT + P	Project Menu	Activates the Project Menu
ALT + R	Run Menu	Activates the Run Menu
ALT + S	Search Menu	Activates the Search Menu
ALT + W	Window Menu	Activates the Window Menu

Table B-3 lists the editing Hot Keys that can be used while you are typing or editing your programs in the **Edit** window. Remember that some of the editing commands require that you mark the text before using the command.

TABLE B-3 TURBO C++ EDITING HOT KEYS

Hot Keys	Menu Item	Action
CTRL + DEL	Clear	Removes selected text
CTRL + INS	Copy	Copies selected text to the clipboard
SHIFT + DEL	Cut	Removes selected text to the clipboard
SHIFT + INS	Paste	Pastes text from the clipboard
ALT + BACKSPACE	Undo	Restores text to the previous condition
CTRL + L	Search Again	Repeats the last Find or Replace
F2	Save	Saves the file in the active window
F3	Open	Lets you open a file
HOME	(none)	Moves to the beginning of a line
END	(none)	Moves to the end of a line
CTRL + PAGE UP	(none)	Moves to the beginning of a file
CTRL + PAGE DN	(none)	Moves to the end of a file

Table B-4 lists the Hot Keys available for managing the various windows that you will be using in the TURBO C++ IDE.

TABLE B-4 TURBO C++ WINDOW MANAGEMENT HOT KEYS

Hot Keys	Menu Item	Action
ALT + F3	Close	Closes the active window
ALT + F5	Execution window	Displays the Execution window
F5	Zoom	Zooms or unzooms the active window
F6	Next	Cycles through the open windows

Table B-5 lists the Hot Keys that make accessing TURBO C++'s on-line help fast and easy.

TABLE B-5 TURBO C++ ON-LINE HELP HOT KEYS

Hot Keys	Menu Item	Action
F1	Contents	Opens a context-sensitive Help screen
SHIFT + F1	Index	Brings up the Help Index
CTRL + F1	Topic Search	Calls up Help on selected C++ syntax and functions in the Editor only

Table B-6 lists the Hot Keys available while running or debugging your programs in TURBO C++ for Windows.

TABLE B-6 TURBO C++ FOR WINDOWS RUNNING AND DEBUGGING HOT KEYS

Hot Keys	Menu Item	Action
Alt + F4	Back Trace	Undoes last instruction execution.
Alt + F5	User Screen	Shows the Execution window.
Alt + F8	Run Until Return	Runs until return from function.
Alt + F9	Execute to	Runs to a specified address.
Alt + X	Quit	Quits debugger and returns to TURBO C++.
Ctrl + F2	Program reset	Resets the running program.
Ctrl + F4	Evaluate/Modify	Evaluates an expression.
Ctrl + F7	Add Watch	Adds a watch expression.
Shft + F3	Copy	Copies selected text to clipboard.
Shft + F4	Paste	Pastes clipboard text to cursor location.
F2	Toggle Breakpoint	Sets or clears a conditional breakpoint.
F2	View Module	Module pick list.
F4	Go to Cursor	Runs the program to the cursor position.
F7	Trace Into	Executes one statement at a time, tracing into functions.
F8	Step Over	Executes one statement at a time, stepping over functions.
F9	Run	Runs the active program

Table B-7 lists the Hot Keys available while running or debugging your programs in TURBO C++ for DOS.

TABLE B-7 TURBO C++ FOR DOS RUNNING AND DEBUGGING HOT KEYS

Hot Keys	Menu Item	Action
Alt + F4	Inspect	Opens an Inspector window
Alt + F7	Previous Error	Takes you to the previous error.
Alt + F8	Next Error	Takes you to the next error.
Alt + F9	Compile to OBJ	Compiles the active file to .OBJ
Ctrl + F2	Program reset	Resets the running program.
Ctrl + F3	Call Stack	Brings up the stack of used functions.
Ctrl + F4	Evaluate/Modify	Evaluates an expression.
Ctrl + F7	Add Watch	Adds a watch expression.
Ctrl + F8	Toggle Breakpoint	Sets or clears a conditional breakpoint
Ctrl + F9	Run	Runs the active program.
F4	Go to Cursor	Runs the program to the cursor position.
F7	Trace Into	Executes one statement at a time, tracing into functions.
F8	Step Over	Executes one statement at a time, stepping over functions.
F9	Make EXE	Makes (compiles and links) the active program.

TURBO C++'s Hot Keys are often the easiest and fastest method to activate a command or function in the IDE. Most of them are listed on the right side of their command in the pull down menus. So if you forget one, you can look it up in the menus.